Chance or Dance

CHANCE OR DANCE

An Evaluation of Design

Jimmy H. Davis and Harry L. Poe

★

TEMPLETON FOUNDATION PRESS

WEST CONSHOHOCKEN, PENNSYLVANIA

Templeton Foundation Press
300 Conshohocken State Road, Suite 670
West Conshohocken, PA 19428
www.templetonpress.org

Templeton Foundation Press helps intellectual leaders and others learn
about science research on aspects of realities, invisible and intangible. Spiritual realities include unlimited love, accelerating creativity, worship, and
the benefits of purpose in persons and in the cosmos.

Designed and typeset by Gopa and Ted2, Inc.

Library of Congress Cataloging-in-Publication Data

Davis, Jimmy H., 1948-
  Chance or dance : an evaluation of design / Jimmy H. Davis
and Harry L. Poe. — Rev. ed.
    p. cm.
  Rev. ed. of: Designer universe.
  Includes bibliographical references (p.   ) and index.
  ISBN-13: 978-1-59947-133-4 (pbk. : alk. paper)
  ISBN-10: 1-59947-133-7 (pbk. : alk. paper) 1. Religion and science.
2. Intelligent design (Teleology) I. Poe, Harry Lee, 1950-
II. Davis, Jimmy H., 1948- Designer universe. III. Title.
  BL240.3.D37 2008
  215—dc22
                                    2007040519

Printed in the United States of America

08 09 10 11 12 13   10 9 8 7 6 5 4 3 2 1

For our students,
past, present, and future,
who will continue the dialogue
about design

CONTENTS

Illustrations

PREFACE TO THE REVISED EDITION

AFTER THE RELEASE OF the first edition of this book, we noted with surprise how many reviewers stated that we believe that intelligent design is science. While we stated that we believe in design as an affirmation of faith, we also stated that we do not believe that the intelligent design movement has yet made the case that intelligent design is science. Our surprise comes in observing how many people active in the conversation about science and faith have a tendency to confuse all statements about design with the intelligent design movement. This observation coincides with another current tendency to confuse any affirmation of creation with scientific creationism. We believe these two trends represent a problem in the intellectual discussion of ideas, and we have issued this revised edition in part to address this situation.

Since the first edition of this book, several important developments have taken place around the idea of design. Intelligent design has been ruled not to be science by a U.S. District Court, and Antony Flew has accepted belief in theism because of the argument of complexity. These and other developments in the intelligent design debate warrant this revised edition. We appreciate the willingness of Templeton Foundation Press to make this revised edition possible.

PREFACE

IN JUNE 2000, two important conferences examined the idea that the universe bears evidence of design. The conference "Evidence for Design: Finding New Ground for Dialogue" took place June 23–27, 2000, under the auspices of the John Templeton Foundation's Science and Religion Course Award program administered by the Center for Theology and the Natural Sciences at Berkeley. This conference was held in Chicago through the facilitation of the Zygon Center for Religion and Science, which is a partnership program of the Lutheran School of Theology at Chicago and the Center for Advanced Study in Religion and Science. The conference "Design and Its Critics" took place June 22–24, 2000, at Concordia University in Mequon, Wisconsin. This conference sought to bring together both proponents and critics of "intelligent design" to make their best cases.

The two conferences approached the subject from different perspectives. The Concordia conference included critics of intelligent design, yet the conference provided a forum for advocates of intelligent design. Leading lights of the intelligent design movement took part, including Michael Behe, William Dembski, and Paul Nelson. The Chicago conference did not include any atheists on its program, but it did not advocate an intelligent design position either. Longtime participants in the science and religion dialogue took part, including Ian Barbour, Owen Gingerich, and Philip Hefner. Ironically, the Chicago meeting had no representatives of the intelligent design movement, nor did the Concordia meeting have representatives of the Christian scientific/theological community that criticize the movement. Despite the irony, both meetings were quite appropriate for their purpose. The Concordia meeting sought to deal with objections to design from the perspective of those who do not believe in a Designer. The Chicago meeting sought to explore other ways of conceiving design than the way suggested by the intelligent design movement.

Due to the limitations imposed on us by the laws of physics, we could attend only one of the meetings. We had explored the views of the leading figures in the intelligent design movement by bringing the mountain to us. Through the Staley lectureship, we were able to bring Michael Behe and William Dembski to Union University. Through a generous grant from the American Scientific Affiliation funded by the John Templeton Foundation, we were able to bring Paul Nelson and Jay Budziszewski to Union. These men graciously allowed us time alone to interview them on the question of design. As a result, we chose to attend the Chicago meeting to hear a different voice on design. We experienced the same courtesy in conversation with Barbour, Gingerich, and Hefner.

The two meetings seemed to be striving toward different objectives. The Concordia meeting seemed to strive toward offering compelling evidence that the universe can be explained only in terms of intelligent design and the existence of an intelligent Designer. The intelligent design movement is concerned that people believe in God as the cause of the universe and everything in it. They hope to demonstrate the relationship between God and nature through traditional scientific empiricism. Their argument is with naturalists who do not believe such a Being exists.

The Chicago meeting seemed to strive toward identifying alternative ways of reconciling modern scientific understandings of nature with the existence of a Creator. Besides a more traditional theism of Gingerich and an interest in process by Barbour, the Chicago group also heard a feminist perspective from Mary Hunt and an interfaith perspective from Ghulam-Haider Aasi. To a certain degree, the Chicago meeting reflected a concern for the implications of design for people of faith. Both Hunt and Hefner spoke in terms of how people will respond to the world in which they live. Hunt voiced a concern for balance in the cosmos, whereas Hefner argued for thinking of one's place in the "project" that makes up the cosmos. Another theme became apparent in the course of the four-day conference. Participants seemed reluctant to think of God as a designer because design suggested a finished product. A finished product suggested a limit to human freedom. The eighteenth-century versions of the design argument sought to explain the design of the universe in determinate terms that corresponded to Newtonian physics. We now see that at least one stream of theologians and scientists want any view of design to reflect a quantum view of indeterminacy. It is the old problem of tying theology too closely to a replaceable scientific interpretation that may slip out of fashion and take the theology with it.[1]

The two conferences represent a snapshot of the diverse perspectives one encounters when thinking about the universe as a place that bears evidence of design. The two conferences do not even exhaust the major positions found within traditional Christianity, much less the major religions of the world. The Reformed tradition, which has played such a significant role in Western culture and American society in particular, has never regarded "proofs" for the existence of God favorably. The attempt to provide empirical evidence for God meets as much resistance from a good Calvinist as it does from a good naturalist. Karl Barth, the Swiss neo-orthodox theologian who had such an influence on American Protestant theology in the twentieth century, stood squarely in the Reformed tradition. The success of neo-orthodoxy explains in part the resistance to the brand of natural theology that the intelligent design movement explores.

This book does not propose to break new ground so much as it hopes to make some established pathways clear. We expect our audience will primarily be drawn from Christians who take an interest in the relationship of modern science to their biblical faith. Agnostics and atheists may read the book. People of other religious faiths or people with a nontraditional view of Christianity may read the book. By and large, however, we expect most of our readers will share a broad though common faith with different denominational and theological expressions. We write from the perspective of faith. Not only do we believe that the universe was designed, but we also know the Designer. How compelling is the evidence, however, for someone who does not know the Designer? Can someone come to know the Designer by observing the design? Does the evidence compel only one conclusion about the origin of the design?

This book explores why the notion of the design of the universe suddenly reappeared at the end of the twentieth century after its supposed demise at the hands of Darwinian naturalism. The first three chapters of the book explore the different ways in which people have considered design over the last three thousand years or so. While the brief study is not exhaustive, it does provide a condensed overview of many of the major positions that have influenced the course of thought in the West. We mention briefly how different religions and philosophies have thought about design. We then explore how philosophical views have influenced both the theology and the science of the West.

Chapters four through six explore three major realms of scientific study in which major breakthroughs have provided renewed speculation on design.

The chapters explore cosmology, math and physics, and chemistry and biology. In the course of this survey, we introduce the new terminology of the design discussions: anthropic principles, irreducible complexity, and specified complexity. The discussion suggests that science has been quite successful at describing processes, but has failed at explaining origins.

We have attempted to keep the technical discussions to a minimum. Unfortunately, it is impossible to discuss this subject without some basic knowledge of the scientific, philosophical, and theological issues at stake. By writing at a basic level, we have failed to give adequate depth to our subject for the well-informed professional. We hope we have succeeded in making the material accessible, however, to those who lack training in these fields. While the molecular biologist may consider our biology section thin, we hope he or she will benefit from an equally thin treatment of the philosophy.

ACKNOWLEDGMENTS

ONE OF THE GREAT pleasures of writing this book has been the many conversations about this subject that we have had with guests at Union University and at meetings elsewhere. In particular, we wish to express our appreciation to Arthur Holmes, Michael Behe, Ian Barbour, William Dembski, Owen Gingerich, Paul Nelson, Robert Russell, John Brooke, Jay Budziszewski, Gayle Woloschak, Alesia Maltz, Mark Noll, John Polkinghorne, Arthur Peacocke, John Albright, Richard Randolph, Harold McKone, and Mil Thompson. We have also relied upon the continuing conversation and insights of our colleagues with whom we teach and work at Union University, notably: Brad Greene, Greg Thornbury, Randall Bush, Wayne Wofford, Michael McMahon, James Huggins, and David Ward. It would be difficult to carry on a writing project of this nature without the support and encouragement of David Dockery, our president, Carla Sanderson, our provost, and Barbara McMillin, our dean. Finally, we express our gratitude to Pam Dennis, who also read the manuscript and offered many stylistic suggestions.

This revised edition of *Designer Universe* came about through the encouragement of Paul Wason of the John Templeton Foundation. We appreciate his interest in our work and the support of the John Templeton Foundation that we have received for our work over the years. It was a pleasure to work with Laura G. Barrett, associate publisher of Templeton Foundation Press, in the development of this revised edition. We also appreciate the help of Natalie Lyons Silver, managing editor at Templeton Foundation Press, for her help during the acquisition process. We wish to express our appreciation to Len Goss, our editor at Broadman & Holman, who first asked us to write the earlier edition of this book as a sequel to the first book we wrote together, *Science and Faith: An Evangelical Dialogue*. This topic is one we would have enjoyed pursuing at length in the earlier book, but space did not permit; therefore, we appreciate the opportunity that Broadman & Holman gave us with the first edition of this book. The title of the first edition was the choice of the publisher, but the title of the revised edition derives its name from the 1994 C. S. Lewis Summer Institute, which had the theme "Cosmos and Creation: Chance or Dance?" It was a pleasure to work again with Jonathan Gillette, who illustrated the book, and Melissa Mann, who burned the CD of our illustrations. Our research could not have been completed without the conscientious aid of Paul Sorrell in the Emma Waters Summar Library of Union University, who secured many rare volumes for us through interlibrary loan. We also appreciate the cheerful work of our student research assistant, Tammy Meyers.

A project of this sort could never be completed in the course of normal business hours. We have taken our work home to our families, who have given us more than support and encouragement. Our wives, Christine Menzel and Mary Anne Poe, have read the manuscript thoroughly and made numerous suggestions for its improvement besides correcting earlier drafts. We could not have completed this project without their presence and interest in the project. We proudly acknowledge their contribution to the book.

Jimmy H. Davis
Harry L. Poe
Jackson, Tennessee
July 27, 2007

CHANCE OR DANCE

1. THE APPEARANCE OF DESIGN

Harry Lee Poe

DURING THE LAST DECADE of the twentieth century, scientists and theologians began to use the word "design" when speaking of the universe. People had used this word or at least this idea to speak of the universe for thousands of years in different parts of the world. Most scientists and theologians in the West, however, had discarded the idea of the design of the universe more than one hundred years earlier. Why, after all this time, has the idea of the design of the universe and everything in it once again come into the conversation of scientists and theologians?

The idea of design provides a way of coming to the idea of God from the back door. The idea of design suggests the existence of a designer. If the universe was actually designed, how did it come to be designed? More importantly for personal beings like people, if the universe was actually designed, who designed it?

It does not take a philosopher, scientist, or theologian to discuss the idea of design. People around the world do it every day. In fact, even when the academic community of scientists and theologians had discarded the idea of design, the overwhelming number of lay people in the West clung to it. The great philosophers of the last twenty-five hundred years, going back to Plato and Aristotle, developed elaborate logical arguments to prove the existence of God by appealing to the idea of design. The average person, however, discusses the same idea without the need for such a carefully thought-out argument.

Plato often used dialogues to present his philosophical arguments. He set the philosophical conversation in the context of a conversation between two people so that he could present both sides of a question and systematically answer the objections to his argument. When most people first encounter the design idea, they hear it in the form of a dialogue. I do not recall how old I was when I first heard the idea of design explained to me, but I clearly recall the terms of the explanation.

"Momma," I asked. "Where did the sky come from?"

"God made the sky," my mother replied.

"Momma," I continued. "Where did the sun come from?"

"God made the sun," my mother replied.

"Momma," I persisted. "Where did the trees come from?"

"God made the trees," my mother patiently answered. "God made everything."

In its simplest and most common form, the idea of design is not an argument to prove the existence of God—it is an explanation of who God is. It assumes the existence of God and proceeds to explain how God relates to everything else. But people talk about the idea in more sophisticated terms in the everyday as well.

Before taking the path that would eventually lead me to write books that deal with theological themes, I had intended to pursue a career in law. In the early 1970s I served for a year as law clerk to Fletcher Mann, a brilliant trial lawyer in South Carolina. He was involved in what was then the largest antitrust suit ever tried in the United States. It involved a large number of textile mills primarily in the South and in Europe. In the midst of the suit, which dragged on for years with hundreds of millions of dollars at stake, Mr. Mann turned to me and mused:

> I remember the most peaceful, serene day I ever spent. It was an early fall day and I was with your parents at your grandmother's mountain house. I was stretched out in that big Pawley Island rope hammock they had on the front porch. The sound of the river rushing over the rocks around three sides of the house was like music. From there I could look straight up the Jones Gap with those mountains in full color on both sides. The temperature was just perfect and the air smelled so sweet and fresh. I remember thinking, on a day like this, how can anyone doubt the existence of a great and good Supreme Being?

The discussion suggests that it is easy to believe in a great, good creator when everything looks beautiful. The discussion seems almost glib, because it ignores those days when the storms rage and everything lies in darkness. What happens to the discussion on those days? The problem of evil, pain, and suffering inevitably raises its head when scientists, theologians, and philosophers discuss the question of design. Notice the context in which Mr. Mann raised the question of design. Everything was not beautiful and sweet smelling. He was living out of a suitcase in Rock Hill, South Carolina, eating a steady diet of motel food, enduring an endless contest of wits with a stable full of high-priced lawyers from New York. The litigation had gone on for years and would go on for years more. It was in the midst of the strife and the darkness that he remembered an experience that became as real as in the moment it occurred.

Since the last paragraph was published in the first edition of this book, Mr. Mann has died. Before he died, however, he took great pleasure in giving copies of this book to his friends. He won the court case, but by the time the book was written, twenty-five years had passed. Both of Fletcher Mann's legs had been amputated and he was waiting to die. Loss of limbs and the impending loss of his life had not diminished in the slightest his sense of awe in the face of the handiwork of God.

Mr. Mann did not raise the question of design to prove the existence of God to me. At that point, the question of design did not involve the theoretical idea of what kind of God exists. Instead, he was reliving the experience of having met the Designer on a balmy fall day in the mountains. It did not matter what might happen on any other day. The Designer penetrated his soul and gave him a peace that he could draw on for the rest of his life. He had experienced the personal implications of the existence of a Designer who relates personally to what he has designed. To that extent, what he had to say was not intended to persuade me or change me. On the other hand, on a lousy fall day in Rock Hill, it did persuade him and change him. The idea of design sometimes has a purely personal quality to it.

When scientists, philosophers, and theologians speak of design, they usually think in terms of a formal proof for the existence of God. They may digress and discuss the possibility of ever proving anything before settling on the idea that they mean the demonstration of a preponderance of evidence that would demonstrate the strongest possible probability that something may be so. The first time I ever heard such a formal proof for the existence of God, it did not come from a Christian theologian, philosopher, or scientist. In fact, it did not come from a Christian at all.

I first heard the design argument for the existence of God from Swami Chinmayananda. He had formerly had a successful law practice in India before his experience of enlightenment during a mountain retreat. The year was 1972; the place, the campus of the University of South Carolina. I chaired the Lectures Series Committee of the University Union, and my committee had agreed to help the Indian students by providing travel expenses to allow the Hindu teacher to visit Carolina and give a lecture. As chair of the committee, I was invited to eat with Swami Chinmayananda and the Indian students. He was a charming and engaging man who spoke with me for several hours. He agreed to give one public lecture for the student body but devoted the rest of his time to the students from India.

He chose as his topic the theme "Why God?" The provocative title was intended to stir interest during that fall election campaign when Nixon and McGovern battled it out. The large lecture hall in Currell College was almost full to hear Swami Chinmayananda explain what he meant by "Why God?" He proceeded to give what I now know to be three of the classic proofs for the existence of God: the argument from first cause, the argument from necessary being, and the argument from design. We will explore these proofs later.

He presented the arguments quite clearly, with wit and contemporary illustrations, but I learned several years later that they were the same arguments Thomas Aquinas had elaborated seven hundred years earlier. These arguments of Thomas Aquinas were the same ones Aristotle had elaborated sixteen hundred years before that. Aristotle, Thomas Aquinas, and Swami Chinmayananda had radically different understandings of God. Aristotle and Swami Chinmayananda did not share the biblical concept of creation held by Thomas Aquinas. Yet, all three found the idea of design compelling. They lived, thought, worked, taught, and wrote in quite different cultures, times, and places. Nonetheless, design was inescapably obvious to them and helped them make sense of their world. In spite of many varied understandings of the nature of the universe and the nature of God, some understanding of design forms an aspect of most of the world's great cultures, past and present.

A WORLD OF VIEWS

People do not always mean the same thing when they speak of design, just as they do not always mean the same thing when they use the word "God." Before exploring why the design argument would reappear after so many thinkers assumed it had been stony cold dead for a hundred years, it may prove helpful to understand how other peoples in different times and places have viewed design.

People living in the West tend to make enormous assumptions about what "everyone knows" or what other people think. In terms of design, people with quite different views of reality have recognized design in nature, yet they have given different accounts of it. Judaism, Islam, and Christianity share a common understanding of why nature might appear to have characteristics of design. The people of these faiths believe that a personal being created all of physical reality with a purpose for all things from beginning to end. The Bible and the Qur'an relate God's relationship to the physical order as its Creator. These three religions have different perspectives on the person of Jesus Christ and the way to salvation, but they agree about God as Creator. Even people in the West who do not have personal faith in God tend at least to have a general awareness of the view of God and creation held by these three great monotheistic religions. While the Christian perspective will be discussed in more detail later, several other religious perspectives will help to illustrate that the idea of design is not simply a culturally derived concept of the West.

Hinduism

As I mentioned earlier, the first person to explain to me the design argument for the existence of God was a Hindu teacher. I did not know much about Hinduism when I heard him speak, but his lecture seems even more fascinating now that I have studied a little about Hinduism. Unlike the three monotheistic religions, Hinduism does not conceive of God as a personal, self-conscious being. Westerners often think of Hinduism as a polytheistic religion in which people believe in many gods. This view is not quite accurate. They do believe in many gods in the sense that they conceive of gods. They do not believe in many gods in the way Christians conceive of God. Instead of the word "god," it may be more helpful to use the Hindu word *Brahman*. Brahman is Absolute Reality. Brahman is everything physical and everything spiritual, because ultimately there is no difference between the physical and the spiritual. These are merely two different expressions of Brahman. Whereas Christians, Jews, and Muslims believe that people are made in the *image* of God, Hindus believe that people *are* God or an expression of Brahman.

Behind what we think of as the objective, physical reality of a person or a tree or a solar system or a pebble lies the Absolute Reality of Brahman. The person, the solar system, the pebble, and the tree all have the same ultimate nature as expressions of Brahman. They have no separate and individual identity distinct from one another. The great Jewish philosopher Martin Buber made a significant contribution to Western thought in his discussion of the "I–it" relationship. Buber's distinctions between subject and object are ultimately meaningless in Hindu thought. Hindu thought has a different expression to describe the unity of all things as expressions of Brahman: "That thou art."

Walk barefoot along a sandy beach on a summer afternoon with the sun beating hot upon your face, the waves of the ocean crashing on the shore, a gentle breeze breaking the heat, and a sea gull screeching overhead. Feel the sand between your toes. That thou art. See the glare of the sun millions of miles away. That thou art. Hear the waves as they scatter their spray. That thou art. Feel the coolness of the breeze. That thou art. Watch the gull as it darts and dives for a fish. Thou art both the gull and the fish! All is One. All is Brahman.

Though all is One, not every expression of Brahman has experienced the enlightenment necessary to realize its own unity with Brahman. Every form of life, whether human, animal, or plant, undergoes an endless series of rebirths or reincarnations as other forms of life unless the series of births is broken by enlightenment. The law of Karma determines future destiny. According to the law of Karma, the form of one's next birth is determined by one's behavior in the present life. Whatever one experiences in the present, whether good or evil, pleasure or suffering, is the consequence of actions in a previous existence.

The ultimate goal of Hindu faith comes in freedom from the endless series of death and reincarnation. Freedom may come by any of three different routes: *Karma Marga* (Path of Duties), *Jnana Marga* (Path of Knowledge), and *Bhakti Marga* (Path of Devotion).[1] The *Karma Marga* involves keeping the rituals and ceremonies, dietary laws, and ethical values of the Hindu tradition. The *Jnana Marga* provides an intellectual approach to breaking the series of reincarnations through attaining the bliss that comes through realizing the illusion of physical reality. A variety of "schools" or systems of thought have developed through the centuries to help people experience the bliss that comes in knowing one's identity with Brahman. By far the most popular of the three ways to liberation, however, is the *Bhakti Marga*. This path involves personal devotion to one of the thousands of gods or deities known to Hinduism.

If all is One, then how do Hindus think of the deities whom they worship and adore? The philosophical understanding of the unity of all things as the Absolute Reality is a fairly recent aspect of Hinduism, perhaps no more than two thousand years old. By comparison, one might think of the incarnation of God in Christ as a fairly recent aspect of Abrahamic faith. The previous stories of the deities continued as an aspect of Hinduism after the understanding of deity changed. Rather than an earlier understanding of separate or independent beings, modern Hinduism would tend to see the deities as the expression of Brahman in purest form, not subject to the Karma of reincarnation.

Besides the 330 million household deities to whom Hindus may show devotion, three great deities receive the greatest honor and attention: Brahma, Shiva, and Vishnu. Veneration of these gods predates the Arayan invasion of northern India thirty-five hundred years ago, which resulted in one of the earliest periods of development in Hindu thought. Shiva is known as the Destroyer, Vishnu is known as the Preserver, and Brahma is known as the Creator. Of the three, Brahma receives the least attention, though he is probably the most ancient of the deities.[2]

As Creator, Brahma might be thought of as the most obsolete or unnecessary of the deities in modern Hindu thought. In ancient times, the epics and other sacred writings described the creation of the physical world in varied ways. Deities of the Vedic or early Hindu period included Varuna, the sky god, who created the universe and maintains it by ritual order. Agni, the god of fire, produced humanity and sustains creation as mediator between humanity and the universe. As Hinduism embraced the idea of the One, the universe came to be viewed as the result of a human sacrifice by Purusha, from whom all the gods came.[3] In time, the view developed that all reality emanates from the One. The view that all reality consists of a single unity is referred to as "monism."

From this brief and superficial overview, we can see that Hinduism as a whole and individual Hindus may tolerate a wide-ranging understanding of deity. Within this wide tradition, what did Swami Chinmayananda mean when he used the design argument to prove the existence of God within a Hindu understanding of God? In a sense, he argued for design without an actual creation! Here we should distinguish between the universe as the creation of God and as the expression of Brahman. Creation implies an object separate from the Creator. Creation is an artistic idea that takes different forms. We may think of the artistic expression of the potter who fashions a lump of clay into a beautiful vessel in which the mind of the artist skillfully takes shape in physical form. We may also think of the creative expression of the dancer who moves his or her own body gracefully into a thousand different shapes before the dance is done. The monotheism of Judaism, Islam, and Christianity involves faith in the potter, while the monism of Hinduism involves faith in the dancer. The pot and the potter are separate, but the dance and the dancer are inseparable.

Observations. In the discussion about evidence of design of the universe, we do well to recognize that different groups in the conversation mean different things when they say "design." Just as "God" means different things to people of different religions, "design" means different things to different groups. It is not merely a matter of different religious perspectives. An engineer will understand design in a way different from that of a biologist. Design may have a mechanical quality or a more artistic quality. It may mean a sense of order or purpose. It may mean a recognizable pattern. As we explore the question, we will begin to see that design itself may be as elusive as God.

A-theistic Religions

Two great religions have come out of Hinduism that step beyond the monism of Hinduism. Buddhism and Jainism both deny the existence of a creator god and Absolute Being. While Hinduism allows for the continuing adoration of and devotion to individual gods, most forms of Buddhism and Jainism deny the existence of these beings. Worship and prayer to such deities serves no purpose. The path to liberation from the endless cycle of birth, death, and rebirth comes through the denial of the individual self, usually through an ascetic regimen. More important, however, is the ethical approach to life, known as the eight-fold path in Buddhism and the twelve vows of Jainism.

Like Hinduism, Buddhism and Jainism have a major concern for how one escapes the law of Karma and the otherwise endless repetition of death and reincarnation. Although both Buddhism and Jainism deny the existence of a god in the sense of a self-conscious, self-expressive, personal supreme being, they have different views of the nature of reality. Jainism acknowledges a dualism of matter and mind (or soul).[4] Buddhism, on the other hand, acknowledges only soul and denies the validity of differentiation between anything. Whereas the Hindu would acknowledge the underlying unity of all things with the statement "That thou art," Buddhism would deny the distinction of anything. Buddhism might say, "That isn't and neither are you!"

Observations. In such a religious context, what implications for design appear? Without a creator, does it make sense to speak of design? Though we usually think of design as relating to how things began, it also concerns how things operate and where they are going. The concern of Jainism, Buddhism, and Hinduism with the law of Karma is a concern for how moral life operates and what will be the ultimate end of people. These religions assume the operation of Karma as a fundamental principle of reality.

Mahavira, the founder of Jainism, believed in both the material and spiritual realms. He believed that the way to escape the cycles of birth and death lay in mortification of the flesh, or extreme asceticism. Gautama, the founder of Buddhism, denied the existence of the material world. He further denied the existence of individual souls. Escape from the cycle of birth and death came intellectually, since no flesh actually exists that one may mortify. In both cases, these religions believe in a moral law that operates throughout all reality. This moral law or order represents design, though it is interpreted within these religious traditions as design without a designer.

Jainism and Buddhism include multiple groups with variations of these beliefs. These religions also have popular forms that differ from the traditional formulations. In both communities, popular religion provides for prayer and the recognition of deities! One must consider whether this situation suggests a projection of the personal on the universe, as Freud suggested, or a recognition of the personal at the heart of the universe.

Religions of Harmony

Taoism of China and Shintoism of Japan both strive for harmony in this life. This goal contrasts with the ultimate concern for escape from life implied by the religions of Karma. Both religions co-mingle freely with Chian or Zen Buddhism. In antiquity, both China and Japan had accounts for the divine origins of things, but these religions have a greater concern for the state of the cosmos than for the origin of the cosmos. The pragmatism of Confucian philosophy also influenced how the two religions developed to stress national character.

The ancient religion of China understood that deities filled the whole cosmos. Shang Ti ruled as the supreme deity, but many other deities were associated with natural forces and physical locations. These deities required propitiation in order to insure prosperity, success, wealth, health, and all that might imply harmony within all dimensions of life and the cosmos. Deities included both helpful and harmful spirits. Around 1000 BC, Chinese thinkers developed a new way of conceiving the relationship between these two opposite groups of spirits known as *yin* and *yang*. The yin represents the dark forces and the yang represents the light forces. Tao came to involve the complex interrelationship of opposite forces at all levels of nature throughout the cosmos. By extension, the yin represents the dark, evil, negative, wet, cold, passive, and feminine principle of the cosmos, whereas the yang represents the light, good, positive, dry, warm, active, and male principle of the cosmos.

People at all levels of society had relative degrees of status or spiritual power. The emperor had the greatest *te*, or the greatest concentration of inherent virtue and power; therefore, he played a crucial role in maintaining the balance or harmony of the opposite forces by sacrificing to the deities. Because the ancestors of the emperor dwelt with Shang Ti, their influence in heaven was considered critical to the maintenance of harmony. The practice of ancestor worship developed with the emperors who sacrificed to their ancestors and consulted them for advice. By 1000 BC, ancestor worship had become a common feature of Chinese religion for people at all levels of society.

Tao involves a way of behaving as well as an understanding of the forces behind all phenomena. Tao has a philosophical side that approximates Western ideas of naturalism and relativism. Yet, the religious side of Tao makes it quite different. The religious side of Tao strives for communication between people and the supernatural powers. Unlike the religions of Karma, Tao describes a universe of ceaseless mutation and development in which people experience an infinite process of transformation.

Like ancient China, ancient Japan conceived of a cosmos filled with deities. But it also regarded many other things as possessing a superior power called *kami*. *Kami* is a quality found throughout the cosmos that elicits awe and wonder, fear and dread, and attraction. Rudolf Otto commented on these same qualities in *The Idea of the Holy*, which we will examine later. The presence of *kami* accounts for the origin of heaven and earth but, more importantly, for the origin of Japan. Originally a single mass, heaven and earth were separated by something like a reed-shoot, which grew up between them and caused them to split. The reed-shoot was then transformed into one of the first *kami*. The first man and woman came about by spontaneous generation. The Japanese islands formed from the coagulation of drops of water that fell from the spear of the *kami* Izanagi after he had dipped it in the ocean of chaos.

Izanagi and his consort Izanami descended to Japan and had many *kami* offspring who continue to be worshiped in Japan. In addition, Izanagi and Izanami produced the sun goddess Amaterasu. Because of the disorder present in the islands of Japan, Amaterasu sent her grandson Ninigi to rule Japan. His great-grandson succeeded him as the first human emperor of Japan, from whom the present emperor is descended in unbroken line. Other *kami* produced the *samurai* class within Japanese society, as well as all other Japanese people.

Concern for harmony and balance that *kami* ancestors might help assure provided a logical connection for the introduction of ancestor worship from China along with Confucianism. With the introduction of Buddhism from China, the *kami* were recognized as manifestations of Buddha.

Observations. The concept of harmony, balance, and order (as opposed to chaos) stressed by Taoism and Shintoism correspond to the concept of design. In this sense, the two religions recognize a fundamental pattern of order despite the presence of competing forces. The occurrence of disequilibrium does not negate the concept of harmony. Instead, it heightens the recognition of the presence of that harmony. Disaster does not mean that the world does not operate according to a prescribed "Way" or Tao.

Dead Religions

Some religions that thrived for a thousand years or more have since died out. The three great religious systems of the West gradually faded as their adherents adopted the monotheism of Christianity. To the south of the Mediterranean Sea, ancient Egypt had a flourishing civilization for thousands of years, along with an elaborate religion that faded after the conquest of Egypt by Alexander and later by Rome. Long before Christianity became a legal religion in the empire, Egypt became a center of Christian faith. To the east of the Mediterranean Sea, ancient Greece enjoyed a rich civilization and religion for a thousand years before its conquest by Rome. The Hellenistic world also became an early center for Christianity in spite of periodic persecution by the Romans. To the north, the Celtic religion of Gaul, Germany, and the British Isles emerged from prehistory. Yet, these fierce tribes abandoned their ancient religion and embraced the preaching of poor, wandering monks. Each of these ancient religions viewed the world as having an intentional, divine origin.

The Egyptians believed that Ptah ordered the world to arise from the mud after first conceiving it in his heart. Egyptian religion, however, involved a collection of deities from two kingdoms. Thus, the Egyptians had other stories of creation. Atum, the hill god, emerged from the primordial waters so common in ancient stories of creation. To him was attributed the creation of air, sky, earth, and dew. From him descended the gods and goddesses of these domains. His son Shu became the air god and his daughter Tefnut became the dew goddess. Their son Geb became god of the earth and their daughter Nut, goddess of the sky. From this brother and sister came Osiris and Isis.

The ancient Greeks believed that all of creation came out of one shapeless mass known as Chaos, within which the seeds of future things slept. What would become earth, sea, and sky lay mixed together in Chaos until separated by one of the ancient gods.[5] By another account, Earth (Gaea), Darkness (Erebus), and Love (Eros) were the first beings to emerge from Chaos. Love came from the egg of Night that floated on Chaos.[6] Love produced life through the use of his torch and arrows. Reus, the grandson of Earth (Gaea), fashioned people from the ashes of the Titans, whom he destroyed with thunderbolts.[7] By another account, the Titans Prometheus and Epimetheus were assigned the responsibility for making man. It was left to Zeus to make woman, who was intended as a curse for man or as a blessing, according to two different stories.

The Norse versions are the best known of the Celtic accounts of the origin of the world. The brothers Odin (Woten), Vili, and Be made the Earth from the body of the giant Ymir, whom they slew. With his blood they made the seas, with his bones they made the mountains, with his hair they made trees, with his skull they made the heavens, and with his brains they made storm clouds. Midgard (middle earth) was made with Ymir's eyebrows, and this realm became the dwelling place of people. Before heaven and earth were made, there was a bottomless pit and a world of mist in which flowed a fountain that fed twelve rivers. These rivers froze not far from the fountain and filled the pit with ice. South of the world of mist lay the world of light, which blew a warm wind to melt the ice. The vapors from the melting ice formed a cloud from which the frost giant Ymir, his children, and his cow sprang. The great cow Audhumbla licked the ice for nourishment. As the cow licked the ice one day, the head of a man appeared. She kept licking until the whole man appeared, who was actually a god. He took one of the giants as his wife and from their union came Odin and his brothers. The gods made man from an ash tree and woman from an elder tree.[8]

While Midgard was home to people, Asgard was home to the gods, Jotunheim was home to the giants, and Niffleheim was home to the dwarves. The Celtic peoples believed that the day would come when all of the world would be destroyed along with the gods. After that, however, the hidden and remote Alfadur (the Almighty) would make a new heaven and earth free of misery.[9]

Observations. These ancient and geographically isolated religions have remarkably similar styles in spite of the differences in content. They all contain a close identification between deities and natural phenomena. One may wonder if the ancients actually thought of the deities as the natural phenomenon itself (the sun, the sea, the earth, the storms) or as the being that exercised control over that aspect of nature. All three religions have views of nature that suppose design, but not necessarily creation. Sometimes the present world is fashioned out of something that already exists.

Monotheistic Religions

The three great monotheistic religions of Judaism, Christianity, and Islam share a common understanding of the origin of the world with respect to design. Followers of these faiths believe in one eternal Supreme Being who created all things. Western culture uses the generic term "God" to refer to the Creator, but the holy books of these three faiths use many names to speak of God. God spoke the cosmos, which began with a chaotic state, into existence. God ordered the chaos, however, by dividing it into the fundamental elements of light (fire), heaven (air), earth, and water. He then ordered these to bring forth the various forms of life. Finally, God made humans in his own image.

The problem of pain, suffering, or disharmony that so concerns all of the religions we have examined arose because of the human dissatisfaction with its place in the order of the cosmos. The knowledge of God came to Christians and Muslims through Judaism and the Law and the Prophets of ancient Israel. From an oral tradition as well as from its final written form stretching over a thousand years, the Bible makes clear that God not only planned and created the universe, but also that he remains intimately involved and concerned with the affairs of people. As such, God has a moral expectation of the behavior of people that conforms to a plan for humanity.

Christians, Jews, and Muslims believe that people have one life to live, and then they face the judgment of God. People are judged according to their conformity to the moral standards of God. For Jews, people attain eternal life with God by keeping the law as given to Moses and interpreted by the

rabbis. For Muslims, people attain eternal life with God by keeping the law
as given to Muhammad. For Christians, people attain eternal life through
receiving the Holy Spirit of God into their lives by faith in Jesus Christ,
who then transforms them. By receiving God's Spirit in this life, they avoid
the judgment of God and are counted righteous because of the righteous-
ness of Christ that the Holy Spirit applies to them.

Observations. The monotheistic religions make a sharp distinction between God and nature, of which people are a part. They also distinguish
between God and all other spiritual beings, of which there are many. God
made all spirits, life, and the material world originally from nothing instead
of from himself. Besides an intentional creation of the material world, God
also has a moral plan for the world and a purpose for people. Thus, nature
is an expression of the creative mind of God, but it is not God.

PHILOSOPHICAL PERSPECTIVES

In addition to the religious perspectives on the concept of design, many
important philosophical perspectives have addressed this issue. In most cultures, the areas of philosophy, science, and religion are indistinguishable.
They represent interrelated aspects of a unitary outlook and approach to life.
This can sometimes cause confusion for the modern Western observer, who
may confuse the science of another culture for an aspect of its religion. Philosophy may also be confused for religion. For instance, statements in the
Bible about the movement of the heavenly bodies represent ancient Hebrew
science rather than the faith of the Hebrew people.

The fragmentation of science, philosophy, and religion began in ancient
Greece with Plato and Aristotle and other philosophers. These two philosophers in particular had a profound influence on the development of Christian theology and modern science, even though they were not Christians.
What they had to say about design had a direct relation to how Christians
would talk about design for centuries. They had entirely different perspectives on reality from each other, yet they both had a concept of the design
of the universe.

Plato

Plato studied under Socrates, who believed in only one God, which put him
at odds with the traditional polytheism of Athens where he lived. Socrates
was condemned to death for corrupting the morals of the youth of Athens

by his perceived atheism during a famous trial at the court of the Aereopagus on Mars Hill. Plato followed Socrates in his attitude toward the ancient gods, though he was much more careful in how he articulated his views. He was an idealist, which meant that he believed ideas took priority over the physical. Ideas were more real to him than their actual physical counterparts. He believed that all actual physical things correspond to an ultimate and absolute ideal upon which all examples of that thing are based. For instance, for all the many chairs in the world, he believed that only one perfect ideal chair existed in the realm of the ideal for which all the actual chairs are vague copies or corruptions.

Plato's concept of ideals or universals relates directly to his conception of the design of the world of experience. He explored this issue in *Timaeus*, which he wrote in the form of a dialogue between Socrates and his student Timaeus. In the course of the dialogue, he introduces the argument of first cause as a means to discuss the issue of design. He acknowledges several questions that need an answer. Was the universe created? If not, how could it exist? Has the universe always existed or did it have a beginning? In this regard, he makes a distinction between "that which always is and has no becoming; and . . . that which is always becoming and never is."[10] Put more simply, he distinguished between what never changes (that which always is and has no becoming) and what does change (that which is always becoming and never is). The Demi-urge is the being who mediates between the external ideals and the physical world of change.

The visible, tangible, material world corresponds to Plato's world of becoming. The physical world is in a constant state of change. For this reason, it is always *becoming* something different from what it was. Because it always changes, it never *is* or it never reaches a stopping point at which it is complete. The world of ideals, however, is a world that the senses cannot apprehend. It is not tangible; neither does it change. The ideals are perfect and complete. Plato argues that things that change or *become* require a cause. On the other hand, things that do not change are eternal; therefore, they do not require a cause. Based on the idea of a first cause that set change and becoming in motion, Plato argued that the physical world of change had been created. On the same basis, however, he argued that the changeless world of ideals had eternal existence and had not been created.

Plato's understanding of design proceeds from his understanding of the changing and the unchanging. He argued that in crafting a world, the Demi-urge looked to a pattern that was eternal and perfect because it did not change. In this sense, the physical world of change is the *image* of the eternal, unchanging world of *ideal*. The ideal provided the pattern or design by which the Demi-urge crafted the physical world.

In other places, Plato discussed such ideas as goodness. For purposes of this dialogue, he assumed the values he argued for elsewhere. Because the Demi-urge is good, he would only craft the most perfect possible world. Because intelligence is better than unintelligence, and since intelligence is only present in soul, the Demi-urge crafted the universe with an intelligent soul. To be the fairest of all possible worlds, for Demi-urge would not craft less than the fairest, there can be only one universe. Plato spoke of the universe in relation to the Ideals in the same way that the New Testament speaks of Christ in relation to God: the "only-begotten."[11]

Plato argued that the universe, a *living* creature, came about by design.[12] All of its features are intentionally so for specific reasons, the logic of which he spelled out. For instance, it was made in the form of a globe with a smooth surface. It is a globe since that shape represents the most perfect of figures, and it is smooth because it has no need of eyes, ears, arms, feet, or any other appendages.

Because the world he crafted experiences change, the Demi-urge designed a way for it to bear the image of eternity. This moving image of eternity is called "time." Time does not exist in eternity because time relates to motion and change. In eternity, the ideals are all at complete rest; therefore, they do not experience time. They have no previous state (past) nor any subsequent state (future).

Most of what Plato had to say represents classical philosophy, but it also includes the necessary intersection with theology and science. Plato dealt with the most current science of his day, which involved astronomy and geometry, to describe the motions of the heavenly bodies in relation to the great globe of the universe (which to him was little more than the inner solar system and the patterns of the constellations). His description of the relationship of the Ideals to the universe he conceived of as possessing a soul represents Plato's speculative theology.

By Plato's account, the Demi-urge crafted the gods of ancient Greece just as he created their physical counterparts in the heavens. Plato's understanding of the Greek gods would correspond more to the biblical idea of angels, in that they stand on a different plane between the Ideals and humans and are crafted, while the Ideals are eternal. The Demi-urge also created a star for each man he crafted. First, he separated the soul of each man from the soul of the universe. Then he implanted each male soul into a physical body. By the laws of destiny, each man who lived well would return to dwell in his appointed star at death. Those who failed in life would be born a second time as a woman. Failing in the form of a woman, humans would continue rebirth as lower and lower forms of animals until they overcame by reason their failure and ascended by further rebirth.

Observation. Plato did not write his argument to prove the existence of God or design. He and his audience would have assumed these in some form. He used the assumption of design to argue for the priority of mind over matter, ideal over image. In so doing, he argued that the Demi-urge did not create out of nothing. Rather, the Demi-urge crafted an ordered (designed) universe out of the chaotic preexistent elements.

Aristotle

Aristotle studied under Plato, but he developed an approach to philosophy entirely different from that of Plato. Plato placed his stress on the world of eternal unchanging perfect ideals, on the mind as the point of contact with the ideals, and on reason as the more reliable form of knowledge. Aristotle, on the other hand, placed his emphasis on the physical world that people know through their senses. This is a remarkable shift, since Plato had taught that our senses give us only imperfect knowledge of an imperfect world that he regarded as opinion.

The question of design arises in Aristotle's book on *Metaphysics* in his discussion of *substance*. Because of his interest in the physical world and the reliability of sensory knowledge, he explored what made up the physical world and where it came from. "Substance" is the term Aristotle used to describe what makes up the world of experience. An apple has substance, but my idea of an apple does not. Substance is subject to change. As we have seen with Plato, accounting for change was a major philosophical problem for the ancient world.

Change involves two contrary states and a third thing. The contrary states are of four kinds: 1) *thisness* or existence, which consists of beginning and destruction; 2) *quantity*, which consists of increase and decrease; 3) *affection*, which consists of alteration from this to that; and 4) *motion*, which consists of movement from here to there. Aristotle argued that the contraries do not change but represent the criteria for recognizing the change. The change occurs in the third thing, what Aristotle calls "matter." The contrary state of beginning never changes to destruction. Furthermore, beginning does not continue. It eventually becomes destruction. The apple, on the other hand, experiences both contrary states, changing all the time. All things that change have matter.

The philosophical question behind all of this discussion relates to the origin of things. Where did the matter come from? What causes it to change? Aristotle believed that the elements present in things provided causes, but he also believed some external or moving cause was involved. He identified different elements and different kinds of moving causes for different things, but this only moved the question back further. What was the original cause that set all things in motion? Aristotle believed with Plato that an unmoved mover set things in motion. The unmoved mover is Aristotle's conception of God.

The unmoved mover, however, is not a creator. Aristotle believed the substance of the universe to be eternal. The unmoved mover merely set it in motion. The unmoved mover, as the greatest good and most beautiful thing, thinks only of itself. The unmoved mover acts upon the cosmos in bringing about the first motion in the same way that the object of thought acts upon the thinker. Because God is in such a state of goodness and beauty, he compels the motion of the universe in response to him in the same way that something or someone beautiful might attract a person's attention. In responding to the excellence of God, the universe moves with a circular motion because the circle is the closest that substance can come to emulating the goodness of God. Aristotle's God might be said to set things in motion quite unintentionally. Though profoundly self-conscious while spending eternity thinking of himself, he or it has no awareness of anything else.

Observations. Other than getting the ball rolling, Aristotle's God serves little function. Once substance was set in motion, God could retire to think about himself while the eternal universe took over. In this view, design appears as the eternal ordered patterns of motion and principles that govern substance in response to the goodness of God.

Conclusion

The concept of design with respect to nature has appeared around the world in past and present cultures. This brief survey has looked at only a few examples, chosen primarily because of their contact or interaction with other cultures. This study could easily have included perspectives from the great cultures of Central and South America. This issue concerned both the Aztecs and the Incas. A study that focused only on the views of the many indigenous cultures of North America would prove highly interesting. Sub-Saharan Africa has also contributed a rich array of perspectives on the concept of design in nature. What they all have in common with the views briefly discussed here is the perception of design, order, purpose, or balance within nature.

We have also seen that different cultures have recognized different things about design. For some, design has to do with the ordered movement of the heavenly bodies, the cycle of the seasons, and the passage of time. For some, design has to do with the presence of underlying principles for living or moral law. For some, design is understood as purpose, where the end goal rather than the beginning of the process takes priority. For some, design means that the appearance of things suggests they result from intentional craftsmanship. For some, design involves the harmony and balance of nature.

We have seen that however design is conceived by different cultures, it appears as a basic assumption of the worldview from which it comes. People assume it as self-evident truth. Furthermore, it does not serve as proof for the existence of God. Where it is discussed in relation to God, it tends to be used to explore the question of what kind of God exists and what kind of universe exists.

In the religions concerned with Karma and in the monotheistic religions, design has great implications for the ultimate goal of things. The law of Karma is seen to operate with rules of morality designed to move humanity toward an ultimate goal of union with Brahman. Christianity, Judaism, and Islam recognize the law of God as the standard by which people are judged. These three religions view history as moving toward an ultimate end when those judged righteous will dwell with God forever, whereas those judged unrighteous will be expelled to outer darkness forever.

This brief survey provides a picture of how things stood a thousand years ago. Since then, the development of modern science and the secularization of Western society have resulted in the separation of science, philosophy, and theology in the West. This fragmentation of knowledge has led to a general view that these disciplines have nothing to say to each other. Their different methodologies and theories of knowledge certainly reinforce the idea that they have nothing to contribute to each other's understanding of the world.

Despite the pervasive perception all over the world of the presence of design in nature, the idea of design has been viewed with profound skepticism by the intellectual community in the West since the time of Charles Darwin. Design has generally been regarded as a code word for Christianity, though, as we have seen, it is one of those rare features of faith common to virtually all religions. At the close of the twentieth century, however, a group of scientists, philosophers, and theologians once again began exploring the relevance of the idea of design when speaking of the cosmos. This time, the discussion is not merely about design but about *intelligent design*. This time, the discussion involves a serious examination of the complex structures of life, the cosmic context in which life has emerged, and probability theory. Before exploring new developments in the intelligent design argument, however, we will examine how the idea of design changed from an assumption of faith to an intellectual argument for faith and the role this argument played in the secularization of the West.

2. THE DESIGN ARGUMENT

Harry Lee Poe

I N THE FIRST FEW centuries after the resurrection of Christ, the Hebrew tradition of divine revelation and the Greek tradition of philosophy began to mingle. It had begun to happen among the learned Jewish scholars in the years prior to the birth of Christ. Especially among the Jews of the Diaspora who settled in the great centers of learning like Alexandria, Greek thought came to play an important part in the Jewish understanding of Scripture. Philo of Alexandria (20 BC–AD 40) stands out as one of the greatest thinkers of his day. One of his exercises involved reconciling Plato's understanding of God and creation found in *Timaeus* with the biblical understanding of God and creation.

Philo found Plato's concept of an eternal God who existed alone and then brought the world into existence compatible with biblical teaching. He also found the nonphysical existence of this God compatible with biblical teaching. The problem lay in Plato's understanding that in addition to this God, eternal ideas existed. Philo could not accept eternal ideas that existed alongside and independently of God. He reconciled the problem by making the eternal ideas the thoughts of God, thus eliminating their independent existence but retaining their eternal existence.

This Alexandrian philosophical tradition entered Christian theology through Clement of Alexandria (d. 215?) and his pupil Origen (c. 182–c. 251). Clement sought to interpret Christianity through Hellenistic philosophy as Philo had done for Judaism. He saw the philosophy of the Greeks as the corollary to the law of the Jews. Most strongly influenced by Platonic and Stoic philosophy, Clement had less interest in the physical earthly life of Jesus than in the eternal *Logos*. Origen followed Clement's approach and developed a complete theological system that employed an allegorical interpretation of Scripture in order to bring the Bible and philosophy into harmony. His work gave theology scientific standing by the standards of the day as he sought to demonstrate that philosophy could serve as the hand-maiden of Christianity.

Origen's scheme relied heavily on Platonic concepts. He viewed the spiritual world as the "real" world, while the physical world merely pro-vided a context for punishment and salvation. This scheme necessarily made the physical world of less interest to Origen, who conceived of major events as taking place in the spiritual realm. Following Plato, he believed that all people preexisted in the spiritual world where sin origi-nally occurred and that they took on physical form in proportion to their sin. The least sinful are the angels whose bodies are the stars. The most sinful are the demons who inhabit depraved bodies. While this scheme worked well with Platonic philosophy, it represented a major departure from the Jewish and Christian understanding of creation and the worth of the physical world.

Not all Christian theologians embraced philosophy as eagerly as did Clement and Origen. Tertullian of Carthage (c. 150–c. 225) took quite a different view. He refused to bend Scripture to conform it to a philosophical understanding of reality. He stressed the irreconcilable differences between philosophy and revealed faith in several of his writings. In his *Apology*, he remarked, "So, then, where is there any likeness between the Christian and the philosopher? between the disciple of Greece and of heaven? between the man whose object is fame, and whose object is life?"[1] In *The Prescription against Heretics*, he asked his frequently quoted questions, "What indeed has Athens to do with Jerusalem? What concord is there between the Academy and the church? What between heretics and Christians?"[2]

As time passed, however, theologians found that they could not leave philosophy alone. They lived in a world in which people thought about the world. Because the Christian faith was concerned with the world, theolo-gians had to think about the world as well. Especially in a world in which few people were Christians and Greek philosophy provided the foundation for knowledge and understanding the world, Christian theologians had to discuss faith in dialogue with philosophy. People who converted to Chris-tianity brought their old philosophical thought patterns and categories with them when they converted. Even Tertullian brought Stoic ideas with him when he became a Christian.

SCIENCE AND CREATION

Perhaps the most famous convert out of paganism and Hellenistic philosophy was Augustine of Hippo (354–430). The question of the origin of the physical world formed the critical question in Augustine's conversion; his answer to that question would form the central element of his theology and the theology of the Christian West for the next thousand years. Before becoming a Christian, Augustine had embraced the religious teachings of Manichaeism as well as the philosophical teachings of Platonism and Stoicism as filtered through Neoplatonism. In his pre-Christian quest for meaning, Augustine encountered the struggle between science and faith in the contest between philosophy and Manichaeism.

Though raised by a Christian mother, Augustine embraced the dualistic religion of Manichaeism as a youth. For Augustine, the problem of evil clouded his view of a designed universe. As he looked about, he saw evil scattered throughout the beauty and goodness and truth he desired. He asked himself how a good God could be responsible for an evil world. Manichaeism allowed him to believe in God, goodness, beauty, and truth, while at the same time attributing the evil he saw to another god. Light, goodness, beauty, truth, and spirit belonged to the God he loved. Darkness, evil, ugliness, error, and matter belonged to the god he despised.

The Manichaeans taught that the present universe resulted from an intrusion of evil into the bounds of goodness. People represent a comingling of good and evil. The comingling began when Darkness attacked Light. The five powers of darkness defeated the five powers of light and devoured part of their light. The Father of Greatness sent the Living Spirit to overcome the powers of darkness, whose carcasses became the heavens and the earth. The purest part of the Light that the powers of darkness had devoured became the sun and the moon. The appearance of another messenger of Light induced the Darkness to produce Adam and Eve in the form of the Father of Greatness. Adam and Eve enclosed the remaining Light that the Darkness had available to it. Each subsequent birth further dilutes the Light and advances the power of Darkness. Buddha, Jesus, and Zoroaster were all sent as messengers to bring the knowledge to people that would allow them to escape the bondage of the material world. The final messenger was Mani, who established the Manichaean religion.[3]

The Manichaean religion allowed Augustine to make sense of the existence of evil and good by allowing for two independent, eternal "forces."

The Manichaeans had an explanation for the relationship between the spiritual and the physical, yet they taught that both had "material" substance. The Manichaeans provided an explanation for the origin of the cosmos and for the behavior of the heavenly bodies.

The study of Cicero had produced in Augustine a thirst for wisdom. This thirst, coupled with his training as a rhetorician, led Augustine to ask the critical question about his own religion.[4] After reading how the Greek philosophers could accurately calculate the phases of the moon, the eclipses of the sun and the moon, the equinoxes, and other movements of the heavenly bodies, Augustine began to doubt the Manichaean "fables" about the nature of the cosmos.

The Manichaeans taught that Christ dwelt in the sun, his wisdom dwelt in the moon, and the Holy Spirit dwelt in the air. The Father dwelt in a secret light. The part of the divine Light entrapped in the material world is released by "the elect," those faithful of the Manichaean religion who have attained enlightenment and live the ascetic life. All that passes from the elect in the course of their bodily functions rises upwards as vapor through the air (Holy Spirit) to the sun and moon. The waxing and waning of the moon was explained as the result of the moon receiving souls from matter (waxing) and transporting them like a ship to the sun (waning). The sun served as the final ship to transport souls to their final destination with the Light. Besides being a ship to transport souls, the sun also formed a triangular window in heaven through which the light of Christ shines, no matter that the sun appears to be round. This feature of Manichaeism survives graphically on the reverse side of the Great Seal of the United States, where the all-seeing eye peers through the triangular window with light emanating around it (see fig. 2.1).

Fig. 2.1. The Manichaean belief in the sun as a triangular window

From the philosophers, Augustine learned that the heavenly bodies moved in ordered patterns according to predictable "laws." The philosophers recorded their rules and calculations so that anyone who took the time to learn them could use them with the same results.[5] Mani, the founder of Manichaeism, wrote extensively on this subject, but his teachings seemed to Augustine to be at odds with the scientific calculations of the secular philosophers. He raised his questions with Faustus, a leading bishop of the Manichaeans, but found that Faustus was generally ignorant of the liberal arts and unable to give a satisfactory response. Guided by the best science of his day, the Earth-centered cosmos of Ptolemy, Augustine rejected his religion because it could not reconcile its teachings about the cosmos with the teachings of the philosophers (see figs. 2.2 and 2.3).[6]

Whereas philosophy helped Augustine reject a religion, it did not provide him with a religion that satisfied his spiritual awareness. The problem of evil continued to be his gnawing concern about the nature of the cosmos. A great obstacle for him consisted in his inability to conceive of "spiritual" substance.[7] As a Manichee, Augustine believed that nothing existed unless it had "material" substance. He also believed that evil existed as a material substance that intruded upon the good.[8] Any evil he did occurred because of the evil intrusion or invasion upon him. Though many philosophers, and Platonic philosophers in particular, had a negative view of the physical world, Augustine learned from them a different way of conceptualizing reality.

Until he began to explore Platonic thought, Augustine conceived of God as a great corporeal mass, yet a "vain phantom."[9] He also conceived of evil as another

Fig. 2.2. Ptolemy's scheme for understanding the relationship of the earth, moon, and sun. Adapted from Ptolemy, The Almagest, *Great Books of the Western World, ed. Robert Maynard Hutchins, vol. 16 (Chicago: Encyclopedia Britannica, 1952), 173.*

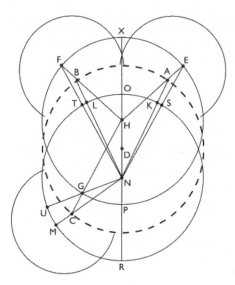

Fig. 2.3. Ptolemy's scheme for understanding the eccentric motion of mars in relation to earth. Adapted from Ptolemy, The Almagest, *Great Books of the Western World, ed. Robert Maynard Hutchins, vol. 16 (Chicago: Encyclopedia Britannica, 1952), 325.*

great corporeal mass, equally infinite with God, but on a smaller scale.[10] Through the philosophers, Augustine came to reject his lingering understanding of evil as a substance that has independent existence of its own. He came to regard corruption as the diminishing or deprivation of something good. Things deprived of all good cease to exist. As long as things exist, they are good because corruption involves damaging that which is good. Evil, therefore, cannot be a substance, otherwise it would be good.[11] With this insight, Augustine revised his view of the universe, the value of physical substance, the nature of evil, and ultimately, the nature of God. He now saw how what he regarded as evil might be present, yet uncreated and not self-existent. Just as he could now envision evil as not "existing" but as describing the deprivation or twisting of God's good creation, he could also envision how God could be spiritual substance. From a corporeal mass that filled part of infinite space not relegated to evil to a god who filled all of infinite space, Augustine finally arrived at a God who transcends all of time and space.[12]

Until this point in his pilgrimage, Augustine paid little attention to Christianity as a viable alternative to Manichaeism. His reading of the Bible had led Augustine to think that Christians believed that God had a body like humans, with arms, hands, eyes, and a mouth with which he spoke. At least the Manichaeans conceived of God as a corporeal mass rather than as a human! Augustine also rejected the idea of an incarnation of God in the

flesh as Jesus, since the flesh would have defiled the Savior according to Manichaean views of the body.[13] The cross had no attraction for him because,
as a Manichee, Augustine believed the crucifixion had no objective reality.
Instead, it served merely as a metaphor for human suffering.

Science and faith coincided for Augustine through the preaching of
Ambrose of Milan. As a teacher of rhetoric, Augustine went to hear Ambrose
because of his reputation as a public speaker. When he heard him expound
on the Bible, however, he came to understand the figurative meaning of the
biblical references to God in human terms.[14] Ambrose's allegorical interpretations of Old Testament texts in particular helped Augustine see that the
Christian faith had a legitimate position, if not a conclusive position.

In the end, Augustine found that the science of his day helped him clarify
his thinking but that it could not take him to God. It could help him think
about God, but it could not provide a way to God. He gladly accepted the
rules that govern the order of the heavenly bodies, and this overwhelming
evidence of order forced him to reconsider his concept of God. Philosophy
brought Augustine just so far, however. Finally, Augustine went beyond the
logic of philosophy, drawn by his attraction to the source of the good, the
true, and the beautiful. From his consideration of evil, he felt drawn to a
consideration of the beautiful: "I was caught up to you by your beauty and
quickly torn away by my weight."[15]

Years after his conversion, Augustine reflected on how much the philosophers had achieved in understanding the operation of creation, yet how
little they knew about the Creator. He marveled at what seemed so evident
to him after his conversion but what eluded the great philosophers. When
Augustine finally became a Christian, his conversion did not come as an
intellectual accomplishment, though his mind had been active throughout
the process. His mind could take him just so far; in the end, he felt God
reaching out to him. He felt as if he were being told to cast himself upon
God, who would catch him.[16]

Augustine considered creation a self-evident truth, yet a truth that people choose not to know. He believed that the heavens and the earth and
all of creation cry out that they were created, but people do not necessarily
receive what is evident.[17] The beauty and goodness of creation, which should
draw people toward God, becomes corrupted by the human mind, which
settles for the lesser good and the lower beauty when it could gain access to
God.[18] He perceived that the human mind, so drawn by the beauty of creation, tends to love the creature more than the Creator.[19] Once turned away

from the Creator, the soul deprived of the greatest good expresses the corruption that the word "evil" describes.[20] For Augustine, the failure of creation to point to God comes not from the inadequacy of the handiwork of
God to proclaim him as the Creator, but in the failure of the human mind
to accept the truth.

Observations. Design played an important part in Augustine's grasp of
God, but for him, the focus came in order and beauty. The design he experienced came as the work of an artist. He always accepted the reality of some
kind of God, but he struggled with the nature of the real God. At one point
as he pursued Manichaeism, he embraced a theology that accepted a form
of design that accounted the physical world as the product of evil infring-
ing on goodness. This approach made sense to him because he struggled
with the problem of evil. How could a good God create a world where evil
appeared at every step?

In his Manichaean solution, Augustine reasoned that God could not have
intimate contact with the physical world without suffering pollution. In
his Christian conclusion, Augustine believed that God must have intimate
contact with the world to account for the very presence of its goodness and
beauty that suffer from corruption.

Though Augustine expressed a lofty understanding of Scripture as revelation from God, he embraced the learning of the philosophers as legitimate knowledge and truth despite its limitations. While the science of the
philosophers could not carry Augustine to God, it could offer insights that
aided in the interpretation of Scripture. In the end, however, knowledge of
God requires something else, because God is Spirit. Perception of the handiwork of God provides evidence that cannot be understood fully until faith
enlivens the heart to perceive what was always clearly evident. Knowledge
of God, however, comes only from God. Augustine's theological perspective of the knowledge of God, with its strong Platonic undertones, would
become the dominant and normative understanding of Western Christianity for eight hundred years.

Proving the Existence of God

In the late Middle Ages, the understanding of design came to have a new
function related to matters of science and faith. Instead of a declaration about
God and the universe, design came to form the critical aspect of an elaborate argument for the existence of God that built upon the ancient Greek

philosophy of Aristotle. In the first part of his greatest work, the *Summa Theologica*, Thomas Aquinas (d. 1274) explored five proofs for the existence of God. These five proofs, however, do not stand alone. They compose elements of a single, unified argument that reflected the unity of creation.

The argument of Thomas may be briefly stated:[21]

1. The first argument relates to motion and change, which was a serious problem for the ancient Greeks. This argument refers to a *Prime Mover* and is based on the idea that objects remain at rest unless set in motion. An object cannot move itself; therefore, whatever moves must be moved by something else. An infinite regression of movers would not be possible, because such a situation would never account for the act of motion that set the potentiality of motion into motion: "Therefore it is necessary to arrive at a first mover which is moved by no other. And this everyone understands to be God."

2. The second argument relates to *efficient cause*. Thomas identified four kinds of cause. *Formal cause* referred to the form or nature of a thing and involved defining what something is, such as a water molecule. *Material cause* referred to the processes and constituents that cause a thing to be, such as the chemical elements that combine to form water molecules. *Final cause* referred to the goal or purpose for which something existed, such as the purpose of water to sustain life. Thomas distinguished between these three understandings of causality and efficient cause. By efficient cause, he meant the agent that caused a phenomenon to be, such as heat, which causes water to evaporate.[22] Thomas argued that every effect must have an efficient cause other than itself. As in the argument related to the Prime Mover, Thomas contended that an infinite regress of causes would not be possible: "Therefore it is necessary to admit a first efficient cause, to which everyone gives the name of God."

3. The third argument relates to possibility and necessity. This argument is also known as the argument from *necessary being*. Thomas argued that everything in nature has the possibility "to be or not to be," as Hamlet would muse. The paper on which these words are printed illustrates how something can be, but because there was a time not too long ago when the page did not exist, it also illustrates how something in nature can *not* be. Since everything cannot be, then

there could have been a time when nothing existed. If such a situation existed, it would be impossible for anything ever to exist, since things only begin to exist because of something that already exists. Thomas then argued for two types of beings: the possible and the necessary. A necessary being, however, would not be necessary if it had its cause in another. This would repeat the problem of an infinite regress of beings that have their necessity caused by another: "Therefore we must admit the existence of some being having of itself its own necessity, and not receiving it from another, but rather causing in others their necessity. This all men speak of as God."

4. The fourth argument relates to the graduation or relative value ascribed to things. Things are referred to as "more" or "less" in relation to some other thing, ultimately to that which is "most" and "least." Something is called "hotter" as it more resembles that which is "hottest." This situation leads us to believe that there must be those superlatives that perfectly exhibit their being. Thomas argued that "the maximum in any genus is the cause of all in that genus; as fire, which is the maximum of heat, is the cause of all hot things. . . . Therefore there must also be something which is to all beings the cause of their being, goodness, and every other perfection. And this we call God."

5. Not until the fifth and final argument does Thomas introduce design in terms of "the governance of all things." Thomas argued from the assumption that all non-intelligent things act toward an end or goal that is evident from their acting to obtain the best result. From this assumption, he concludes that things achieve their end "not by chance, but by design." Thomas further argued that things that lack knowledge could not move toward a goal or purpose unless directed by an intelligent being: "Therefore some intelligent being exists by whom all natural things are ordered to their end; and this being we call God."

Thomas offered these five proofs in response to what he considered the two strongest objections to the question of the existence of God. The first objection relates to the presence of evil in the world. If God is infinite goodness, then no evil should be found in the world. The presence of evil, therefore, provides evidence that God does not exist. The second objection relates to natural causes. This objection states that the supposition of God is not necessary, since all natural phenomena can be reduced to one principle called "nature" and all voluntary phenomena can be reduced to one principle called human reason or will. The five proofs of Thomas are intended to be understood in reference to these two objections to the existence of God rather than as freestanding proofs. The argument has a context related to the problems of evil and naturalism.

After stating his proofs, Thomas drew two conclusions that represent the force of his argument. The first conclusion comes as a restatement of the teaching of Augustine nearly eight hundred years earlier:

> As Augustine says (*Enchir.* xi): "Since God is the highest good, He would not allow any evil to exist in His works, unless His omnipotence and goodness were such as to bring good even out of evil." This is part of the infinite goodness of God, that He should allow evil to exist, and out of it produce good.[23]

The second conclusion demonstrates the relationship between the five proofs:

> Since nature works for a determinate end under the direction of a higher agent, whatever is done by nature must be traced back to God, as to its first cause. So also whatever is done voluntarily must also be traced back to some higher cause other than human reason or will, since these can change and fail. For all things that are changeable and capable of defect must be traced back to an immovable and self-necessary first principle, as was shown in the body of the Article [argument].[24]

A critical element, if not *the* critical element, of the combined arguments of Thomas involves his rejection of an infinite regress. This argument depends on a beginning. Thomas is known as the theologian who introduced the philosophy of Aristotle into Christian theology, but an essential aspect of Aristotle's understanding of the order of the universe lay in his concept of the eternity of the universe. Though Thomas borrowed heavily from Aristotle, especially in terms of his theory of knowledge, Thomas departed from him on several key items of doctrine. He utilized Aristotle's methodology and system to a large extent, but he drew some different conclusions.

Thomas accepted the doctrine of a temporal beginning to the universe by faith based on the traditional understanding of the biblical account of creation in Genesis. He did not, however, believe in the philosophical necessity of a temporal beginning of the cosmos for God to be the one who created out of nothing. On philosophical grounds, he could argue that God eternally created the world out of nothing, which would result in an eternal universe that had a first cause! First cause speaks to origins rather than to time from a philosophical point of view.[25]

This point has important contemporary significance 750 years after Thomas Aquinas because of the current debate over the meaning of time in cosmogony. The big bang theory suggests a beginning to the universe, though it does not necessarily require a beginning of matter. The theological implications of a beginning along the lines suggested by Thomas Aquinas have not escaped Stephen Hawking, who is now exploring a way to account for a finite universe that also has no boundary! Hawking explains the significance of such a view:

> The idea that space and time may form a closed surface without boundary also has profound implications for the role of God in the affairs of the universe. With the success of scientific theories in describing events, most people have come to believe that God allows the universe to evolve according to a set of laws and does not intervene in the universe to break these laws. However, the laws do not tell us what the universe should have looked like when it started—it would still be up to God to wind up the clockwork and choose how to start it off. So long as the universe had a beginning, we could suppose it had a creator. But if the universe is really completely self-contained, having no boundary or edge, it would have neither beginning nor end: it would simply be. What place, then, for a creator?[26]

Observations. Thomas had confidence in the senses to perceive the real world and to communicate that reality to the mind. What people know, they know through their bodily senses. This confidence results in a number of assumptions about nature. Thomas assumes the existence of the physical world; thus, he argues from a position that not all people share. Beyond this assumption, he assumes the order and purpose of the universe. Living in the ordered society of the feudal Christendom of the thirteenth century with its strict hierarchy, order and purpose would have seemed a self-evident truth. In a different society, however, the existence of order and purpose may seem a larger question than the existence of God.

THE REJECTION OF ARISTOTLE

The philosophy of Aristotle came to dominate the scientific and theological thought of the late Middle Ages after Thomas Aquinas used Aristotle to provide the intellectual foundation for his system. Augustine and his preference for Plato fell from his once preeminent position. Thomism and the Thomists who followed Thomas Aquinas soon captured the universities and, through those powerful institutions, gave shape to the intellectual revivals that would blossom as the Renaissance and the Reformation.

John Calvin

In many ways, the Protestant Reformation of the sixteenth century represented a return to Augustinian theology after several centuries of the triumph of Thomism. Far too many dynamics were involved to reduce the Reformation to a simple return to Augustine, but Augustine clearly had a strong influence on the leading reformers. Perhaps the most prominent expositor and popularizer of Augustine was John Calvin. Calvin had many other significant influences on his theology besides Augustine; a great deal had happened in the eleven hundred years between the two theologians. But in the matter of design, Calvin took his cue from Augustine.

The opening of Calvin's *Institutes of the Christian Religion* begins with a discussion of human knowledge of God. Calvin believed that all people are born with a knowledge of God. This prior knowledge of God leaves all people without excuse when they fail to worship God or give their lives to his service. This knowledge exists more as a memory than as a clear vision, but it is sufficient to provide some concept of God.[27] This *a priori* knowledge is not the only knowledge people have of God. Calvin also taught that the whole structure of the universe manifests God's perfections and that "on each of his works his glory is engraven in characters so bright, so distinct, and so illustrious, that none, however dull and illiterate, can plead ignorance as their excuse."[28]

In opening his discussion of the knowledge of God, Calvin employs a variety of evocative phrases and terms that support the idea of God as the great Designer: "the elegant structure of the universe," "divine skill manifested so conspicuously," "well-ordered array," "ingenious contrivance," "architect."[29] He does not hesitate to say that nature presents "innumerable proofs" of God that may be understood technically through the sciences or casually by the most illiterate observer. Calvin acknowledged that the study of astronomy, medicine, and the natural sciences provided insight into the wisdom of God. He also argued that anyone could observe the underlying order of the universe reflected in the motion of the heavenly bodies.

In addition to the knowledge of God that comes through the technical or casual pursuit of the sciences, Calvin also argued that knowledge of God comes to a person by "descending into himself." There people will find "in their own persons a factory where innumerable operations of God are carried on. . . ."[30] Augustine had illustrated this descent within himself through his *Confessions*, but he took that insightful journey within after his conversion. Here lies the problem. Calvin observed that while knowledge of God may be possible by inward examination, people suppress the knowledge they may find there. People not only suppress the knowledge of God they might find within, but they also ignore the majesty of the evidence of God's power in nature. In spite of the

> mirror of his works, so great is our stupidity, so dull are we in regard to these bright manifestations, that we derive no benefit from them. For in regard to the fabric and admirable arrangement of the universe, how few of us are there who, in lifting our eyes to the heavens, or looking abroad on the various regions of the Earth, ever think of the Creator?[31]

The culprit in the undermining of the very fabric of the universe is none other than the human imagination. Calvin illustrated his critique of the human imagination by reference to Plato, the Stoics, the Epicureans, Socrates, and Xenophon, who speculated about God. The knowledge of God available to people by science and spiritual introspection inevitably ends in a perversion of the truth of God by the human imagination. Thus, the patterns and arrangement of the universe prove futile in demonstrating true knowledge of God to the one who will not know the truth. Appealing to Scripture, Calvin argued,

> Wherefore, the apostle, in the very place where he says that the worlds are images of invisible things, adds that it is *by faith* we understand that they were framed by the word of God (Heb. xi. 3); thereby intimating that the invisible Godhead is indeed represented by such displays, but that we have no eyes to perceive it until they are enlightened through faith by internal revelation from God.[32]

Observations. Calvin affirmed that nature bears the imprint of God's handiwork, but he denied that this proof actually proved the existence of God to someone who did not already have faith in God. Despite the evidence of God's creative activity, the mind that lacks faith cannot recognize the evidence.

René Descartes

While Protestants such as Calvin distanced themselves from the philosophical approach of Thomas Aquinas, which relied on Aristotle's understanding of knowledge, a growing number of Catholics began to challenge the Aristotelian dominated realm of science. Galileo ran afoul of the academic authorities not because his science contradicted the Bible, but because it contradicted Aristotle! René Descartes (1596–1650) also rejected the philosophy of Aristotle that stressed the reliability of sensory knowledge.[33]

Like Calvin, Descartes felt drawn toward Augustine with his Platonic philosophical foundation. Unlike Calvin, he went in quite an unorthodox direction with his emphasis on the mind. Descartes was consumed with the idea of absolute certainty as the only valid basis for human knowledge. Descartes hoped to develop a unified science of nature based on mathematics, but his method was based on doubt. The method he proposed involved four rules: 1) accept nothing as true which his mind could not accept clearly and distinctly without doubt, 2) divide the difficulties of a question into the smallest number of parts to allow for the most adequate examination, 3) examine the parts of the question beginning with the most simple and moving toward the most complex, 4) make such thorough observations and recordings of data as to allow for no omissions.

Descartes' method depends on doubting everything except that which is so clearly and distinctly true that it will not allow for doubt. By identifying what cannot be doubted, he then expected to build on that foundation of certainty to develop a unified theory of knowledge that included physics, metaphysics, and the other sciences. In applying the method, Descartes had to doubt the existence of the physical universe, of God, and even of himself. In analyzing the extent of his doubt, Descartes concluded that he could not doubt his own existence. He found his own existence to be that clear and distinct certainty for which he searched as a starting place for knowledge. As he thought about what he doubted, he realized that he was the something that was thinking. To think, he had to exist. The Latin version of this conclusion, *cogito ergo sum* (I think; therefore I am), stands out as one of the great philosophical maxims of all time. He held to this conclusion with absolute certainty.

While his method provided Descartes with certainty that he existed, it did not provide certainty that his body existed. He demonstrated to his satisfaction the existence of the mind as a substance, but he also concluded that the body must be a distinct substance from the mind. With this line of thought, Descartes developed a dualism of mind and body, the spiritual and the physical. This dualism depended upon Descartes' assumption that all things involve only two essential attributes: thought and extension. This means that all properties of thinking things may be described in terms of ways of thinking. All properties of extended things may be described in terms of ways they are extended.

Descartes proceeded to prove the existence of God from his own existence, since his own thinking existence was the only clear and distinct certainty he had. Not until he had proved the existence of God could he then move to prove the existence of a physical universe. Here we see the arguments of Thomas Aquinas turned upside down. Thomas sought to prove God's existence based on the existence of a physical universe, but Descartes would not allow the presupposition that the universe actually exists!

Descartes' argument for the existence of God begins with the idea in his mind of God. While Thomas argued that the physical universe must have a first cause, Descartes applied the same logic to his thoughts. His idea of God represented an effect that must have a cause. Every idea is an idea of something, whether it actually exists or not. The degree of reality of an idea depends on the reality of the object of thought. Because the idea of God is an idea of infinite perfection, its cause must lie outside Descartes, whose doubts betray his imperfection. Since imperfection could not be the cause of perfection, then a perfect Being independent of Descartes must exist. This Being is God.

From the existence of God, Descartes argued for the existence of a physical or external world beyond the mind. As part of the perfection of God, Descartes stated that God cannot deceive nor would he want to deceive his creatures. Because ideas of a physical world do not have perfection as one of their attributes, such ideas do not necessarily have an objective reality. Nonetheless, creatures have a tendency to believe that an external, physical world exists. This tendency to believe in a physical world would be misleading if such a world did not exist. In such a case, God would be guilty of creating creatures who are easily misled.

As a result of his approach, Descartes concluded that knowledge of the physical world does not come through the senses. Knowledge of matter represents an intellectual concept constructed in the mind. While he believed in the existence of many minds, Descartes believed that the physical world existed as a single, continuous, material extension. He could not accept the idea of a void, so he concluded that all physical substance represents a unified extension that operates mechanically.

Observations. Descartes' method proceeded from a basic skepticism that doubted the existence of nature and the physical world. Such skepticism did not allow for the assumptions from which Thomas developed his arguments. A world that did not exist had no motion, no cause, no order, no purpose. By making a radical distinction between mind and body, Descartes laid the intellectual foundation for the separation of science and faith. Rather than proving the existence of God from nature, Descartes proved the existence of nature from his belief in God.

Blaise Pascal

Perhaps the brightest star in the intellectual galaxy in the generation after Descartes was Blaise Pascal. Like Descartes, Pascal (1623–1662) made significant contributions to mathematics, philosophy, and theology. Like Descartes, Pascal challenged the old Aristotelian system.

In the area of experimental physics, Pascal demonstrated the probability that a vacuum could and did exist in nature. Aristotle had taught that nature abhors a vacuum. Pascal's work on the vacuum began when he heard of Torricelli's experiment with the barometer. When Torricelli placed a tube of mercury upside down in a bowl of mercury, some of the mercury remained in the bottom of the tube while a space remained above the mercury (see fig. 2.4). Pascal simply asked 1) why the mercury would remain in the tube above the bowl while its open end was submerged in the mercury, and 2) what filled the space in the tube above the mercury? Because of Aristotle's view of the impossibility of a vacuum, the prevailing wisdom of the day concluded that some invisible substance filled the space.

In *Experiences nouvelles touchant le vide*, published in 1647, Pascal described the series of experiments he had performed with tubes of different sizes and shapes filled with various liquids. His experiments led to the formulation of basic laws related to air pressure, including his conclusion that vacuums can and do exist. When challenged on his conclusions on Aristotelian grounds, Pascal responded with a statement on scientific method that further shook

Mercury

*Fig. 2.4. Torricelli's barometer
experiment*

the old Aristotelian consensus. He distinguished between observable facts of
an experiment following from the hypothesis or contradicting the hypothesis. If the facts follow from the hypothesis, they merely demonstrate the
possibility or probability of the hypothesis. If a single fact contradicts the
hypothesis, however, then the hypothesis has been falsified. The facts of the
experiment can never lead to absolute proof of a hypothesis, because other
possible experiments that might lead to falsification might be performed if
they could be conceived. In his experiments, Pascal demonstrated the falsification of Aristotle's hypothesis about vacuums, but he only demonstrated
the probability of his own hypothesis about the existence of vacuums.

His experiment with vacuums led to several important insights that contributed to theology and science, including the emerging mechanical view
of nature that replaced the mysterious, invisible substance that had filled the
empty spaces of Aristotle's universe. Pascal's contributions to science virtually eliminated the place for traditional authority (as opposed to experimentation) in science. Old understandings of the workings of nature fell away
as experimentation led to new understandings. The Greek philosophers no
longer held a special place in presupposing the nature of the universe when
the study of nature could be expected to lead to new understandings. Pascal's emphasis on probability in scientific experimentation also influenced
his understanding of religious knowledge.

Pascal's theory of knowledge owes a great deal to a religious conversion
he underwent on November 23, 1654. Pascal became an active part of the
Jansenist movement within the Catholic Church. Though fully within the
church, Jansenism had many features that seemed to coincide with Protes-
tantism. Pascal wrote a series of eighteen letters published as the *Lettres provinciales* during 1656–57 in which he defended one of the leading Jansenist
philosophers and theologians against attack within the academy. Despite
the efforts of Pascal, Antoine Arnauld was condemned by the faculty of the

Sorbonne, Jansenism was condemned by the pope, and *Lettres provinciales* was placed on the Index of Forbidden Books.

Pascal the mathematician thought geometry offered the best method for knowing truth. The discovery of the truths of geometry depends on the use of axioms that everyone accepts as true. These axioms represent principles so clear that nothing clearer can aid in proving them. From these first principles, it is possible to derive the propositions of geometry through a logical system of thought. Axioms cannot be proven by appeal to more basic fundamental principles; therefore, people can never know with absolute certainty the truth of the geometric principles. Nonetheless, this method allows the greatest certainty that people may obtain through their mental capabilities.

Because of the inability to arrive at the truth of first principles, skepticism constantly hovers at the edge of Pascal's method. Pascal does not attempt to minimize the skepticism. Instead, he argues that the skepticism occurs because people refuse to recognize that first principles (axioms) come through instinct and revelation rather than through the same processes of thought and experimentation that lead to knowledge derived from first principles. Pascal argued that "feelings" play a crucial role in understanding the fundamental truths upon which all other knowledge depends.

Descartes made a radical distinction between the physical and the spiritual, between mind and body. Pascal, on the other hand, insisted that knowledge of the physical world ultimately depends upon intuition and revelation as much as religious knowledge does. He explored this theme in his unfinished work known simply as *Pensées* (*Thoughts*). In a world in which one's mental faculties always lead to skepticism, Pascal had little regard for the attempt to prove the existence of God from nature. One either knows intuitively through revelation that God made all of nature, or one does not. On this subject, Pascal deserves to be quoted at length:

> I admire the boldness with which these persons undertake to speak of God. In addressing their argument to infidels, their first chapter is to prove Divinity from the works of nature. I should not be astonished at their enterprise, if they were addressing their argument to the faithful; for it is certain that those who have the living faith in their hearts see at once that all existence is none other than the work of the God whom they adore. But for those in whom this light is extinguished, and in whom we purpose to rekindle it,

persons destitute of faith and grace, who, seeking with all their light whatever they see in nature that can bring them to this knowledge, find only obscurity and darkness; to tell them that they have only to look at the smallest things which surround them, and they will see God openly, to give them, as a complete proof of this great and important matter, the course of the moon and planets, and to claim to have concluded the proof with such an argument, is to give them ground for believing that the proofs of our religion are very weak. And I see by reason and experience that nothing is more calculated to arouse their contempt.

It is not after this manner that Scripture speaks, which has a better knowledge of the things that are of God. It says, on the contrary, that God is a hidden God, and that, since the corruption of nature, He has left men in darkness from which they can escape only through Jesus Christ, without whom all communion with God is cut off. *Nemo novit Patrem, nisi Filius, et cui voluerit Filius revelare.*[34]

This is what Scripture points out to us, when it says in so many places that those who seek God find him. It is not of that light, "like the noonday sun," that this is said. We do not say that those who seek the noonday sun, or water in the sea, shall find them; and hence the evidence of God must not be of this nature. So it tells us elsewhere: *Vere tu es Deus absconditus.*[35]

Everyone has the same evidence. Some believe and some do not. Those who believe do not do so because the evidence is more compelling for them, but because they believe. Once they believe, the evidence becomes compelling.

Order, purpose, and design do not represent proof of the existence of God. Instead, faith in God allows one to grasp the order, purpose, and design of nature. Ultimately, Pascal considered all knowledge to be religious knowledge. From his description of the method of geometry, Pascal considered reliance on intuition and revelation to be a most reasonable course. In his famous wager argument, he explains the reasonableness of faith. Pascal challenges skeptics to consider what they might gain by faith in God as opposed to what they might lose. If they choose God, and God exists, they have gained eternity. If they choose God, and God does not exist, they have lost nothing. On the other hand, if they do not choose God and God does not exist, they have lost nothing. If they do not choose God but God does exist, they have lost everything.

In this argument, Pascal's mathematical and methodological stress on probability plays a great part. He does not intend his wager argument to be grounds for faith as much as to demonstrate the reasonableness of faith, for he goes on to discuss the problem of the person who now recognizes the reasonableness of faith and the desirability of faith, yet who lacks faith. He offers the example of others who have struggled with faith: "Follow the way by which they began; by acting as if they believed, taking the holy water, having masses said, etc."[36] In short, faith will come to those who seek it.

Observations. Pascal regarded faith in God as the basic axiom from which all certain knowledge proceeds. Skepticism performed a useful function by demonstrating the limits of human reason and the need people have for God. He had little confidence in formal proofs for God. Having experienced a conversion, he believed that knowledge of God does not come through the reason of philosophy but through the reason of the heart.

3. The Mechanical Universe

Harry Lee Poe

THE SEVENTEENTH CENTURY BEGAN in England with monarchs who claimed to rule by divine right. It ended with monarchs who reigned at the pleasure of Parliament. The century began with Englishmen living in a New World. It ended with Englishmen living in a "new universe" created by Isaac Newton. Newton did not create his universe *ex nihilo*, but glued together all the pieces that scientists of the previous few centuries had been constructing.

With his laws of gravity, Newton drew a picture of the universe as a great machine with interconnecting parts, symbolizing the progress of the exploding industrial age. The theological and political ideas of the seventeenth century were dominated by advocacy and reaction to reformed thought, picturing the universe as a vast kingdom presided over by a sovereign king who had absolute power over everything. With the triumph of Puritans and Parliament over King Charles I in the 1640s, reformed thinkers had the opportunity to put into practice their theory of government. The experiment took place not only in England, but also in New England and in the city of Geneva, where John Calvin had developed his understanding of reformed theology. When the experiment failed, the influence of reformed thought declined not only in politics and theology, but also in the universities. When the Commonwealth government collapsed and King Charles II was restored in 1660, the former Puritans were expelled from their posts in the universities.

As the Great Fire of London swept the city clean to make way for the new pattern of architecture devised by such men as Christopher Wren, so the Restoration, with its new kind of democratized monarchy, swept church, state, and academy clean of old ideas. Isaac Newton (1642–1727) was born during the period of the Commonwealth, but he came to intellectual flower during the reign of the "merry monarch," Charles II. The reign of Charles

II allowed broad latitude in the matter of morals in keeping with the king's own sexual exploits. Though John Bunyan wrote *The Pilgrim's Progress* during this period, he did so from a jail cell where he sat imprisoned for the crime of preaching. *The Pilgrim's Progress* looked back to the earlier allegorical literary tradition of the Middle Ages for its inspiration. The Restoration gave birth to a new intellectual tradition whose literature would flow well into the eighteenth century with such bawdy classics as *Moll Flanders*, *Fanny Hill*, and *Tom Jones*. As Shakespeare had captured the climate of his day, so these early novels captured their times as well.

Until Newton, all professors of mathematics at Cambridge were required to come from the clergy since mathematics was considered a philosophical discipline. Like astronomy and chemistry, it fell within the category of natural philosophy. Science as we know it today did not exist as a discipline distinct from philosophy. The word "science," when it was used, simply meant knowledge. The medieval assertion that theology was the queen of the sciences referred to theology as the fountain of knowledge in general. Cambridge University granted Newton the chair of mathematics, although he did not have the requisite theological qualifications or the orthodox faith of the Church of England. Newton was not a Cartesian and had a profound interest in the relationship between the physical and the spiritual, but with Newton's appointment, the academy took the bold step to make the clean division between mind and body, spirit and matter, which Descartes had advocated only a few decades earlier.

The climate for the constructive engagement of theology and natural philosophy was far worse on the Continent. While England had been engaged in its own Civil War for several years in the 1640s, Europe had been inflamed with a major war that devastated most of Germany and sapped the energies of France and the Lowlands. The Thirty Years War destroyed the earlier enthusiasm the Europeans had for matters theological. The pious motives of theological conviction with which the war began dissolved into cynical plays for power and the establishment of nation-states by the war's close. The early distinction between Catholic, Calvinist, and Lutheran disappeared as rival religious positions made treaties against a common nation that may have been of the same religious persuasion. With the growth of cynicism, religion as seen in traditional Christian faith played a smaller and smaller part in the intellectual discussions of the day. During the Enlightenment in France, the discussions of natural philosophy and moral philosophy would continue, but without the need for reference to God.

Newton's great rival in Germany also made his own contribution to the design discussion, even though he did not take part in it himself. His work would have implications several generations later. Gottfried Wilhelm Leibniz (1646–1716) prepared the way for evolutionary thought with his *principle of continuity*: things pass from one state of being to another state through an infinite number of intermediate states. All of reality, whether consciousness or motion, exists as a continuum. He rejected Aristotle's notion of a finite universe and replaced it with the notion of infinity that he expressed symbolically through differential calculus, which he invented in 1676. He attempted to apply the function of an infinitesimal algorithm within infinitesimal calculus to all realms of discourse, whether theology, philosophy, mathematics, physics, metaphysics, or moral philosophy.

Leibniz embraced a mechanical understanding of the universe within the infinite continuum of change. He believed that all matter was composed of yet smaller matter in an infinite regression, just as he believed that all lines were composed of an infinite number of points. Furthermore, he described each sub-part of matter as having within it a degree of *force* in constant agitation. This internal force interacts with external forces in the phenomenon of motion. Upon analysis, the ball that strikes a wall and bounces back does not suddenly stop moving and then start moving again in another direction. Instead, it goes through a continuous process of change very quickly. The change in motion involves the elasticity of the ball (or any other matter) as its internal force interacts with the external force. The loss of motion occurs gradually, but very quickly.

Leibniz's ideas of infinity and force in the seventeenth century would have a profound impact on the intellectual environment. He removed the intellectual stigma of an infinite regress that insisted upon a first cause. His concept of force internal to matter made it possible to conceive of a motion without a prime mover. Leibniz was not a naturalist himself, but his ideas made it possible to conceive of naturalism. In the next generation, David Hume would demonstrate how devastating these simple ideas could be to the design argument.

From Locke to Deism

All of the thinkers discussed so far have approached the issue of design from the perspective of faith. They have all believed that God designed the world, though they have disagreed as to what they meant when they used the word "God." They have also disagreed about what one may know of God from the presence of the physical evidence of the world. Those who have shared a common Christian faith have not reached the same conclusions about what the physical world can tell us of God. They have subscribed to different philosophical perspectives through which they have interpreted the physical world and through which they have interpreted the Bible. Even in their disagreements, however, they have assumed that God designed the world. In the eighteenth century, that cultural consensus began to collapse.

In the seventeenth century, the first tremors of that collapse had begun to be felt. Thomas Hobbes, who had gone into exile in France with the Stuarts during the time of the Puritan dominance in England and the Thirty Years War on the Continent, began to discuss political and moral philosophy in ways that did not reflect the traditional role of God. The same latitude allowed in moral behavior gained acceptance in discussions of theology. The old precision of the Puritans seemed out of place. Amos Funkenstein has argued that a change in the theological perspective of the intellectual tradition occurred beginning in the seventeenth century with men like Galileo, Descartes, Leibniz, Newton, Hobbes, and Vico. Funkenstein refers to this development as a "secular theology."[1] They either had no theological training or their training was minimal. Yet, they persisted in discussing the theology of their work. Their theology, however, focused on the world as they understood it from their work.

John Locke (1632–1704) also contributed to the intellectual climate in which people considered the evidence of design in the universe. Raised in a Puritan family, Locke remained a committed Christian all his life, though he insisted on testing even the truth of faith through reason. He set the stage for the English love of empiricism with his "Essay Concerning Human Understanding," in which he argued that people acquire all of their ideas from experience. Experience involves both sensation through the body and reflection through the mind. Locke rejected the Platonic notion of innate ideas that people bring into life. The ability of the mind to organize sensations into ideas comes from its ability to make associations or analogies between things and build upon these. His views on knowledge have been regarded as an answer to Descartes, because Locke argued for the unity of body and mind. Furthermore, Locke assumed the existence of the physical world. A variety of internal inconsistencies in Locke's thought made it quite possible for later thinkers to accept his priority of knowledge through the senses without accepting his understanding of the unity of mind and body. As we shall see, committed Christians like Bishop Butler would use Locke's empiricism to ground Christian faith in physical evidence, while Hume would use the same approach to discredit the claims of Butler.

During this same period, deism came into prominence. Deism traveled through the intellectual circles of Britain after the Restoration but lacked a systematic approach or unified program. The most prominent early advocate of deism, Lord Herbert of Cherbury (1583–1648), had no clear followers except Charles Blount (1654–1693), who took up deism after Herbert's death. Deism took many forms, but generally it involved belief in a Supreme Being who established the natural and moral order of the universe. The deists generally regarded the scriptures of all religions as human inventions and unnecessary to true religion. They rejected miracles and all forms of the supernatural as contrary to reason. What can be known of God is known by reason. Most of the deists would also have denied the incarnation of God as Jesus Christ. The title of the most famous work by John Toland (1670–1722) sums up the attitude of many deists: *Christianity not Mysterious: Or a treatise Shewing That there is nothing in the Gospel Contrary to Reason, Nor above it: And that no Christian Doctrine can be properly call'd a Mystery* (1696).

While deists believed in a God who could be known by reason, they had a strong revulsion for the church and its priests. In a sense, the deists represented the same revolutionary spirit in the theological/philosophical area that had been shown by the British Parliament in the Glorious Revolution when they deposed their king. Deism represented an individualistic approach to religion. This revolutionary spirit appeared most clearly among the French deists, Voltaire (1694–1778) and Rousseau (1712–1778), and the American deists, Benjamin Franklin (1706–1790) and Thomas Jefferson (1743–1826). While the deists had no common creed, they all shared a strong confidence in human reason.

BOYLE, BUTLER, AND EMPIRICISM

Robert Boyle (1627–1691) promoted the design argument, but he also advanced the mechanical view of the universe. He inherited a great fortune from his father, the first Earl of Cork, with which he pursued a career that would contribute to the development of experimental science. He improved the air pump and demonstrated that air has both weight and elasticity. His mechanical view of the universe provided the deists with philosophical ground on which to stand, but his fortune provided an endowment to support a lectureship for the defense of Christianity. The Boyle Lectures produced many a hard-crafted argument over the years. They did not always produce their intended result, however, for Benjamin Franklin claimed that he became a deist as a result of reading some of the Boyle Lectures! Despite important lectures based on design by such figures as Richard Bentley and William Derham, the lectures tended toward the highly rationalistic, like the deists they tended to combat. Anthony Collins, a prominent deist, joked that no one doubted the existence of God until Samuel Clark's lecture proposed to demonstrate it.[2]

Perhaps the most influential work by a deist was *Christianity as Old as the Creation: Or, The Gospel a Republication of the Religion of Nature* (1730), written by Matthew Tindal (1657–1733). This book drew over 150 responses, among which was *The Analogy of Religion* (1736) by Bishop Joseph Butler. Butler (1692–1752) was every bit the rationalist but wanted to make a case for revelation. He based his argument on the design of the universe evident in nature.

Butler adopted the empiricism of Locke and set about to make religion a matter of sober reason. In this regard, he shows an acceptance of Descartes' dichotomy of mind and body in an interesting way. He would not accept the place of "religious affections" in his approach to religion. Emotion and "enthusiasm" had no place. Thus, he made a strong distinction between reason and emotion. He ordered John Wesley out of his diocese in 1739 to protect his people from the Great Awakening. Though Butler developed his argument in a highly rationalistic way, he rejected rationalism as the final judge of knowledge and gave that dignity to empiricism. What can be known must ultimately be demonstrated by the sensory experience of empiricism. The data for science and religion must be the same! Our knowledge of God does not come from ideas of God implanted into us before birth, but from observation of the physical world that God made. Once supplied by data through the senses, human reason has the capacity to analyze and draw reliable conclusions from the data. Butler viewed the mind as entirely trustworthy.

Butler's argument from design depends on the assumption that if the evidence so analyzed measures up to the standards of reason, the prudent person must assent.[3] This approach relies on probability as assessed by a prudent person rather than on absolute proof, since Butler would argue that we do not have absolute proof for anything. The prudent person would not require more than reasonable evidence. While attempting to construct an argument for revelation within the context of a design scheme, Butler also insisted that revelation falls under the judgment of reason both in terms of the meaning of revelation and the morality of revelation. Though he worked in a design context, Butler did not have as his aim an argument to demonstrate the existence of God based on design. He and his opponents assumed the existence of God and the orderly design of nature. He wrote primarily against the deists within their philosophical frame of reference to make a case for specific revelation and redemption through the incarnate Christ.

Butler stressed that God has established universal laws of nature that people may recognize through sensory observation and understand through reason. As governor of the universe, however, God has established laws that govern every other aspect of human experience as religion or moral law. Laws in one realm have their counterpart in the other realm because they form part of a single universal scheme of God's governance. Through experience, we have developed *probabilities* of the course of nature so that we know how to dress in January and July. We may experience a warm day in January and a cold day in July, but we have probability as a guide that serves us well if not absolutely. We may discern the laws of nature and draw applications that guide our lives based on probabilities. If we conduct our everyday life according to probability, then we behave prudently. We would be imprudent if we did not also conduct our religious life by probability. If the evidence for Christianity is only probable, rather than absolute, the prudent person has a moral obligation to follow its dictates.

By *analogy*, Butler makes the transfer from everyday life to the religious life. The combination of the probabilities of nature and the cumulative history of the experience of the human race provide the data from which analogies may be drawn. Because God governs both the natural and the moral realm, we may derive analogies of one from the other. Pain serves a function in nature to warn animals of potential danger. It serves as a means of guidance through the avoidance of pain. By analogy, we may see that God has provided the same principle of pain through punishment in society to give guidance to society. Butler's use of analogy depends upon the acceptance of the idea that God governs all realms of reality by the same universal laws. Probability reveals the law in one realm, and analogy provides the basis for recognizing it in another realm. The laws of nature and of religion (morality) may be understood as representing the same basic principles.

Butler's discussion of immortality illustrates how analogy provides evidence for immortality.

In nature we may observe that many creatures undergo dramatic changes in the course of their lives; for example, the maggot becomes a fly and the egg hatches into a bird. The embryonic changes of humans further illustrate this point. The evidence suggests by analogy that people will live on in some altered state beyond death. Nature's laws of motion and momentum demonstrate that a body persists in its course. We know that people also have powers of momentum related to human capacities such as action, love, and suffering. The evidence suggests by analogy that some dimension of the human personality will persist after death. Furthermore, Butler argues that we lack any evidence to indicate what happens at death other than the observable physical results. He stresses that the body is merely the medium of the self and not the self per se. While we have no empirical evidence that life ends at death, we have no empirical evidence that it does not. In the absence of data one way or the other, analogy provides the most reliable evidence that life persists.

Special revelation represents the third area in which analogy provides access. The first area of nature led to the second area of natural theology. These lead to the third area of revealed religion. Butler illustrated the application of analogy to special revelation through the concept of mediation, a notion that deists had little use for. Butler observed that people experience mediation all the time in everyday life whenever one person helps another person. To object to mediation by Christ is to object to all mediation as such. In social experience we observe judges who grant leniency and creditors who extend credit. God's extension of mercy to provide spiritual help to those in trouble is analogous to this common experience. In nature we observe that medicine provides remedy and healing for different illnesses and afflictions. By analogy, Jesus Christ provides the remedy for the sickness of sin. Having established analogy as a principle in the area of natural theology, Butler demonstrates the reasonableness of its extension to special revelation as well.

Observations. Butler's approach builds on the assumptions of the best science and philosophy of his day. As such, his theology is bound to the intellectual context of the mid-eighteenth century. He adapted empiricism to the formulation of theology within a rationalistic framework hostile to emotion. Religion was primarily for him a matter of morality. His argument from analogy assumes the order of nature and society in a way that deists would approve. The existence of God and God's design of the universe are assumed.

Eliminate any of his assumptions and his whole system collapses. We shall see that David Hume attacked Butler's concept of analogy without allowing him to assume either the existence of God or the order of the universe.

HUME'S NATURALISM

Newton could look at the vast engine of the universe and conclude, "He must be blind who from the most wise and excellent contrivances of things cannot see the Infinite Wisdom and Goodness of their Almighty Creator, and he must be mad and senseless who refuses to acknowledge them."[4] The same data by itself, however, left room for other interpretations. In *Dialogues Concerning Natural Religion* (1779), David Hume (1711–1776) took quite a different position.[5] Hume inherited the skepticism of Calvin, Descartes, and Paschal, but he inherited none of their faith. Once the Cartesian dichotomy between mind and body had entered the intellectual environment, the skeptic could only appeal to common experience. Transferring experience of the physical world by analogy to the spiritual world created particular logical problems. Hume pressed this issue particularly with the standard argument of natural theology that the universe gives evidence of mind or intelligence behind its order and purpose.

Hume suggested the analogy of the design of the universe with reference to human creativity as it had developed:

> Throw several pieces of steel together, without shape or form; they will never arrange themselves so as to compose a watch: Stone, and mortar, and wood, without an architect, never erect a house. But the ideas in a human mind, we see, by an unknown, inexplicable economy, arrange themselves so as to form the plan of a watch or house. Experience, therefore, proves, that there is an original principle of order in mind, not in matter. From similar effects we infer similar causes. The adjustment of means to ends is alike in the universe, as a machine of human contrivance. The causes, therefore, must be resembling.[6]

Having stated the conventional analogy of mind behind the universe, Hume points out that experimental facts depend upon similar causes that produce similar effects. Any alteration in circumstances raises doubts about the event. Such changes will require renewed experimentation to determine what effect the changes have had on the event. It is one thing to compare the universe to houses, ships, furniture, and machines, but quite another to infer a similarity in cause. Hume challenged the traditional attribution of mind to the underlying cause of the universe. People have many examples of house, ship, furniture, and machine by which to infer that they result from the action of a mind. Since we have but one universe, we do not have an adequate experimental basis to draw a similar conclusion. By experiment we have knowledge of the place of mind in the construction of a house, but in that experiment we have access both to the house and to the builder. With the case of the universe, it is the existence of the mind of the builder that lies in doubt. Furthermore, Hume disallows the argument that the mind behind the universe represents self-evident truth. If it can be doubted, as Hume has done, then it is not self-evident. If any other explanation comes to mind, then it is not self-evident.

By pressing the analogy of the mind, Hume suggests that people have made themselves the model for the universe. This anthropomorphic approach amounts to little more than what Freud would call over a century later a "projection" upon the universe. Hume argued that the existence of intelligent mind behind the material universe represents an unnecessary intrusion into the natural order. In describing God as the first cause or the prime mover, one must next explain why God does not have a cause other than himself. Hume argued that one may just as easily argue that the universe has no cause other than itself. It is not necessary to go so far as to posit a God when one may stop with the physical world.[7] It is not necessary to look for some ordering principle outside of matter when the principle of order may just as easily be seen as an aspect of matter itself. In this line of discussion, Hume began to build a case for looking no further than the tangible evidence in arriving at an explanation: "An ideal system, arranged of itself, without a precedent design, is not a whit more explicable than a material one, which attains its order in a like manner; nor is there any more difficulty in the latter supposition than in the former."[8]

Even if one were to allow as self-evident the existence of God, the evidence of the material world does not necessarily lead to the God of the Bible.[9] Using the analogy of the house, ship, or city, many people are involved in the construction of these human artifices. If the universe is like a human artifice, then why would we not suppose the existence of many gods? Even if the universe arose by the design of some single deity, one is left to creative imagination to determine what kind of deity designed it. An infant deity might have made this universe as a first, inferior attempt and soon abandoned it. An inferior deity might have made this universe, thought of with contempt for its shoddy workmanship by superior deities. An old, retired deity who has since died might have made this universe in senility. Without a basis for comparison and experimentation, it would be impossible to say what kind of God might have made a universe like ours.

Instead of granting that the universe resembles a machine or other human artifice, Hume argued that the universe seems more to resemble a life-form, either animal or vegetable.[10] While the ancient philosophers spoke of design, they also seem to have had a preference for understanding the world as a great body whose mind was God. Hume allows the reasonableness of this inference, since people expect to find a mind where they find a body, but the experience of humans does not reasonably transfer by analogy as evidence to support the existence of God. The sense of order that some attribute to design, Hume attributes to the "inviolable laws" inherent in matter itself. If the universe bears a greater resemblance to life than to machines, then its origin would more probably come from generation than from design.[11] Referring to his earlier example, Hume declared that the world resembles an animal or vegetable much more than a watch. The internal organization of life that causes a tree to have the same order as the tree from which it sprang would explain why the universe would have a sense of order. It is the order of its nature. Hume allows that order in human experience does arise from reason as well as from generation, but without more data, the explanation for order in the universe is simply a matter of arbitrary choice.

In a universe of finite matter but infinite duration, Hume argued that every possible order and position would occur an infinite number of times. People currently experience just one of those infinite possibilities that the universe has undergone. Whenever the universe reaches a state of order, it would have the appearance of design. Hume assumed that motion and force belonged to matter as an aspect of its nature; thus, the universe required no prime mover to set the universe in motion. Hume reasoned that

> thought has no influence upon matter, except where that matter is so conjoined with it, as to have an equal reciprocal influence upon it. No animal can move immediately any thing but the members of its own body; and indeed, the equality of action and re-action seems to be a universal law of nature. . . ."[12]

Hume next moved to the necessary existence of God and the problem of evil. As for the necessary being upon whose existence the universe depends,

Hume reasoned that any being who can be conceived of as not existing could hardly be called necessary.[13] The problem of evil involves more discussion. After a general survey of human misery and the natural order of the strong preying upon the weak, Hume questioned the validity of attributing to God such moral qualities as justice, benevolence, and mercy:

> His power we allow infinite: Whatever he wills is executed: But nei-
> ther man nor any other animal are happy: Therefore he does not
> will their happiness. His wisdom is infinite: He is never mistaken
> in choosing the means to any end: But the course of nature tends
> not to human or animal felicity: Therefore it is not established for
> that purpose.[14]

Hume argued that the only purpose of nature with respect to life is the preservation of individuals and the propagation of species. Hume would not allow the appeal to a final judgment and heavenly reward to resolve the problem of divine benevolence, since these would be unprovable hypotheses. He insisted that "The only method of supporting divine benevolence . . . is to deny absolutely the misery and wickedness of man."[15] No one can deny this misery because pain is "infinitely more violent and durable" than pleasure.[16] Any resolution to these difficulties must come from faith, not from experience of the material world.

Observations. Hume laid the intellectual foundations for naturalism that would blossom through the work of Charles Darwin. He suggested that all of nature could be explained by nature itself. It need not have had a cause any more than God would have had a cause. What appears to be design could be nothing more than the natural state of nature that could produce life to observe it. Rather than supporting the Christian understanding of God, Hume suggested that an argument from nature could more strongly support a Hindu understanding of God in which nature represents the body and God the mind.

PALEY'S WATCH

William Paley (1743–1805) developed perhaps the most famous argument from design in his *Natural Theology: or Evidences of the Existence and Attributes of the Deity Collected from the Appearances of Nature* (1802). As we have observed, several others before Paley had used the watch as an analogy of the mechanical nature of the universe. Paley built upon this well-known analogy and began his book without any other introduction than the analogy itself:

In crossing a heath, suppose I pitched my foot against a stone, and were asked how the *stone* came to be there; I might possibly answer, that, for any thing I knew to the contrary, it had lain there for ever: nor would it perhaps be very easy to show the absurdity of the answer. But suppose I had found a *watch* upon the ground, and it should be inquired how the watch happened to be in that place; I should hardly think of the answer which I had before given, that for any thing I knew, the watch might have always been there. Yet why should not this answer serve for the watch as well as for the stone? Why is it not as admissible in the second case, as in the first? For this reason, and for not other, viz. that, when we come to inspect the watch, we perceive (what we could not discover in the stone) that its several parts are framed and put together for a purpose, e.g. that they are so formed and adjusted as to produce motion, and that motion so regulated as to point out the hour of the day: that if the different parts had been differently shaped from what they are, of a different size from what they are, or placed after any other manner, or in any other order, than that in which they are placed, either no motion at all would have been carried on in the machine, or none which would have answered the use that is now served by it. To reckon up a few of the plainest of these parts, and of their offices, all tending to one result – we see a cylindrical box containing a coiled elastic spring, which, by its endeavour to relax itself, turns round the box. We next observe a flexible chain (artificially wrought for the sake of flexure) communicating the action of the spring from the box to the fusee. We then find a series of wheels, the teeth of which catch in, and apply to, each other, conducting the motion from the fusee to the balance, and from the balance to the pointer; and at the same time, by the size and shape of those wheels, so regulating that motion as to terminate in causing an index, by an equable and measured progression, to pass over the given space in a given time. We take notice that the wheels are made of brass in order to keep them from rust: the springs of steel, no other metal being so elastic; that over the face of the watch there is placed a glass, a material employed in no other part of the work, but in the room of which, if there had been any other than a transparent substance, the hour could not be seen without opening the case. This mechanism being observed (it requires indeed an examination of the instrument, and perhaps some previous knowledge of the subject, to perceive and understand it; but being once, as we have said, observed and understood), the inference, we think, is inevitable, that the watch must have had a maker: that there must have existed, at some time, and at some place or other, an artificer or artificers, who formed it for the purpose which we find it actually to answer; who comprehended its construction, and designed its use.[17]

Paley's argument operates by analogy, like Butler's argument. One can anticipate where he is going with his argument. The universe and everything in it is even more complex than a watch and bears even more evidence of contrivance than a mere watch; therefore, we conclude that the universe must have had a maker (see fig. 3.1). By analogy, his argument also involves a first cause and a prime mover who set it all in motion. The argument hinges on design rather than on existence. He did not question the origin of the existence of the material world. Rather, he questioned how a world with the appearance of *design* came to be. Infinite regress becomes a much thornier problem when exploring the explanation for something with the appearance of design.

Having established the basic principle of his argument, Paley applied the analogy to case after case in the natural world, beginning with the comparison of the eye to a telescope (see fig. 3.2). He then discussed how the eyes of different animals differ, yet are perfectly suited to that animal's way of life. From the eye, he moved to the ear, and from ears, to reproduction, which duplicates the organization of design. The presence of flaws or imperfections in nature does not offer counterevidence against a designer any more than the failure of a watch to keep good time offers evidence that the watch had no designer. Because of the frailty of the parts, the watchmaker will regularly clean the watch and make repairs.

Most modern treatments of the development of the design argument discuss Hume after Paley to show how Hume destroyed Paley's argument, even though these discussions acknowledge that Hume wrote before Paley. John Hick states that Paley did not deal with any of Hume's criticisms of the design argument, and Hugh Ross writes as if Hume actually wrote after Paley.[18] Paley actually addressed the issues raised by Hume. Hume's argu-

Fig. 3.1. Paley's Illustration
of the Parts of the Watch

Fig. 3.2. Paley's Illustration
of the Parts of the Eye

ment would not gain its real force until joined with Darwin's theory, as we shall see. Hume had argued that any universe would have to have some form that might be mistaken for design. Paley countered with his litany of specific examples from biology to show that such features as eyes are not simply some random form that fills an empty cavity in the head. Paley also responded to Hume's suggestion that in an infinite amount of time, all the possible configurations could occur that might account for the kind of universe in which we live. Paley simply replied that no experimental evidence existed to support such a conjecture. Paley speculated on what we might say of the person who explained the existence of mills and engines by arguing:

> That a mass of metals and other materials having run when melted into all possible figures, and combined themselves in all possible forms and shapes, and proportions, these things which we see, are what were left from the accident, as best worth preserving. . . . I cannot distinguish the hypothesis as applied to the works of nature,

from this solution, which no one would accept, as applied to a collection of machines.[19]

BRIDGING THE GAP

The picture of God as a designer and watchmaker has an interesting influence on how some people view God's relationship to nature. The deists had followed that line to conclude that God had established laws for the physical and moral governance of the universe but that he remained removed from the day-to-day operations. This view, known as *uniformitarianism*, gained growing acceptance in scientific circles by the early 1800s. It did not represent the exclusive view, but it represented a growing perspective. In this climate, Francis Henry Egerton, Eighth Earl of Bridgewater, commissioned a series of eight essays known as the *Bridgewater Treatises* that appeared in the 1830s to refute uniformitarianism.

Not all of the *Bridgewater* contributors took a design approach to their argument, but several did.[20] Perhaps the most significant of these was geologist William Buckland (1784–1856) of Oxford University. Buckland began by establishing a link with the earlier Boyle Lectures through his quotation from William Derham's *Physico-Theology* as an opening epigram. In his Preface, he further made clear that he hoped to do through geology what William Paley had accomplished through biology: the "demonstration, of the continuous Being, and of many of the highest Attributes of the One Living and True God" through an "examination of the evidences of Design" found in the fossil record.[21] Geology itself was in its infancy as a science when Buckland wrote (see fig. 3.3). Buckland had the added difficulty of fashioning his argument around the fossils of extinct animals that would suggest an age of the Earth far in excess of the six thousand years commonly held by the religious community at the time he wrote. As the solution to this difficulty, Buckland suggested a gap of time between the creation of the universe in Genesis 1:1 and the fitting out of the Earth in Genesis 1:2.

Buckland offered an intriguing answer to Hume's complaint about the universal presence of pain and death. He argued that the sudden death of animals, either by falling prey to a carnivore or by some natural disaster, represents an act of kindness by God. Rather than subjecting creatures to the slow process of sickness and decay, God provided a way for them to experience sudden and unexpected death.[22]

Paley, Buckland, and others did answer Hume's views, and they did so

Fig. 3.3. Buckland's Examination of the Fossil Record

in the way most attractive to the English of their day. They compiled case after case of empirical evidence to support the position of design. Hume had a theory, but he lacked empirical evidence. Butler, standing in the tradition of Locke, had held the day on the priority of empirical evidence over rationalism as the final determination of knowledge. Hume had only offered a theory that nature had within itself the power to produce the marvels that appear to be designed. Paley and Buckland, on the other hand, produced specific cases involving the structure of living things to demonstrate the necessity of design. As John Hadley Brooke and Geoffrey Cantor have observed, "David Hume's critique of natural theology was not only indecisive but ingeniously contested."[23] Hume's views could not have standing unless someone produced the missing empirical evidence to support a natural explanation for the structures of biology.

LEAVING EVERYTHING TO CHANCE

Between 1831 and 1836, Charles Darwin (1809–1882) took an extended voyage to the Southern Hemisphere aboard the *H.M.S. Beagle*. In the course of his journey as the ship's naturalist, Darwin collected the empirical data he would use as evidence to support a natural explanation for the adaptation of life-forms to their environments as well as an explanation for the complex organs that have special functions for a species. The theory of evolution did not originate with Charles Darwin, but he did succeed in providing it with an experimental basis that captured the imagination of the scientific community.

As far as Darwin's theory relates to design, its most significant feature lies in the concept of *natural selection*. The variety of forms of life relates to the urge to survival. Each generation of life produces variety in its offspring, however subtle the variation may be. Those variations that are more conducive to their environment have the greater chance of survival and produce offspring that build on these variations while adding new ones. Over a period of thousands of generations, the varieties that are less conducive to their environment die out, while the successful varieties thrive until they eventually become a new species. The changes that occur take place by chance, rather than by design. The successful changes lead to ever-advancing forms of life, while the unsuccessful changes lead to extinction.

While many criticisms of Darwin's theory arose at the time of the publication of his book *The Origin of Species* (1859), the criticism that has the most direct application to the question of design concerns the presence of complex organs. The eye represents, perhaps, the most obvious of such organs. The eye had been the first organ to which Paley had pointed to demonstrate design within life-forms. Now Darwin's critics again pointed to the eye to ask how it could occur as a slight variation between generations. It would have to appear in its completed form or else serve no function at all for untold generations until all the pieces necessary to make an eye work had come about through variation between generations. Darwin admitted that the eye gave him "a cold shudder."[24] As we shall see, the problem of the eye and the explanation of complex organs by appeal to natural selection alone would reappear in the closing days of the twentieth century.

Darwin defended natural selection with the theory that the earliest stages of the development of the eye must have been useful in some way in the struggle for survival. He suggested a possible sequence of development that would have involved "functional eyes" that could be illustrated from several forms of life. In other words, Darwin appealed to Butler's old analogical approach in the absence of clear evidence! While this approach did not prove his case in the matter of complex organs, it satisfied his supporters. Those dissatisfied with his case would have to wait for new evidence. In the meantime, Darwin provided Hume's theory of naturalism with an empirical base. Hume had not destroyed Paley's argument, but Darwin's evidence for Hume's theory took the punch out of Paley's argument so that it fell into disfavor.

Darwin's was not the only interpretation of the data about evolution. Alfred Russell Wallace was working on the same idea at the same time as Darwin. Wallace, in fact, wrote a paper on the subject that compelled Darwin to go public with his views quickly or be left at the starting gate by Wallace. The two men issued a joint paper on evolution for the Linnaean Society in 1858. Wallace had quite a different perspective on what conclusions could be drawn from the data of evolution. He believed that God guided the process of evolution as his instrument for creation. Wallace pointed to such *orthogenetic trends* as the increasing size of the human brain over a period of thousands of years during which the functions of such a brain were not utilized. Natural selection would suggest that the development of an ability over such a long period of time could not occur if it did not give people an advantage in survival. That the capacity of the brain for speculative thought would not be utilized by humans for thousands of years suggested to Wallace both purpose and design. He interpreted this data as evidence of a superior intelligence that guided the development of people "in a definite direction, and for a special purpose."[25] The agreement of Wallace and Darwin on the data and their disagreement on the question of mechanism behind the data suggest that evolution involves both scientific and philosophical implications.

Observations. By the time Darwin wrote *The Origin of Species*, science had come into its own as a distinct field of thought from philosophy. Until the middle of the nineteenth century, those disciplines now grouped under the umbrella of science had a different umbrella over them known as natural philosophy. When science ceased to be called natural philosophy, it appeared that a formal break had occurred that separated science from the philosophical discussions that had accompanied it since the time of the Greek philosophers. Descartes had suggested this separation in his dichotomy of body and mind, empirical data and rationalistic thought.

The change of name, however, merely veiled a relationship that continues to this day. Much of what passes for empirical science is actually rationalistic philosophy. *The Encyclopedia of Philosophy* acknowledges this situation in the way it attends to Darwin. It treats Darwin in two articles. One article discusses Darwin and his contributions as a scientist. A second article discusses the philosophical view known as "Darwinism." Today the philosophical views embodied in Darwinism form a major aspect of the worldview assumptions of modern life. The science of Charles Darwin describes the change in life-forms that has taken place over time. Yet, the issue of change and accounting for why change should occur goes back to the Greek philosophers, as we have seen. The philosophy of Charles Darwin gives a naturalistic explanation for his observations. Just as the Aristotelian philosophical assumptions of the academy provided a framework for science to develop in the late Middle Ages, the philosophical assumptions of Darwinism have provided a framework for science to develop in the twentieth century. Just as the philosophy of Aristotle became enmeshed in the science of the Renaissance, the philosophy of Darwinism has become enmeshed in the science of the twentieth century so that the philosophical assumptions are regarded as scientific dogma.

PHILOSOPHY OF LANGUAGE

By and large, philosophy in Britain had conceded the playing field to empiricism by the early 1930s. C. S. Lewis studied philosophy at Oxford just before and after World War I. By the time he had done additional study in literature and become a tutor at Oxford, the entire conception of philosophy had changed. Under the influence of *logical positivism* in Vienna after World War I, philosophy took a new direction that focused on "cognitive meaning" or empirically verifiable experiences. For a word to have meaning, it must have a physical object to which it refers. Many of the things about which people talk may be satisfying to them, but the positivists would argue that they had no cognitive meaning. They applied this principle to religious issues such as the existence of God. In a famous parable, John Wisdom illustrated the religious problem:

> Two people return to their long-neglected garden and find among the weeds a few of the old plants surprisingly vigorous. One says to the other "It must be that a gardener has been coming and doing something about these plants." Upon inquiry they find that no neighbor has ever seen anyone at work in their garden. The first man says to the other "He must have worked while people slept." The other says, "No, someone would have heard him and besides, anybody who cared about the plants would have kept down these weeds." The first man says, "Look at the way these are arranged. There is purpose and a feeling for beauty here. I believe that someone comes, someone invisible to mortal eyes. I believe that the more carefully we look the more we shall find confirmation of this." They

examine the garden ever so carefully and sometimes they come on new things suggesting that a gardener comes and sometimes they come on new things suggesting the contrary and even that a malicious person has been at work. Besides examining the garden carefully they also study what happens to gardens left without attention. Each learns all the other learns about this and about the garden. Consequently, when after all this, one says "I still believe a gardener comes" while the other says "I don't" their different words now reflect no difference as to what they have found in the garden, no difference as to what they would find in the garden if they looked further and no difference about how fast untended gardens fall into disorder. At this stage, in this context, the gardener hypothesis has ceased to be experimental, the difference between one who accepts and one who rejects it is not now a matter of the one expecting something the other does not expect. What is the difference between them? The one says, "A gardener comes unseen and unheard. He is manifested only in his works with which we are all familiar." The other says, "There is no gardener." With this difference in what they say about the gardener goes a difference in how they feel towards the garden, in spite of the fact that neither expects anything of it which the other does not expect.[26]

The parable suggests that when people have the same empirical data available, they may disagree over the interpretation of the data. Wisdom argued that the interpretation of the data in this situation has to do with the feelings of the observers rather than the data they observe. This line of thought represents the development in philosophy from logical positivism, which looked for the empirically verifiable fact about which language could speak with meaning, to *linguistic analysis*. Linguistic analysis replaced logical positivism in the 1930s and regarded language as a game by which people express their feelings. This philosophical stream would blossom at the end of the twentieth century as a full-blown cultural trend known as postmodernism.

Observations. Notice that the parable allows the existence of the garden but questions the existence of the gardener. The parable acknowledges the appearance of design. The objection to design does not lie within the data itself. The objection lies within the philosophical assumptions of the interpreter of the data.

TENNANT'S REVIVAL OF DESIGN

Though interest in the design argument faded significantly in the new theological/philosophical/scientific climate of the early twentieth century, a major revision of the design argument appeared in Britain at Cambridge at the same time the philosophers of Oxford were capitulating to naturalism. F. R. Tennant (1866–1957) revived not only the design argument, but also the ancient tradition of education. He was trained in chemistry, biology, psychology, theology, philosophy, and logic.

A rabid empiricist in the British tradition, Tennant refuted the rationalism of Plato, Augustine, and Calvin that would attribute reason and knowledge of universals to people at birth. He insisted that knowledge requires sensory data. He further rejected other classical modes for establishing the existence of God. He gave no ground to mysticism, with its claim to ineffable experience of the divine. He denied the existence of any "religious organ" or biological structure that accounted for human knowledge of God (people involved in genetic research at the end of the twentieth century again began to postulate the existence of a "religion gene"). Tennant rejected Rudolf Otto's concept of the universal religious experience. He argued that Otto's "numinous" (Otto's term for religious experience) was too vague and nebulous to serve as valid data for resolving so weighty a matter as the existence of God. He was also averse to admitting data so open to alternative explanations by abnormal psychology! Finally, Tennant would not admit revelation as knowledge of God for apologetic purposes, since so much of the Bible involves moralization that might be accounted for in the natural development of cultures. We should take note that whereas Tennant strove to demonstrate the existence of God and ascribed to Christ the reverence due the one who had the keenest insight into God's purpose, he belonged to the liberal wing of the church. As such, he accepted many of the German higher critical ideas of biblical interpretation then in fashion.

Tennant believed that empirical evidence provided the only legitimate basis for the establishment of theistic religion. The argument rested on the demonstration of two points: the existence of the soul and of God. He reasoned that without a soul, it makes little difference whether God exists! He based his argument for the existence of the soul on the experience of consciousness and self-consciousness. Consciousness involves being aware, but self-consciousness involves being aware of being aware. Because of this reflexive awareness, the memory of the awareness builds a collection of data upon which the self-conscious person may draw. Awareness remains even after the object of awareness has gone! At this point, Tennant makes a bit of a logical stretch by assigning this ability to bring order and continuity to life experience as residing in the soul. He defines *soul* as an observable trait of people that involves the qualities related to the awareness of experience.

Tennant's argument for the existence of God does not depend on his argument for the existence of the soul except in his own mind. His argument involves a revival of the design argument in terms of *cosmic teleology*. The term "teleology" comes from the Greek word *telos*, which means end, goal, or final outcome. Cosmic teleology implies that the entire universe seems designed to lead to a certain goal. In this case, Tennant argued that the universe was designed in such a way as to make life in general, and intelligent life in particular, come to pass. He builds on the tradition of Paley and the authors of the *Bridgewater Treatises*, but he relies heavily on the work of L. J. Henderson. In the same way that Darwin provided empirical evidence to support Hume's idea for the natural explanation of life, Tennant presented an empirical case for the divine origin of life.

L. J. Henderson published a book in 1913 titled *The Fitness of the Environment* in which he explored for page after page the adaptations of inorganic aspects of nature that made life possible. Tennant took up Henderson's data in constructing his own argument that too many variables had to be exactly right in order for life to appear, and the likelihood of these happening by chance is too improbable to consider. On this basis, he argued that some Designer must have arranged all of the necessary conditions to make life possible. While evolution may describe how changes occur in life-forms, it does not account for how life emerged in the first place. One thing the fossil record does not allow is an infinite regress.

This argument is susceptible to the criticism that Tennant does not have a large enough experimental model to predict whether life may emerge by chance. With only one universe, he cannot make a comparative analysis. Hume had made this criticism of the design argument 150 years earlier. Tennant responded to this critique by distinguishing between pure mathematical probability and probability as experienced in the world of fact. This second kind of probability Tennant identified with the induction method of scientific inquiry that cannot be fully explained by reason. At this point, Tennant's rigid empiricism lies on the slippery slope of openness to "hunches" for which successful scientists are so famous, and to the intuitive domain of religious knowledge.

Observations. The commitment to natural theology with its most cherished child, the design argument, has carried with it an increasing commitment to empiricism as the principal and most reliable form of knowledge. In the seventeenth century, the advocates of design saw specific revelation as the highest form of knowledge, but by the time of Tennant, we see that the leading natural theologians did not even consider specific revelation a possibility.

We have also seen that the design argument depends to a great degree on the probability of whether the structures of the universe can best be accounted for by chance or by design. Opponents of design have argued since the eighteenth century that we do not have a large enough experimental basis for study since we only have one universe. We are restricted to what actually happened and cannot consider what might have happened. As we shall see later, the development of the computer in the latter twentieth century has created the possibility of experimenting with innumerable models of the universe. This possibility for research has led in part to a renewed interest in the design argument.

We have also seen that the design argument has developed over the centuries from a general statement about what the casual observer might notice about the universe and its structures to what the trained specialist in precise fields of science might investigate under the most rigorous of circumstances. As we shall see, the new examination of design focuses on scientific research and its implications.

As we saw briefly, as philosophy capitulated to empiricism in Britain in the form of linguistic analysis, it focused almost exclusively on the meaning of language. In this discussion, philosophers moved in their consideration from questions of verification (how to prove something true) to questions of falsification (how to prove something false). In the new conversation about design, we will see that William Dembski focuses a great deal of attention on how one might establish the criteria for determining if the evidence for design makes a convincing case.

We now turn to an examination of developments in science that have sparked the new interest in design.

4. A Fine-Tuned Universe

Jimmy H. Davis

"Do I feel lucky? Well do you . . . ?"
—Clint Eastwood, *Dirty Harry*

D O PEOPLE FEEL LUCKY when they look into the night sky and see the Milky Way, the Big Dipper, and the North Star? Do they feel lucky when photographs from the Hubble Space Telescope reveal how vast the universe is? Do they feel lucky when they turn their gaze to the Earth and see its blue sky, green land, and emerald oceans? Do they feel lucky that there is a place (the Earth) in the vastness of space that has life—not only life but also intelligent life?

A Very, Very, Brief History of the Universe

Before we answer Dirty Harry's question about how lucky we should feel about the universe, we need to review the current scientific thinking on the origin (cosmogony) and structure (cosmology) of the universe. The current scientific understanding is called the big bang theory.[1] According to this theory, the universe began about 13.7 billion years ago, extremely small, very hot, and very dense. Since that beginning, the universe has been expanding and cooling. This tiny universe contained the four fundamental forces that regulate the structures of the nucleus (strong and weak nuclear forces), atoms (electromagnetic force), and clumps of matter (gravity). The theory postulates that atomic nuclei began to form about three minutes after the big bang, atoms began to appear about 500,000 years later, and galaxies began to emerge about a billion years after the big bang. Since first-generation stars are thought to contain only hydrogen and helium, no rocky planets existed in the first galaxies. Throughout the different star life cycles, elements such as carbon and iron were synthesized by nuclear fusion. Upon the death of the first stars through supernova explosions, elements beyond iron were synthesized. About 9 billion years after the big bang, second-generation stars and their planets condensed from the dust clouds that resulted from the death of the first generation stars. Life appeared about 10 billion years after the Big Bang.

Observations. The scientists who proposed the big bang model did not start out with a religious belief in creation and then look for scientific evidence to support it. Rather, the scientists were following a naturalistic or materialistic path of discovering what happens to matter under the influence of the four forces over long periods of time. Thus, many scientists were surprised and disturbed to discover that the big bang model pointed toward biblical themes: a beginning for the universe (creation) and a creator who planned (designed) a universe perfect for human life. The more information scientists collected within the materialistic framework, the more data they had that was consonant with biblical faith. Let us review facets of these findings: a created universe, a fine-tuned universe, and an uncommon Earth.

A Created Universe

From the ancient Greeks until the early 1900s, the prevailing scientific view was of a static, eternal universe. This view posed a major challenge to the Christian view of a created universe. In fact, Thomas Aquinas (1224–1274) had to conclude that knowledge of creation did not come by science but by faith when he harmonized the Greek thought of Aristotle (384–322 BC) with Christian thought. In spite of Thomas' conclusion, by the early 1900s several observations were beginning to challenge the model of a static, eternal universe:

Radioactivity. With the discovery of radioactivity in 1896 by the French physicist Antoine Henri Becquerel (1852–1908), scientists realized that some of the elements that make up the universe do not last forever. Since these elements are still present, can the universe be eternal?

Relativity. In 1915, the German physicist Albert Einstein (1879–1955) published the *General Theory of Relativity*. Einstein realized that his proposed understanding of the universe led to the idea of an expanding universe with a beginning. Einstein believed in a static universe, and he modified his equations (adding the cosmological constant) to remove the expansion of the universe and its beginning. Einstein later said that this modified proposal was the greatest mistake of his life.

Red Shift of Galaxies. As the elements within the sun are heated, they emit light. Each element emits light at characteristic wavelengths. The wavelengths of the light emitted by the same element in other stars were discovered to be shifted toward longer wavelengths. Since the color red has the longest wavelength of the visible colors, the observed shift is called a "red shift." In 1929, the American astronomer Edwin Hubble (1889–1953) interpreted the observed red shifts as evidence of an expanding universe.

Using the relativity calculations and the red shift data, the Belgian priest and astronomer Georges Lemaître (1894–1966) proposed that the universe began as a "primeval atom" that exploded to cause an expanding universe. Russian-American physicist George Gamow (1904–1968) refined Lemaître's model into what is today called the big bang model. Thus, scientists using just the concepts of matter and force stumbled upon a beginning for the universe.

Observations. A beginning implies a cause and a cause implies a creator. Having a creator does not imply a personal, caring God. As we saw in chapter one, since ancient times, other accounts for creation have been given besides the one that credits the universe to God. For example, Plato's creation account attributed the creation not to God but to a Demiurge, a subordinate deity who did the manual labor of heaven. But as scientists continued to examine the universe, they found that the universe is not just any old universe but one designed for human life.

A Fine-tuned Universe

We live in an exciting time in which scientists are able to measure many of the parameters that determine the characteristics of the universe. Also at this time, scientists can use computers to examine how changes in these parameters affect the universe's characteristics. Scientists knew that the big bang model implied certain broad constraints on the occurrence of life: the universe must exist long enough for life to occur; certain stars must be stable long enough for life to occur; heavy elements must be present for the formation of planets and the chemicals of life. At the same time, because scientists were considering only matter and force, they assumed that there could be large variations in the values of the parameters without affecting the occurrence of life. From a materialistic point of view, they did not expect to find fine-tuning.

Getting the Right Atomic Parts. Atoms are made of nucleons (protons and neutrons) surrounded by orbiting electrons. The neutron outweighs the proton by 0.138 percent. This mass difference is surprising, as both neutrons and protons are composed of three smaller particles called quarks. Yet, the implication is significant: "[T]here seems no fundamental reason why the neutron should be the more massive of the two. Furthermore, the mass difference is quite small, a mere tenth of a percent. One might think it would make no difference. But it does make a difference. Indeed it is crucial."[2] It is crucial because neutrons decay while protons do not. Beta decay results when a neutron in the nucleus decays to a proton and an electron. The electron is emitted from the atom as a type of radioactivity called the beta particle. If the proton were more massive than the neutron, then the proton would be the particle that underwent decay. In the latter case, hydrogen, which is composed of an electron and proton, would not exist. (Hydrogen is a necessary element for life as we know it.) Also, if protons decayed rather than neutrons, stars would exhaust their fuel within a century, which is too short a time frame for life to form.

Atoms are composed of two charged particles. The electron has a negative charge while the proton has a positive charge. Static cling in clothes from a dryer shows that like charges repel and unlike charges attract. That the charge of the electron is equal to the charge of the proton is surprising, since the electron and proton appear so different. The proton belongs to the family of elemental particles called *hadrons*, which are made of three quarks, while electrons are in the *lepton* family and are not made of quarks. The proton is also about 1,836 times more massive than the electron. What if the charges of the electron and proton were not equal in magnitude? Depending upon the difference, objects could be torn apart by electrostatic repulsion. For an object the size of a person, a charge difference of one part in a billion would cause the object to fly apart. A difference in electrical charge of one part in a billion billion would cause an object as large as the Earth to fly apart. Thus, the electron-proton charge equality must be finely tuned for the universe to exist.

Getting the Right Atoms. Having the correct subatomic particles is not enough. To have life, these subatomic particles need to combine to form

Element	Percent by Mass in Human Body	Significance
Oxygen	65%	Components of major biological systems
Carbon	18%	
Hydrogen	10%	
Nitrogen	3%	
Phosphorus	1.2%	
Sulfur	0.2%	
Potassium	0.2%	Produce electrolytes responsible for fluid balance and nerve transmission
Sodium	0.1%	
Chlorine	0.2%	
Calcium	1.5%	Bones, nerve function
Magnesium	0.05%	
Zinc	<0.05%	Essential trace metals in human metabolism

Fig. 4.1. Most important elements in living organisms

the atoms of life. The atoms needed for life are shown in figure 4.1, with the most abundant elements being oxygen, carbon, and hydrogen. To obtain the right atoms, there must be a balance among the strong nuclear force, the weak nuclear force, and gravity. Another factor in obtaining the right atoms is the relationship among the nuclear energy states of different atoms.

The strong nuclear force, which is the strongest of the four fundamental forces, governs the degree to which protons and neutrons stick together in the nucleus. If the strong nuclear force were 2 percent weaker than it currently is, protons and neutrons would not stick together, and the only atom that could form would be hydrogen; hydrogen has only one proton and no neutrons in its nucleus. With this slightly weaker strong nuclear force, the heavier elements needed for life would not form. If the strong nuclear force were just 0.3 percent stronger than it currently is, the affinity of protons and neutrons for each other would be so great that none of them would occur alone. In this case, the atom hydrogen could not exist, eliminating a vital component of biological systems.

The weak nuclear force is active among subatomic particles and governs the rates of radioactive decay. If the weak nuclear force were stronger than it currently is, all the atoms would be converted to heavier elements, and life-essential elements such as carbon, oxygen, nitrogen, and phosphorus would not exist. If the weak nuclear force were weaker than it currently is, the universe would contain only the lightest elements. In the latter case, the concentrations of carbon, oxygen, nitrogen, and phosphorus would be too small to build biological molecules. Finally, if the weak nuclear force were weaker than it currently is, not enough neutrinos would be produced to cause supernova explosions. Supernova explosions scatter heavy elements into space. Heavy elements are needed to form rocky planets like the Earth.

Gravity is the weakest of the four fundamental forces but operates over long distances. According to current cosmological theory, a star begins as a cloud of hydrogen gas held together by gravity. The force of gravity gradually pulls the hydrogen gas toward the center of the cloud, causing the gas temperature to increase. As the contraction continues, the hydrogen gas reaches a temperature high enough for hydrogen atoms to fuse into helium atoms. The star "ignites" and expands outward because of the forces released by the fusion. Calculations reveal that if the force of gravity were slightly smaller, the friction due to the collapse of the hydrogen cloud would never reach a temperature high enough to cause fusion to occur. According to current theory, stars are needed for life to exist. Conversely, if the force of gravity were slightly larger, the resulting hydrogen clouds would be so large that only very large stars would form. The larger a star, the faster it "burns" its nuclear fuel and the shorter its life span. Thus, in a universe with a stronger gravity, the life span of stars would be too short for life to develop.

According to the big bang model, the nuclei of all the elements above hydrogen are synthesized by nuclear fusion within the stars. Nuclear fusion occurs when two nuclei collide and stick together to form a larger nucleus. For the two smaller nuclei to stick, the energy of the two nuclei plus their energy of motion must be equal to or slightly smaller than a stable energy level for the new atom. One can model the nuclear energy levels by using books and a bookshelf (fig. 4.2). The widths of the books represent the energy of one of the small nuclei. The shelves of the bookcase represent possible allowed energy states of an atom that could result from the fusion. If the combined height of the two books (their combined energy) is greater than the height of the shelf (energy level of new nucleus), then fusion will not occur. If the stacked books can fit on a shelf, fusion will occur and a new atom will be formed.

Fig. 4.2. Nuclear energy levels. The books a, b, and c represent nuclei that can possibly fuse. The four-shelved bookcase represents the nuclear energy levels of a nucleus that could possibly be formed by fusion. The energy of the fused atom is modeled by stacking the books on their sides. Books a and c or b and c could not fit on any of the shelves. These combinations will not result in fusion. Books a and b could fit on shelf 4. Fusion will occur with this combination.

In the nuclear reactions of stars, there is fine-tuning among the nuclei of helium, beryllium, carbon, and oxygen. The relationships among these nuclei[3] are helium-4 plus helium-4 equals beryllium-8; beryllium-8 plus helium-4 equals carbon-12; and carbon-12 plus helium-4 equals oxygen-16.

In the first relationship, beryllium-8 is formed from two helium-4 nuclei. Beryllium-8 has a very short half-life of only 10^{-15} seconds. If beryllium-8 were more stable, fusion to the heavier elements would proceed fast enough to explode before enough heavy elements formed for the occurrence of life. If beryllium-8 were even less stable, no elements beyond beryllium, such as carbon, would form.

The second relationship involves carbon-12. When beryllium-8 and helium-4 collide, they have a combined energy that is just 4 percent less than an energy level in carbon-12. The kinetic energy of their collision provides enough energy to match the carbon-12 energy level. If the combined energies of beryllium-8 and helium-4 were anything other than this precise fit, not enough carbon would be synthesized for life to occur.

The third relationship involves oxygen-16. When carbon-12 and helium-4 collide, they have a combined energy that is 1 percent greater than the energy level of oxygen-16. This energy level mismatch prevents all the carbon from being converted to oxygen. The helium-4, beryllium-8, carbon-12, and oxygen-16 relationships were predicted by the British astronomer Fred Hoyle (b. 1915) in 1954. Hoyle, an atheist, wrote,

> A common sense interpretation of the facts suggests that a super-intellect has monkeyed with physics, as well as with chemistry and biology, and that there are no blind forces worth speaking about in nature. The numbers one calculates from the facts seem to me so overwhelming as to put this conclusion almost beyond question.[4]

Getting the Right Molecules. For life to be possible, atoms must combine to form molecules. Figure 4.3 shows some common molecules found in living organisms. Molecules form when atoms share electrons. Two atoms can share electrons if their outermost electrons have similar energies. The ability of atoms to bind together to form molecules depends upon two factors: the strength of the electromagnetic force and the ratio of the mass of the electron to the mass of the proton. Daily we experience the electromagnetic force through magnetism and electrical interactions such as static cling. If the electromagnetic force were smaller, the atomic nucleus could not hold onto the electrons and there would be no sharing of electrons to make molecules. If the electromagnetic force were larger, elements above boron, such as carbon, would be unstable. In either case, the molecules needed for life would not exist.

The proton is 1,836 times more massive than the electron. The ratio between the mass of the proton and electron determines the paths that the electrons travel as they orbit the nucleus. If the ratio between the proton and electron were slightly larger or smaller, no molecules could form and life would be impossible.

Having Enough Time. Even if we fine-tune all the previously discussed variables to produce the molecules of life, we still need a universe that will exist long enough for life to occur. According to the big bang model, life did not occur until the universe was about 10 billion years old. It is thought that this amount of time is needed for first-generation stars to synthesize all the elements needed to form planets and the molecules of life.

Fig. 4.3. Molecules of life. In the molecules, carbon = C, hydrogen = H, oxygen = O, nitrogen = N, and phosphorus = P. The lines represent the bonds between the atoms.

How long the universe exists is due to the interaction between the size of the big bang and the force of gravity. The big bang causes the space-time fabric of the universe to expand outward. The gravitational attraction between the components of the universe acts like a brake to slow down and possibly reverse the expansion. An everyday analogy of this conflict involves a ball attached to a paddle by a rubber band. When hit by the paddle, the ball flies away, stretching the rubber band. At some point, the outward motion of the ball equals the inward pull of the rubber band. The ball stops moving outward and the pull of the rubber band causes the ball to fly inward toward the paddle. The distance the ball flies before stopping and returning to the paddle depends upon how hard the ball was originally struck. Likewise, the larger the big bang, the longer the space-time fabric of the universe will expand before it can possibly be stopped by the gravitational force.

Calculations have shown that if the big bang were slightly smaller (one part in a billion trillion), the time taken for gravity to stop the expansion of the universe and re-compact the universe (the big crunch) would be less time than it took for life to develop in the current universe. If the big bang were slightly larger (one part in a million), the expansion would be too fast for gravity to collect matter into stars and planets, which, according to the current model, are needed for life to form. In either case, the "birth" of the universe (the force of expansion) had to be finely tuned for life to develop.

Another time factor is the amount of time it took for life to occur on Earth. The current model estimates the time between the formation of the Earth and the appearance of life on the Earth as about 1 billion years, with man appearing about 3 billion years later. Thus, stars with stable energy outputs over billions of years are necessary. The ratio of the electromagnetic force constant to the gravitational force constant determines the type of star that forms. If this ratio were decreased by just one part in 10^{40}, only stars larger than the sun could form. These large stars rapidly burn their fuel and have lifetimes too short for life to develop. For a further discussion, see the section below titled "Uncommon Earth."

Having Enough Space. Another factor in determining whether life can occur is the size of the universe. In the movie *Contact*, a character remarks that if the universe does not have life scattered throughout the galaxies, it was a waste of space. In 1900, astronomers believed that the universe consisted of only the Milky Way galaxy. If life is found only on Earth, then this would seem to be a much more economical universe than a universe with countless galaxies void of life. The Milky Way contains about 100 billion stars. A universe of this size and mass would have only expanded for about a month before the big crunch. Such a small universe might be more economical but would be lifeless.

Another version of the "waste of space" argument involves wondering why the universe contains so much empty space—why the stars are so far apart. If the stars were closer to each other, the stellar gravitational interactions would disrupt planets from their orbits around the stars, flinging the planets into interstellar space to freeze.

Observations. Working within a materialistic worldview, many scientists were very surprised to discover that the existence of life requires a fine-tuning of the universe. Everywhere scientists looked, they found very little leeway in how the universe was put together. Protons, neutrons, and electrons need to be very close to their observed masses and charges for atoms to form. The atoms of life (hydrogen, carbon, oxygen, and so forth) would not be stable if the strengths of the strong nuclear force, weak nuclear force, and gravity were not very near their current values. Changing strength of the electromagnetic force and the sizes of the proton and electron would prevent the molecules needed for life from forming. The size of the big bang and the current strength of gravity were needed to allow enough time for life to appear. Also, all the billions and billions of stars and galaxies are needed to provide enough matter and space for a stable universe to exist long enough for life to exist. No wonder the atheist Hoyle had to struggle with the design reflected by the "superintellect" that "monkeyed" with the universe.

Uncommon Earth

Each year we ask our upper-level students to give a class presentation on selected topics, such as whether there is life on the other planets of the solar system or whether there is intelligent life elsewhere in the universe. The students usually go beyond the science and really want there to be life elsewhere. They are like the characters in the movie *Contact* who think all the space in the universe is wasted if we are the only life. Well, are we lucky to have the Earth, or is it just one of thousands of planets teeming with life?

What is the place of the Earth in the universe? To the ancients, the Earth was the center of the universe. The Earth was unique; it was imperfect and temporal while the heavens were perfect and eternal. The Polish astronomer Nicolaus Copernicus and his followers made the Earth just one planet among others orbiting a minor star in the backwater of the Milky Way galaxy. Astronomers Frank Drake and Carl Sagan, who estimated the number of planets with life and advanced civilizations in the Milky Way galaxy, express this thinking in the Drake equation.[5] The form of the equation is

$$N_* \times f_p \times n_e \times f_l \times f_i \times f_c \times f_L$$

where (with Drake-Sagan estimate of value):

N_* = the number of stars in the Milky Way galaxy (400 billion)

f_p = fraction of stars having planetary systems (1/3)

n_e = number of planets with environments suitable for life (2)

f_l = fraction of suitable planets where life occurred (1/3)

f_i = fraction of inhabited planets where intelligence arose

f_c = fraction of intelligent civilizations that developed communicative technology ($f_i \times f_c$ = 1/100)

f_L = fraction of planet's life with technical civilization (1/100,000,000)

Putting these estimates together, Drake and Sagan calculated that

the number of stars with planets could be 130 billion;

the number of planets with environments suitable for life could be about 300 billion;

the number of suitable planets where life occurred could be 100 billion;

the number of planets with a technical civilization could be 1 billion;

the number of technical civilizations in the Milky Way at one time could be ten.

The Drake-Sagan numbers imply that the Earth is not uncommon. According to Drake and Sagan, the Earth is one of 100 billion planets where life occurred and one of a billion planets where technical civilization developed. "Don't worry, be happy." If an advanced civilization had not developed on Earth, there are a billion other places for it to develop. Such thinking is the basis of the SETI (Search for Extraterrestrial Intelligence) project. Begun in 1990, NASA funded a modest SETI project for a few years. The search is now privately funded.[6]

Recently, scientists have been rethinking the assumptions behind the Drake equation. The Drake equation assumes that the Earth is a common planet reproduced billions of times in the galaxy. Some scientists are beginning to think that the Earth is an uncommon planet in an uncommon area of the galaxy. To decide whether the Earth is an uncommon planet, one needs to consider the type of galaxy the Earth is in, the Earth's star location in the galaxy, the type of star the sun is, the Earth's location in relation to the sun, the location of other planets in the solar system, the size of the Earth's satellite, and the composition of the Earth.

Galaxy Type. Astronomers estimate that there are 100 billion galaxies, each containing billions of stars. The three types of galactic shapes are spiral, elliptical, and irregular. Most galaxies are elliptical. Elliptical galaxies contain older stars that have a low concentration of heavy metals needed for life. Irregular galaxies are usually located near larger galaxies. Their irregular shape is thought to result from tidal interactions with the larger galaxy. Such interactions would create instabilities that would not favor the development of life. The sun is located in the Milky Way galaxy, which is a spiral galaxy. Spiral galaxies are flattened disks that contain large populations of gas, dust, molecular clouds, and young stars that provide the environment for life to occur.

Location in Galaxy. Even spiral galaxies can have dangerous environments. Within the Milky Way galaxy, there are compact, spherical groups of stars called globular clusters. Not only do globular clusters contain the oldest stars in the galaxy, these stars are tightly packed together. In some cases, the stars in a cluster are only a few billion kilometers away from each other. Both the age of the globular cluster stars and the star density disfavor the occurrence of life. The star-packed center of a galaxy is also a dangerous place, with black holes, supernovae, and stellar close encounters. The sun is located far from the galactic center (about 32,600 light years), currently between spiral arms (fig. 4.4). As the sun rotates around the galactic center,

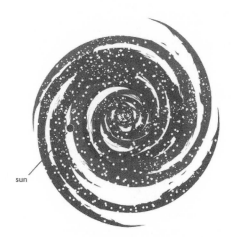

sun

Fig. 4.4. Location of the sun in the Milky Way Galaxy

it is thought that the sun spends 80 million years outside the spiral arms, 40 million years in, and so forth.

Type of Star. A suitable star is one that will burn long enough for life to occur, one that does not rapidly change in energy output, and one without too much ultraviolet radiation emission. The sun is not a typical star; 95 percent of all stars are less massive than the sun. Less massive stars are less luminous; thus, a planet would have to be very close to the star to stay warm. But being close to the star is dangerous because of tidal effects. Also, at close distances, the rotation of the planet becomes locked so that one side always faces the star, as in the case of the planet Mercury. This rotational lock causes one side of the planet to freeze, the other side to burn. Stars much larger than the sun have life spans too short for life to occur. It is estimated that 70 percent of all stars are binary or multiple stars. Binary or multiple stars contain two or more stars orbiting each other. Stable planetary orbits are hard to imagine in such systems. The sun is a single star. It is not the largest or smallest, the hottest or coolest type of star. It contains a lot of metals (building blocks for planets) and has had a stable output for billions of years.

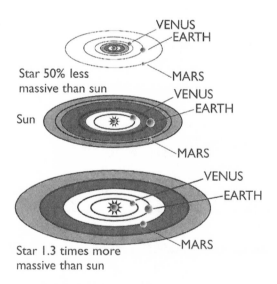

Fig. 4.5. Estimates of habitable zones around stars. Adapted from Peter D. Ward and Donald Brownlee, Rare Earth *(New York: Copernicus, 2000).*

Where the Earth Is Located in Relation to the Sun. Once one has a solar-type star in the outer reaches of a spiral galaxy, one then has to determine if there is an ideal distance for a planetary orbit. The ideal distance is considered to be the distance from the star where the water in the ocean neither permanently freezes nor boils away. This turns out to be a range of distances called the habitable zone (fig. 4.5). A planet such as Venus, located closer to the sun than the habitable zone, would become too hot for life. A planet such as Mars, located farther from the sun than the habitable zone, would become too cold for life. With the Earth at a distance from the sun of 1.0 AU (1.0 AU equals 93 million miles), the width of the sun's habitable zone is from 0.95 to 1.15 AU. Thus, the habitable zone for the sun is very narrow.

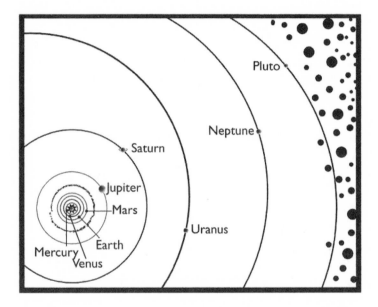

Fig. 4.6. The solar system. Note the relationship between Earth and Jupiter.

Location of Other Planets in the Solar System. Just being in the habitable zone does not appear to be enough to ensure the stability of life. Figure 4.6 shows the relationship of Jupiter to the Earth. Mars is smaller than the Earth. Jupiter, being near Mars, is thought to have attracted building material to itself, resulting in a smaller Mars. Thus, if the orbit of Jupiter had been a little closer to the orbit of the Earth, then the Earth could have ended up as small as Mars. A smaller planet would not support life, since it could not retain its atmosphere.

Although Jupiter could have been a threat to the Earth, Jupiter in the right place can be a guardian for the Earth. Throughout the history of the solar system, planets have been bombarded by asteroids and comets. Too many impacts can melt the surface of a planet and sterilize the planet. What controls the impact rate? Computer modeling indicates that the giant planet Jupiter acts as an asteroid and comet catcher. Jupiter's gravity captures many asteroids and comets, preventing them from reaching the Earth. Is there any evidence of Jupiter-like planets around other stars? Yes, since 1995, at least 209 planets orbiting stars other than the sun have been discovered.[7] Only large planets like Jupiter can be detected. All of these "Jupiters" are in bad orbits. Some are in elliptical orbits far from the star. Elliptical orbits would create unstable gravitational effects that would not "protect" any inner terrestrial-like planets. Others of these "Jupiters" are in circular orbits close to the star. It is speculated that these "Jupiters" formed far from the star and that their orbits decayed. As the "Jupiter" spiraled inward, it would sweep any terrestrial-like planets into the star. All other "Jupiters" detected so far seem to prevent the occurrence of life.

Size of the Earth's Satellite. The Earth has a satellite similar in size to itself. (In the rest of the solar system, only Pluto has a satellite similar in size to itself.) The large moon stabilizes the tilt axis of the Earth and thus stabilizes the climate of the Earth. The tilt of the Earth's spin axis has not varied by more than a degree or two from its present value of 23 degrees. It is calculated that without the moon, the Earth's tilt axis could vary by as much as 90 degrees. Figure 4.7 shows the relationship between the tilt axis of a planet and the amount of solar radiation falling on the planet's poles and equator. At a tilt of 0 degrees, no sunlight would ever reach the poles. At a tilt of 90 degrees, one pole would be exposed to sunlight for half a year while the other pole would be in darkness. Such fluctuations in the tilt axis would make it very difficult for life to exist.

The Composition of the Earth. Even with the right planet around the right star in the right location in a galaxy, the existence of life could still be difficult. The planet must possess a certain composition for life to flourish. The planet needs to contain carbon and other elements necessary for life (fig. 4.7). The Earth contains 0.05 percent carbon by weight, while the rocky asteroids contain 4 percent carbon. It is thought that if the Earth contained as much carbon as the asteroids, the carbon dioxide produced would cause runaway greenhouse overheating.

The planet needs water on and near its surface. The Earth contains 0.1 percent water by weight while the asteroids contain 20 percent water. A planet needs enough water to buffer the global temperature but not too much to

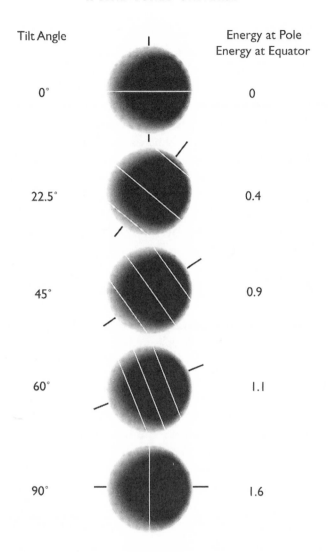

Fig 4.7. The relationship between the tilt angle and the ratio of solar energy falling on a planet's pole and equator. Earth's tilt angle is 22.5 degrees. Adapted from Peter D. Ward and Donald Brownlee, Rare Earth *(New York: Copernicus, 2000).*

prevent shallow seas from occurring. Twice as much water on Earth would likely result in a water world. Such a water world would result in very few nutrients being available in the ocean, since these nutrients come from land erosion. On Earth with its shallow seas, carbon dioxide is turned into limestone in these shallow seas and thus is removed from the atmosphere. A water world would produce a runaway greenhouse effect, since deep waters would not be able to remove carbon dioxide in this way. Instead of a runaway greenhouse effect, the Earth's temperature has remained stable. It is estimated that for the last 2 billion years, oceans have been at an average temperature of less than 50 degrees Fahrenheit.

The planet needs an atmosphere containing oxygen and an ozone layer. The Earth atmosphere contains 20.9 percent oxygen by volume. A greater concentration than this could result in hydrocarbons and plants being burned too easily. The atmosphere's oxygen concentration is maintained through oxidation of minerals and respiration of plants. The ozone layer is a region of the Earth's atmosphere about 19 to 48 kilometers (12 to 30 miles) above the Earth's surface. In this layer, ozone concentrations of up to ten parts per million occur. The ozone layer protects life on Earth by absorbing some of the ultraviolet radiation from the sun.

The planet needs heavy metals such as iron and nickel in its core. This type of core generates a magnetic field that protects the planet from high-energy particles from outer space by repelling these particles. The planet also needs radioactive elements such as uranium. The heat from the radioactive decay in the inner regions of the planet helps maintain a constant planetary temperature.

Finally, a planet needs a thin outer crust of low-density material to allow for plate tectonics to occur. The Earth's continents and oceans rest on a layer of rock called the lithosphere. The lithosphere consists of thirteen rock masses or plates (fig. 4.8). Plate tectonics is the theory that describes the motion of these plates. The boundaries of these plates are where earthquakes and volcanic eruptions tend to occur. The movements of the plates gradually rearrange the surface of the Earth (fig. 4.9). The lithosphere needs to contain water in order for it to be able to bend and break, allowing the

Fig. 4.8. The Earth's crust is divided into thirteen major plates. Arrows indicate the general direction of plate movement.

plates to move. Why is plate tectonics important? The movement of the plates helps regulate the carbon dioxide concentration in the atmosphere and thus the temperature of the Earth. As discussed before, carbon dioxide is removed through weathering by the formation of limestone. Limestone

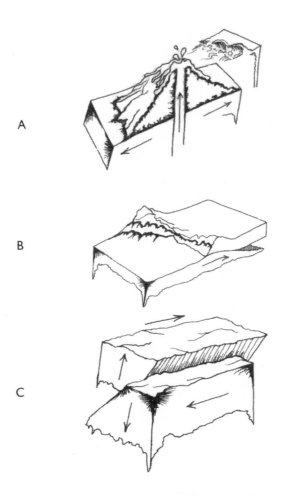

Fig. 4.9. The different ways the plates interact. (A) Diverge along a volcanic ridge where new crust is constantly being formed. (B) Converge so that one plate must be subducted beneath the other. (C) Scrape against another plate to form a fault zone, which may produce violent earthquakes. In each case, the plate motions result from movement of the convecting mantle below.

at plate boundaries is subducted (pulled down) deep into the mantle, where it decomposes to release carbon dioxide. Thus, weathering and subduction work together to keep the carbon dioxide concentration in balance. The movement of the plates creates continents and shallow seas. Without plate tectonics rebuilding the continents, the continental landmasses would ultimately be worn down by erosion. Plate tectonics helps make possible the Earth's magnetic field. The Earth contains a liquid iron-nickel core. Plate tectonics removes heat from this core, setting up convection currents. These convection currents in the spinning core create the magnetic field. In the absence of the magnetic field, high-energy particles from outer space could boil away the Earth's atmosphere. Finally, plate tectonics, through rearranging the Earth's surface, promotes global biodiversity.

Observations. After listing all factors that make the Earth uncommon, it is now obvious that Drake and Sagan overestimated the number of stars and planets that could have life. Rather than being one planet among billions, the Earth now appears to be the uncommon Earth, the rare Earth. Again, Hoyle's superintellect has monkeyed with the universe by placing the sun far from the center of a spiral galaxy; located the Earth in the habitable zone of a typical star; located the Earth at a safe distance from Jupiter; provided the Earth with the moon to stabilize the tilt angle and the climate of the Earth; provided the Earth with the "right" amount of carbon, oxygen, heavier elements, and water; and provided plate tectonics to rebuild and replenish the Earth. The data implies that the Earth may be the only planet "in the right place at the right time."

RESPONSES TO THE DATA

The responses to evidence pointing to a created universe, a fine-tuned universe, and an uncommon Earth depend upon one's worldview. In general, the responses fall into two categories. Some observers regard the universe as the result of purely materialistic processes. Others believe the universe is the result of intelligent design.

Materialistic Processes Responses

Scientists who propose materialistic processes to explain the structure of the universe in many cases do not deny that the universe *appears* to be designed. Nonetheless, they not only deny that God was the designer; they deny that there is any designer. As astrophysicist George Greenstein states,

As we survey all the evidence, the thought insistently arises that some supernatural agency—or, rather, Agency—must be involved. Is it possible that suddenly, without intending to, we have stumbled upon scientific proof of the existence of a Supreme Being? Was it God who stepped in and so providentially crafted the cosmos for our benefit? . . . A heady prospect. Unfortunately I believe it to be illusory . . . . I believe that the discoveries of science are not capable of proving God's existence—not now, not ever. And more than that: I believe that reference to God will never suffice to explain a single one of these discoveries. God is not an explanation.[8]

The following responses cover the range of materialistic explanations for the structure of the universe and the existence of intelligent life. We will divide the materialist responses into two classes: anthropic principles and non-anthropic responses. Since the word "anthropic" means "of or related to human beings," the anthropic principles attempt to give a materialistic reason for the existence of humans. There are at least four anthropic principles: weak, strong, participatory, and final. Non-anthropic responses attempt to provide materialistic explanations for the structure of the universe without the special emphasis on humans.

Accident of Observation. This argument states that because we exist, the universe must be so constructed to support life. Many unlikely (low probability) events had to have occurred or we would not be here. Maybe it was just incredible luck that the universe happened to have the right conditions for life. This argument states that just as someone wins the lottery even though the odds are very small, a universe that supports life occurred even though its odds of occurring were very small. This argument is called the weak anthropic principle (WAP).

The weak anthropic principle is a tautology; it states the obvious. If the universe was not fit for life, then we would not be here. Which is a larger act of faith, believing that the God of the Bible designed the universe or that the universe is the surprise result of a series of chance events?

Many Possible Worlds. Some scientists go beyond the tautology of the weak anthropic principle to state that the universe must have those properties that allow life to occur. This latter statement is called the strong anthropic principle (SAP). What material process can make these properties present? One explanation is to evoke the existence of multiple worlds (universes). One way to deal with the previously discussed very small probabilities is to propose billions of universes with our universe being the one with life. One version of the many-possible-worlds proposal is to assume that the multiple universes followed each other in time. Billions of big bangs would be followed by expansion, then contraction to a big crunch, to be followed by another big bang, and so forth. Each big bang–big crunch sequence represents one universe with its unique set of parameters. We exist in the universe that supports life. As we saw in chapter three, David Hume proposed a similar theory in the eighteenth century.

Another version of the many-possible-worlds proposal is to assume that billions of universes exist simultaneously. Since the word "universe" means the sum total of things, these multiple universes are sometimes called multiple worlds or *multiverse*, and other times are labeled *mini-universes* in a *super-universe*. There are at least three flavors to the simultaneous many-possible-worlds proposal. Two of the flavors arise from the inflationary big bang model, with the third from quantum mechanics. During the earliest time period of the big bang model, energy-matter fluctuations could have formed "bubbles" that individually inflated into mini-universes. One flavor proposes that these mini-universes are stacked one on top of the other in the multi-dimensions of space. Currently there would be no way to communicate between these mini-universes. Recent interpretations of string theory support this view. Another flavor proposes that these bubbles inflated into domains within one universe. Each domain would have its own set of properties. Our domain would be what we consider the universe. These domains are so far apart that again there is no communication between them. One interpretation of quantum mechanics is that every time a quantum event occurs, the universe is split. Since there are billions of atoms and since all atomic and subatomic events are quantum events, this flavor would result in zillions and zillions of universes. To someone with a materialistic worldview, all three of these flavors do provide enough universes to provide enough chances for our universe and life to occur.

The burden of proof resides with those making the many-possible-worlds proposals. How scientific is a proposal that cannot be tested? If there is no way to detect the other worlds, how scientific is this proposal? As Martin Gardner states, "The many-worlds interpretation has been called a beautiful theory that nobody can believe."[9]

Man the Creator. This proposal states that observers are needed to bring the universe into existence and is called the participatory anthropic principle (PAP). The PAP also grows from an interpretation of quantum mechanics that states that the act of observing creates the reality; by choosing to observe the wave properties of the electron, the observer causes the electron to be a wave rather than a particle. A proponent of this interpretation of quantum mechanics as well as of the participatory anthropic principle is the physicist John A. Wheeler. Wheeler states:

> The Universe starts small at the big bang, grows in size, gives rise to life and observers and observing equipment. The observing equipment, in turn, through the elementary quantum processes that terminate on it, takes part in giving tangible "reality" to events that occurred long before there was any life anywhere.[10]

Notice that Wheeler capitalizes the word "universe" in his text.

There are several concerns with PAP. Quantum events are at the heart of Wheeler's PAP. Yet quantum mechanics deals with micro-, not macro-systems. The uncertainty of a quantum event approaches zero as the number of particles increases. The uncertainty involved in observing an electron would not be the same as that for the universe. Intelligence is not an exclusive factor in observing quantum events. Cloud chambers, Geiger counters, and photographic plates can record quantum events. Also, there are minds other than the human mind. Could a moth observe the moon and give it reality?

Creation of God. The participatory anthropic principle is extended by the astronomer John Barrow and physicist Frank Tipler to what they call the final anthropic principle (FAP): intelligence must come into existence, and once it does, it can never die out. They believe that life will spread beyond the Earth to colonize all of space and to keep the universe from destroying itself and life. Using the terminology of the Catholic paleontologist Teilhard de Chardin, Barrow and Tipler state:

> At the instant the Omega Point is reached, life will have gained control of *all* matter and forces not only in a single universe but in all universes whose existence is logically possible; life will have spread into *all* spatial regions in all universes which could logically exist, and will have stored an infinite amount of information, including *all* bits of knowledge which it is logically possible to know.[123] And this is the end.[11]

Note 123 in the Barrow and Tipler quote states, "A modern-day theologian might wish to say that the totality of life at the Omega Point is omnipotent, omnipresent, and omniscient!"[12] Thus, Barrow and Tipler are saying God does not exist now but that all of life is evolving into God.

The critic Martin Gardner offered this evaluation of Barrow and Tipler's work: "What should we make of this quartet of WAP, SAP, PAP, and FAP? In my not so humble opinion I think the last principle is best called CRAP, the Completely Ridiculous Anthropic Principle."[13] By rejecting the notion of an eternal, transcendent Creator God, materialists have to propose more and more irrational options. As the Bible says, "See to it no one takes you captive through hollow and deceptive philosophy" (Colossians 2:8 NIV).

Inflexible Fundamental Constants. Not all who express a materialistic response agree with the anthropic principles. They would criticize the anthropic folks for putting a special emphasis on humans. One response is to use the many-possible-worlds proposal to suggest that this is the only universe where life probably occurred. They further criticize the anthropic principles by saying that the fundamental constants have no choice in their values. They agree with Einstein when he said, "There are no arbitrary constants. . . . Nature is so constructed that it is possible logically to lay down such strongly determined laws that within these laws only . . . completely determined constants occur."[14] Scientists who hold this view are encouraged by the work of those trying to understand the earliest part of the big bang theory. The grand unified theories (GUT) have attempted to model the time in the early universe when the electromagnetic, strong nuclear, and weak nuclear forces were combined. The GUT results imply that the values of the electromagnetic force and the strong nuclear force are linked. If true, the values of these forces could not be individually fine-tuned. As we have previously discussed, string theory is another attempt to understand the early universe. As anthropic critic and physicist Gordon Kane says, "[I]f this theory is right there will be no move to vary any of the constants the anthropic people like to vary."[15] So far, however, string theory has not predicted the value of any of the constants: "[I]f string theory pins down every physical constant, then the fine-tuning for life will turn out to be hard-wired into the mathematics."[16] Thus, design is not removed; design just moves from the constants to the underlying laws. The designer is still in the equations.

Observations. The anthropic principles seem to be proposing a "mystic" design without a designer. Is it scientific to believe that the future designs the past? It is amazing how the many-possible-worlds model is becoming the materialistic response of choice. One sees it in popular magazines such as *National Geographic.* The very vocal critics of design invoke the many-possible-worlds model to say here is a "scientific" alternative to design. This model may feel good to the materialists, but it is not "scientific" if there is no way to falsify the model.

INTELLIGENT DESIGN RESPONSES

This chapter's opening quote from *Dirty Harry* asks how lucky we feel. How lucky should we feel when we consider that the universe is similar to Goldilocks' porridge, with every key parameter about just right? How many coincidences does it take for one to say that luck has nothing to do with it, that someone has designed it this way? Is one coincidence enough, two, three, or the approximately seventy coincidences for the fine-tuning of the universe and Earth?[17] All these coincidences seem to point to either incredible luck or intelligent design. As we saw in the last section, many scientists can never, philosophically, go beyond a naturalistic explanation for the coincidences. Another example is geologist Peter D. Ward and astronomer Donald Brownlee, whose book *Rare Earth*[18] concerns how unique the Earth is; they never once address design issues nor acknowledge others who have made similar arguments within the context of design. As Ward has said, "We are just incredibly lucky. Somebody had to win the big lottery, and we were it."[19]

Surely there is some way to distinguish luck from design? The mathematician William Dembski has written extensively on how people determine whether an event is by chance or by design. As Dembski writes,

> The fact remains . . . that intelligent causes have played, are playing and will continue to play an important role in science. Entire industries, economic and scientific, depend crucially on such notions as intelligence, intentionality and information. Included here are forensic science, intellectual property law, insurance claims investigation, cryptography, random number generation, archaeology, and the search for extraterrestrial intelligence (SETI).[20]

Thus, one sees that design interference is a legitimate concern of many areas of science. However, many scientists have been unable to transfer the design interference techniques to questions concerning the origin of the universe, structure of the universe, or origin of life. How does one determine if an event is designed?

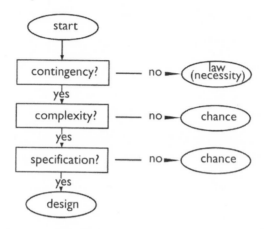

Fig. 4.10. The explanatory filter. Adapted from William A. Dembski, Intelligent Design *(Downers Grove, Ill.: InterVarsity Press, 1999).*

How does forensic science work? When confronted with an event, a scientist must determine whether the event is the result of law, chance, or design. Dembski calls this decision process the *explanatory filter*; a flowchart representation of this filter appears in figure 4.10. Dembski proposes that contingency, complexity, and specification must be present in the event for design to be present. If there is no *contingency*, then the event is the result of an automatic process that had no choice in its output. Here the appeal would be to a natural law where things always occur this way. Next, one needs to establish the presence of complexity. With *complexity*, the event is not so simple that it can be explained by chance. Finally, it is necessary to establish *specification*, a detailed, precise pattern associated with intelligent causes. Thus, Dembski proposes that *specified complexity* is how intelligent design is detected. A single letter of the alphabet, such as C, is specified but not complex. A random drawing from a hat containing the twenty-seven letters of the alphabet could result in the letter C. A string of letters, SDIERMNTY-HJVM, is complex but not specified. A poem of Robert Frost is complex and specified and the result of design.

Let us consider two events: radio signals received from CP 1919 by astronomers in England in 1967 and radio signals received by the SETI investigators in the movie *Contact* (fig. 4.11).

In 1967, graduate student Jocelyn Bell at the University of Cambridge, England, discovered a pattern in the radio signals from the celestial object

Space Source CP 1919	Movie Contact
101010101010101010101010101010101010101010	11011101111101111111011111111111011111
101010101010101010101010101010101010101010	11111111011111111111111111101111111111
101010101010101010101010101010101010101010	11111111011111111111111111111111011111
101010101010101010101010101010101010101010	11111111111111111111111101111111111111
101010101010101010101010101010101010101010	11111111111111110111111111111111111111
101010101010101010101010101010101010101010	11111111111111111011111111111111111111
101010101010101010101010101010101010101010	11111111111111111111101111111111111111
101010101010101010101010101010101010101010	11111111111111111111111111011111111111
101010101010101010101010101010101010101010	11111111111111111111111111111111111111
101010101010101010101010101010101010101010	01111111111111111111111111111111111111
101010101010101010101010101010101010101010	11111111111111101111111111111111111111
101010101010101010101010101010101010101010	11111111111111111111111111111111111111
101010101010101010101010101010101010101010	01111111111111111111111111111111111111
101010101010101010101010101010101010101010	11111111111111111111111101111111111111
101010101010101010101010101010101010101010	11111111111111111111111111111111111111
101010101010101010101010101010101010101010	11111111111111101111111111111111111111
101010101010101010101010101010101010101010	11111111111111111111111111111111111111
101010101010101010101010101010101010101010	11111111111011111111111111111111111111
101010101010101010101010101010101010101010	11111111111111111111111111111111111111
101010101010101010101010101010101010101010	11111111101111111111111111111111111111
101010101010101010101010101010101010101010	11111111111111111111111111111111111111
101010101010101010101010101010101010101010	11111111111110111111111111111111111111
101010101010101010101010101010101010101010	11111111111111111111111111111111111111
101010101010101010101010101010101010101010	11111111111111111110111111111111111111
101010101010101010101010101010101010101010	11111111111111111111111111111111111111
101010101010101010101010101010101010101010	11111111111111111111111111111111111101
101010101010101010101010101010101010101010	11111111111111111111111111111111111111
101010101010101010101010101010101010101010	11111111111111111111111111111111111111
101010101010101010101010101010101010101010	11111111111111111011111111111111111111
101010101010101010101010101010101010101010	11111111111111111111111111111111111111
101010101010101010101010101010101010101010	11111111111111111111111111111111111111
10101010	11111111

In these patterns, 1s represent beats or pulses and 0s represent pauses.

Fig. 4.11. Radio signals

CP 1919. The pattern was a pulse followed by a pause, pulse followed by a pause, and so forth, with a regular period of 1.33730199 seconds between pulses. Bell and her research director Anthony Hewish determined that the signals were not local but were coming from among the stars. Because of the pattern in this radio signal, they considered the possibility that the signal was from a galactic civilization and nicknamed the source LGM for little green men.

In the movie *Contact*, the SETI investigator played by Jody Foster also detected a radio signal from space that was a pattern of pulses and pauses. But this signal had a different pattern from that of the CP 1919 source. The *Contact* source had several pulses, then a pause, followed by even more pulses, followed by a pause, and so forth.

Let us use the explanatory filter to see if we can determine if either the CP 1919 or the *Contact* source was possibly the result of intelligent design. Radio signals from space were first detected in 1932. The sun, Jupiter, the Milky Way galaxy, other galaxies, supernova remnants, radio stars, and gas clouds were all discovered to emit radio signals. The intensity of these radio sources was steady or varied slowly with time; no pulses were detected. Natural processes were proposed as the origin of these radio sources: the movement of charged particles, such as electrons and positrons, through magnetic fields. With the discovery of the pulsing signal in 1967, scientists had to determine whether this pattern was the designed signal from an alien civilization or the result of natural processes. How contingent is the CP 1919 signal? Within weeks, three other sources with pulsing signals were discovered, each with a different period. Also, the signal from all these sources was not complex, just a repeating pattern of ons and offs. Scientists concluded that they had discovered recently predicted celestial objects called "pulsars." Pulsar stands for "pulsing radio source." Pulsars are believed to be neutron stars, the dense, rapidly spinning remains of burned-out supergiant stars. As a neutron star spins, a beam of radio waves sweeps through space. If the Earth is in the path of this beam, a series of pulses followed by pauses results. Over five hundred pulsars have been identified in the Milky Way galaxy.

What about the *Contact* signal? The *Contact* signal contained the following series of pulses separated by a pause: 2, 3, 5, 7, 11, 13, 17, 19, 23, 29, 31, 37, 41, 43, 53, 59, 61, 67, 71, 73, 79, 83, 89, 97, and 101. These numbers are the first twenty-five prime numbers. A prime number is a number, other than 0 or 1, that is only divisible by one and itself. In the case of the *Contact* signal, contingency is present, as no known natural process can produce a sequence of prime numbers. No pulsar could theoretically produce such a pattern of signals. The *Contact* signal contains 1,126 bits representing the first twenty-five prime numbers. Suppose the signal contained only twelve bits (110111011111), representing the first three prime numbers: 2, 3, and 5? This sequence is too short to justify answering "yes" to the complexity question. A random process could by chance produce such a sequence. The *Contact* signal is much longer and is, thus, complex. But, contingency and complexity are not enough to infer design. Specification must also be present. Flipping a coin 1,126 times will result in a complex sequence, but without the pattern shown by the sequence of prime numbers. The *Contact* signal is not only complex but contains the pattern of specified complexity. As the *Contact* character said, "This isn't noise; this has structure."

Observations. Many scholars from science and philosophy are saying that they see specified complexity in the universe's coincidences of having the right atoms, the right molecules, enough time, and enough space for life to occur. They also see design in the Earth's coincidences of the right galaxy type, the location in the galaxy, the type of star, the Earth's distance from the sun, the location of Jupiter, the size of the moon, and the composition of the Earth. Or, as biochemist Michael Behe says, "In other words, we apprehend design in highly improbable (complex) events that also fit some independently identifiable pattern (specification)."[21] Those who detect design include theists, deists, and a-theists. Those in the theist camp include both young-Earth as well as old-Earth creationists. They all believe that design should be reinstated into science, that design is a valid, empirical tool for scientists to use.

The Nature of the Designer

What does the evidence for design suggest about the Designer? As we previously stated, the design conclusions are consonant with the tenets of Christianity, but one has to be cautious when the relationship between scientific theory and theological claims moves from consonance to apologetics. Scientific theories are never complete and do undergo refinements; a faith based on scientific theories appears to crumble when the scientific theory changes. A classic example of this dilemma occurred in the work of Thomas Aquinas, who blended Christian theology with Aristotelian science that included an Earth-centered universe. Refinement of cosmology from an Earth-centered model to a sun-centered model put a tremendous stress on the Thomist theology. A more recent example occurred when Pope Pius XII, in 1951, stated that the beginning of the big bang provided grounds for belief in God. Although the design movement does not prove the existence of the "God of Abraham, Isaac, and Jacob," its findings do provide insight into theological issues.

A Creator

Far from being a challenge to biblical teaching, the current understanding of the big bang theory supports the biblical teaching that the universe had a beginning and that space, time, and matter are finite.

Care for Living Things

The evidence of design suggests a Designer who has great care for living things, especially humans. This care is reflected in the vast amount of energy and matter committed to making the universe a pleasant place for life. For life to exist, the universe needs to be vast (15 billion light years across), with an unbelievable amount of matter and energy (100 billion trillion stars). The uniqueness of the Earth suggests the great care the Designer took in preparing a home for humans. As Hugh Ross stated, "God invested heavily in living creatures. He constructed all these stars and carefully crafted them throughout the age of the universe so that at this brief moment in the history of the cosmos humans could exist and have a pleasant place to live."[22] This arrangement suggests a very caring Creator.

The Designer and God

While the characteristics of the universe give us insight into the nature of the Designer, these characteristics will always be an incomplete view of God.

5. The Comprehensible Universe

Jimmy H. Davis

"One may say the eternal mystery of the world
is its comprehensibility."
—Albert Einstein

I T IS NOT TOO surprising that Einstein was mystified by the comprehensibility of the world (universe). The universe contains objects that range from the very small and invisible to the very large and visible (fig. 5.1).

Object	Exponent	Meaning
Distance from Earth to nearest galaxy	10^{22}	ten sextillion meters
Diameter of Andromeda galaxy	10^{21}	one sextillion meters
Distance from Earth to nearest star	10^{16}	ten quadrillion meters
Diameter of solar system	10^{13}	ten trillion meters
Diameter of sun	10^{9}	one billion meters
Diameter of Earth	10^{6}	one million meters
Height of Mount Everest	10^{4}	ten thousand meters
Height of World Trade Center	10^{3}	one thousand meters
Human child height	1	one meter
Length of insect	10^{2}	one hundredth of meter
Width of paper thickness	10^{5}	ten millionth of meter
Length of bacterium	10^{6}	one millionth of meter
Diameter of large molecule	10^{8}	ten billionth of meter
Diameter of atom	10^{11}	ten trillionth of meter

Fig. 5.1. Relative sizes and distances in the universe

There are all kinds of phenomena to consider: comets, meteorites, moon, rain, ocean waves, diamonds, salt, DNA, plants, and animals. How can we possibly hope to be able to explain all these phenomena? Yet, we are able to comprehend the world using the methods of modern science. In this chapter, we will examine ideas from mathematics, physics, chemistry, and biochemistry that help make the universe comprehensible.

UNIVERSAL, MATHEMATICAL LAWS

"[The universe] is written in the language of mathematics,
and its characters are triangles, circles, and other geometrical figures,
without which it is humanly impossible to understand a single word
of it; without these, one wanders about in a dark labyrinth."
—GALILEO GALILEI, *The Assayer* (1623)

Is Galileo correct in saying that the way to comprehend nature is to use mathematics? Most scientists would answer yes. A key figure in showing that mathematics is the language of nature was Isaac Newton. Newton's triumph was to unify terrestrial and celestial phenomena. Beginning with Aristotle (384–322 BC), people believed that the terrestrial domain was different from the celestial domain. Using qualitative, commonsense arguments, Aristotle observed that the earth underwent change and decay while the heavens seemed to be unchanging and eternal. Motion seemed very different in the two domains. On earth, rest seemed the natural state: a rock rolled quickly down a hill and stopped, an arrow flew from a bow and quickly stopped, and so forth. In the heavens, everything seemed to be in constant motion: the moon, sun, planets, and stars constantly circled the earth. During the late Middle Ages and during the Renaissance, scientists began trying to quantify their observations, with the division between terrestrial and celestial domains continuing. The German astronomer Johannes Kepler (1571–1630) mathematically showed that the planets orbit the sun in elliptical orbits. Meanwhile, the Italian scientist Galileo Galilei (1564–1642) mathematically explained the motion of projectiles and free-falling bodies.

It remained for the English mathematician and physicist Isaac Newton (1642–1727) to show that terrestrial and celestial motion could be explained by the same set of laws of motion (law of universal gravitation and the three laws of motion). While a student at Trinity College, Cambridge, Newton learned of the work of Kepler and Galileo. After taking his bachelor of arts degree in January 1665, Newton fled Cambridge because of the Great Plague to work on some ideas he had been formulating. Returning to his country home, he spent the next eighteen months laying the foundation for trans-forming science. During this eighteen-month period, he invented differen-tial calculus, began developing the laws of motion and gravitation, invented the reflecting telescope, and showed that white light contains all the colors of the spectrum. After the Great Plague, Newton returned to Cambridge, where he was appointed Lucasian Professor of Mathematics in 1669.

Always fearful of criticism, Newton did not immediately publish any of his findings. In 1675, the German mathematician Gottfried Wilhelm Leib-niz (1646–1716) independently discovered differential calculus and imme-diately published his findings. Newton spent the rest of his life fighting Leibniz over who invented differential calculus. In 1684, challenged by the British astronomer Edmond Halley (1656–1742), Newton refined his ideas on motion. After eighteen months of intense work, Newton published in 1687 the *Philosophiae naturalis principia mathematica* (*The Mathematical Principles of Natural Philosophy*), or *Principia*, as it is commonly known. Newton's view of mathematics is reflected in the title of the *Principia*. He viewed mathematics as the undergirding principle of science or natural phi-losophy, as it was then known.

The *Principia* is considered one of the greatest scientific books ever writ-ten. Using the laws of motion and the universal law of gravitation, Newton provided an explanation for what had previously been thought of as dissimi-lar phenomena, such as the causes of tides, the orbits of comets, the preces-sion of the earth on its axis, and the effect of the sun's gravity on the orbit of the moon. Most of the problems of physics and astronomy could now be addressed. The work of Kepler and Galileo had been united and converted into one consistent theory. At last, the earth and the heavens were united into one universe.

As can be seen in Figure 5.2, precise mathematical expressions are used to describe motion. The success of these mathematical expressions led other scientists to look for quantitative expressions in their fields. For example, the French chemist and royal tax collector Antoine Lavoisier (1745–1774) carefully measured the amounts of the chemicals used in chemical reactions. Based on his studies, Lavoisier discovered the law of conservation of mass (the mass of the products equals the mass of the reactants). For this work, Lavoisier is considered one of the fathers of modern chemistry; for his tax collecting, Lavoisier was guillotined by the French revolutionaries.

SECOND LAW OF MOTION

The acceleration of a body is directly proportional to the net force acting on the body and inversely proportional to the mass of the body, or

$$a = \frac{F}{m}$$

where a represents the acceleration,
       F represents the force, and
       m represents the mass.

LAW OF UNIVERSAL GRAVITATION

Every body in the universe attracts every other body with a force that is directly proportional to the product of their masses and inversely proportional to the square of the distance between them, or

$$F = \frac{GM_1 M_2}{r^2}$$

where F represents the force of attraction between two bodies,
      G represents the gravitational constant,
      M^1 represents the mass of one body,
      M^2 represents the mass of a second body, and
      r represents the distance between the two bodies.

Fig. 5.2. Mathematical expressions for motion

Two long-term trends resulted from the success of Newton's work. First, people came to believe that mathematics was the language of nature. Somehow, the phenomena of nature followed a mathematical pattern. An interesting example of this belief involved NASA's *Pioneer 10* and *Pioneer 11* spacecraft. *Pioneer 10* was launched on March 2, 1972, and explored Jupiter, while *Pioneer 11* was launched on April 5, 1973, and explored Jupiter and Saturn. These were the first spacecraft that would leave the solar system and journey into interstellar space. Since there was a remote chance of contact with beings from other stars, Carl Sagan convinced NASA to include a message from Earth to the stars. The message was etched on a six-inch by nine-inch gold-plated aluminum plaque. On the plaque, a man and woman, modeled on classical Greek sculpture, stand in front of a drawing of the spacecraft. Also on the plaque are drawings showing which planet in the solar system launched the spacecraft, the relationship of the sun to four-teen pulsars, and the hyperfine transition of the neutral hydrogen atom.[1] In what language should this plaque have been written? Sagan argued: "The extraterrestrials cannot possibly understand English or Russian or Chinese or Esperanto, but they must share with us common mathematics and phys-ics and astronomy. I believe that they will understand, with no great effort, this message written in the galactic language: 'Scientific.'"[2] At the heart of Sagan's assumptions is "common mathematics" of the binary number sys-tem, which uses only two digits, 1 and 0, and is used by computers for stor-age of numbers.[3]

The downside of the belief that mathematics is the language of nature is the bias that if one cannot describe a phenomenon mathematically, then one does not truly understand the phenomenon. This bias leads to a reduc-tionist view of nature; everything in nature should be describable in terms of physics. Simplistically, one would say that the action of the atoms of chemistry explains biology and that the action of matter and the forces of physics explain chemistry. This reductionism ignores that the whole can be greater than the sum of its parts.

The second result of the success of the Newtonian laws to explain motion in the terrestrial and celestial domains was the view that the same laws apply throughout the universe. The assumption is that the same laws of physics and chemistry apply to a rock on Earth as well as to a star light years away. Is the concept of universal laws valid? We test this concept every day. Dur-ing a twenty-four-hour period, the rotation of the Milky Way galaxy carries the Earth about 12 million miles. Over a century's time, the Earth travels about 400 billion miles. The law of universal gravitation appears to apply to this 400 billion miles of space or we would be floating by now. Likewise, the observed behavior of stars and galaxies thousands of light years away can also be described by the law of universal gravitation.

Newton was a theist who believed that God created and constantly sus-tains the universe.[4] However, others interpreted Newton's ideas as a clock-work-like description of the universe that led to a deistic view of nature: the universe was a machine that had been created by God. Once God had "wound up" the universe, he retired and let his laws keep the universe going. This deistic view gradually gave way to a totally materialistic view: everything can be explained by the interaction of matter and the laws of nature.

Observations. The success of physics has been built on applying math-ematical principles to physical problems. Because we are educated to solve physical problems using mathematical principles, we can easily miss the amazing fact that a mental construct (mathematics) has anything to do with the physical world. Why should anything as simple as the mentally constructed counting systems of arithmetic have anything to do with piles of stones or clusters of stars? This amazing utility of mathematics is a strong argument for design in which the mind corresponds to the universe.

Order among the Elements

"Chemistry studies the material substance of the universe,
 the stuff we can hold, kick, feel, weigh, smell, see, touch, and taste."
—Carl H. Snyder, *The Extraordinary Chemistry of Ordinary Things*

One of the fundamental questions for chemistry is what are the building blocks of matter? Are the building blocks composed of the four elements proposed by the ancient Greeks (earth, fire, water, air)? Or is the number infinite, with each substance made of its own unique building blocks? Gradually, chemists realized the number of building blocks was more than four but less than infinity. Each building block, called an element, is composed entirely of a single type of atom.[5] Since the beginning of recorded history, the number of known elements has grown from an original group of ten that included antimony, carbon, copper, gold, iron, lead, mercury, silver, sulfur, and tin. The ten most abundant elements by mass in the Earth's crust are oxygen (46%), silicon (28%), aluminum (8%), iron (6%), calcium (4%), sodium (2%), magnesium (2%), potassium (2%), titanium (0.6%), and hydrogen (0.1%). As of August 2007, 115 elements have been discovered, with the elements above neptunium being synthetic elements produced by nuclear reactions.

A second fundamental question concerning the elements is: Are the same building blocks common throughout the universe? The spectrum of light from a star carries information regarding the elemental composition of the star. Atoms give off light when they are heated. The color of the emitted light can be used to identify atoms. Two dramatic events on Earth caused by atoms emitting light are the colors of fireworks and the colors of the aurora borealis or northern lights. The colors of fireworks are due to the emissions of light by excited metal atoms (yellow = sodium, blue = copper, green = barium, and red = strontium). Likewise, the colors of the aurora borealis are caused by a similar process involving excited atoms and ions (greenish yellow and deep red = oxygen, red = dioxygen ion, and violet and blue = dinitrogen ion).

When scientists used the same techniques to analyze the spectra of stars, they found that no matter how far away, or how hot, or how massive, all stars contain the same elements as found on Earth. Thus, the same elements (building blocks) have been discovered throughout the universe.

A third fundamental question concerning the elements is: Can the elements be organized? At first, it would seem as if all the elements are different. Consider three solids: potassium, iron, and gold. Potassium reacts explosively with water. Iron slowly rusts in the presence of water. Gold hardly reacts with anything. Consider two gases: hydrogen and neon. Hydrogen reacts explosively with oxygen. (Remember the Hindenburg.) Neon hardly reacts with anything. Now we have two inert substances, but one is a colorful solid while the other is a colorless gas! Where is the pattern? There must be a pattern, or chemistry could not be studied as a science.

One possible way to organize the elements would be to collect all those elements of similar properties. One group of elements was observed to have a characteristic shine, to be good conductors of electricity and heat, and to be malleable and ductile. These elements are classified as metals and include the familiar iron, gold, and silver. Others are labeled nonmetal, which means they have properties opposite of metals and contain the familiar oxygen and nitrogen. Finally, there is a third group labeled metalloid or semimetal having both metallic and nonmetallic properties and containing the familiar silicon of semiconductors.

Since seventeen elements are nonmetals and seven are metalloids, most of the elements are metals. Except for mercury, all the metals are solids. Eleven nonmetals are gases, one is liquid, and five are solids. Vastly different chemistries can be observed for metals (remember potassium, iron, and gold) and nonmetals (remember hydrogen and neon). Thus, the metal/nonmetal/metalloid classification is too broad because of the large variance in physical properties and chemistries of the elements.

As more and more elements were studied, it was discovered that certain groups of elements did react similarly. Lithium, sodium, potassium, and cesium all react with water to produce hydrogen gas. Lithium reacts the slowest, while cesium reacts so violently that the force of the reaction destroys the reaction vessel. Helium, neon, argon, and krypton are all inert,

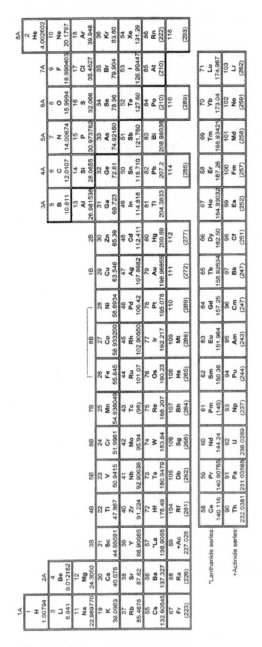

Fig. 5.3. The periodic table of elements

colorless gases. Using information about the similar properties of groups of elements, in 1869, the Russian chemist Dmitry Mendeleyev organized the sixty-three elements known in his day.

When the elements are arranged in order of their atomic number (number of protons in their nuclei), a tabular series of rows and columns results with the elements in each vertical column having similar properties. This tabular arrangement is called the periodic table (fig. 5.3). The elements in a column have similar properties because they have the same number of electrons in their outermost shell (energy level). In the left-most column, including lithium (Li), sodium (Na), potassium (K), and cesium (Cs), each has one electron in its outermost shell. This family of elements is called the alkali metals. The alkali metals are all soft, silvery metals. In contrast to the metal iron, they can be cut with a dull knife. The alkali metals are the most reactive of all metals, reacting with air and water. They are never found as free metals in nature.

The elements helium (He), neon (Ne), argon (Ar), and krypton (Kr) are in the right-most column, with each element having eight electrons in its outermost shell.[6] These elements are called the noble gases and are colorless, odorless, nonreactive gases. The reactivity of an element depends upon the number of electrons in its outermost shell.

The electron configurations of the elements display a periodic variation with increasing nuclear charge (atomic number). Since the physical and chemical behaviors of the elements depend upon the electron configurations, the elements show periodic variations in physical and chemical properties. In this section, we will examine two properties of an atom: atomic radius and first ionization energy.

The atomic radius is a measure of how large an atom is. One way to determine the atomic radius is from measurements of the distances between atoms in molecules. In figure 5.4, the atomic radius is plotted versus the atomic number for the first nineteen elements. Notice that the curve tends to repeat or is periodic. In general, the atomic radius decreases as one moves from left to right across a horizontal row (period); compare Li to Ne and Na to Ar. The atomic radius generally increases as one moves from top to bottom within a vertical column (group); compare Li, Na, and K or He, Ne, and Ar.

The first ionization energy is the energy needed to remove an outermost electron from the neutral atom. The value of the first ionization energy is

Fig. 5.4. Periodic trend of atomic radii

a measure of how reactive an element is. Atoms with a small ionization energy value would be more reactive than atoms with a higher ionization energy value. In figure 5.5, the first ionization energy is plotted versus the atomic number for the first nineteen elements. Again, a periodic trend is observed. The ionization energy tends to increase as one crosses a period from left to right; compare Li to Ne and Na to Ar. The ionization energy tends to decrease as one moves down a group; compare Li, Na, and K or He, Ne, and Ar.

Building on the quantitative approach to the study of matter, on the fact that the number of building blocks (elements) is limited, and on the periodic relationships between the elements, chemists transformed the way people live. Think what life would be like without plastics such as plastic wrap (polyethylene), Styrofoam, PVC pipe, and Teflon-coated cookware. Or if we no longer had synthetic fibers: nylon, Dacron, rayon, or Mylar. How would we deal with everyday pains without aspirin and Tylenol? Could we endure allergy season without antihistamines? Would our homes be as clean without Lysol? Think of all the diseases contained with the antibiotics sulfa, penicillin, and tetracycline. Our clothes and bodies would be a lot dirtier without synthetic detergents and soaps. We would not be able to copy and fax as conveniently without xerography. And finally, I would not be composing this chapter on a computer.

Fig. 5.5. Periodic trend of ionization energies

Atoms to Compounds

Chemists are interested in discovering how atoms react (combine) with each other to form collections of atoms called compounds. By knowing not only which atoms are present but also which atoms are bonded to each other, chemists gain an understanding of why Teflon produces a stick-free surface while polyethylene does not. In this section, we will examine the different ways atoms combine to form compounds.

Chemistry involves the interaction of the electrons of one atom with the electrons of another atom. The nucleus goes along for the ride. Models of several atoms are shown in figure 5.6. The nucleus contains the protons and the neutrons. The electrons are arranged in shells or energy levels.[7] The first (innermost) shell has the lowest energy and can hold a maximum of two electrons (oxygen, sulfur, and neon in the figure). The second shell can hold a maximum of eight electrons (sulfur and neon in the figure), while the third shell can hold a maximum of sixteen electrons. It has been observed that, in an uncombined atom, the outermost shell will never contain more than eight electrons (oxygen, sulfur, and neon in the figure).

An atom is most stable when it contains eight electrons in its outermost shell; hence, the nonreactivity of the noble gases. Chemical reactions involve atoms shuffling electrons until each acquires eight electrons in its outermost

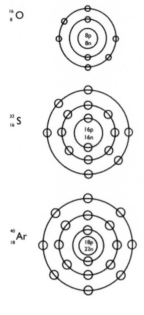

Fig. 5.6. Model of atoms. The central area is the nucleus containing protons (p) and neutrons (n). The electrons are in shells (energy levels) around the nucleus.

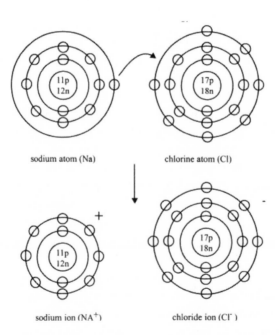

Fig. 5.7. Ionic reaction. The metal sodium transfers an electron to the nonmetal chlorine forming table salt containing sodium and chloride ions.

shells (a noble gas electronic configuration). One way of shuffling the electrons is for one atom to lose electrons to another atom. Metals react with
nonmetals in this manner. Metals lose electrons and become positive ions,
while nonmetals gain electrons and become negative ions. This reaction
results in an ionic compound held together by an ionic bond. Figure 5.7
illustrates the reaction of the metal sodium with the nonmetal chlorine to
form the ionic compound sodium chloride or table salt. Notice that each
ion now has eight electrons in its outermost shell.

Nonmetals react with nonmetals by sharing electrons. The reaction results
in a covalent compound held together by a covalent bond. Figure 5.8, part
A, illustrates the reaction of carbon with oxygen to form carbon dioxide. In
the covalent product, each atom has eight electrons in its outermost shell.
The shorthand notation (O=C=O) is called a structural formula, which

*Fig. 5.8. Covalent reactions. A. The oxygen and carbon atoms share electrons thereby
obtaining eight electrons in their outermost shell. B. The oxygen and hydrogen atoms
share electrons. Oxygen obtains eight electrons in its outermost shell while hydrogen
obtains only two electrons. Two electrons in hydrogen's outermost shell is a stable
arrangement because this arrangement is like the electronic arrangement of Noble
Gas Helium.*

reveals that there are two covalent bonds (double bond) between the carbon and each oxygen. Figure 5.8, part B, illustrates the reaction of oxygen with hydrogen to form water. Observe that in this covalent, compound oxygen has eight electrons in its outermost shell, but hydrogen has only two. Hydrogen becomes like the noble gas helium, which has only two electrons, unlike the other noble gases, which have eight in their outermost shells. The shorthand notation for water reveals that there is one covalent bond (single bond) between oxygen and each hydrogen.

Covalent molecules come in two varieties: nonpolar and polar. Nonpolar molecules result when their atoms have an approximate equal sharing of electrons. Polar molecules result when two atoms share electrons unequally.[8] Chemists model this event by saying that the electrons spend more time orbiting one nucleus than orbiting the other. Oxygen has a greater attraction for electrons than hydrogen does. Thus, the electrons, in water, spend more time near the oxygen nucleus than the hydrogen nuclei. This results in the formation of a partial negative charge on the oxygen and a partial positive charge on the hydrogen. This separation of partial charges causes water to be a polar molecule. Whether a covalent molecule is polar or nonpolar affects many of its properties. Polar molecules are attracted to other polar molecules and to ionic compounds. Nonpolar molecules are attracted only to other nonpolar molecules. These polarity relations determine solubilities. Sodium chloride (ionic) and sugar (polar) dissolve in water (polar). Oil (nonpolar) and dirt (nonpolar) do not dissolve in water (polar). As we shall observe, these polarity relationships determine many of the properties of the molecules of life.

Observations. Because we have been taught since elementary school that there are about one hundred chemical building blocks, we easily miss the astonishing fact that there are so few building blocks. We easily overlook the wonder that the same building blocks are present in the tiniest molecule as well as in the largest galaxy. It is a tremendous help to chemists that once they know the properties of these one hundred or so elements, they can deal with the structure of granite or oil or a star or bones. This order throughout nature implies design.

CARBON, THE ELEMENT OF LIFE

Most of the molecules of life are covalent compounds resulting from the reaction of the nonmetal carbon with the nonmetals hydrogen, nitrogen, oxygen, and sulfur. Although carbon composes only 0.19 percent of the lithosphere and only 0.01 percent of the hydrosphere, carbon makes up 20 percent of living organisms. The chemistry of carbon compounds is called organic chemistry. When these organic compounds are found in living organisms, the chemistry is called biochemistry. The following are some of the properties of carbon that make it an ideal candidate to be the key element in the compounds found in living organisms:

forms stable, covalent carbon-carbon bonds;
forms characteristic three-dimensional structures;
reacts at functional groups;
forms energy-rich compounds.

Carbon-Carbon Bonds. Carbon has the ability to form stable covalent bonds with other carbon atoms, resulting in molecules containing thousands of carbon-carbon bonds (fig. 5.9). Carbon can form both single (saturated) and multiple (unsaturated) bonds with other carbon atoms. These carbon-carbon arrays form the backbones of molecules found in living organisms. Since these carbon-carbon arrays can be linear (chains) or cyclic (rings), a great variety results. Further variety results from the fact that some arrays can be saturated, while others may be unsaturated. When all of these factors have been considered, over 90 percent of all compounds turn out to be organic compounds.

Three-dimensional Structures. Carbon can form a maximum of four bonds. A tetrahedral structure results when carbon has four single bonds (fig. 5.10). The structures of the single-bonded molecules shown in figure 5.9 are not flat but have a zigzag geometry. When carbon is bonded to another atom with a double bond, a trigonal planar geometry results. Two different arrangements are possible in some double-bonded carbon compounds. The cis arrangement (Latin *cis*, "on this side") occurs when two groups lie on the same side of the double bond. The trans arrangement (Latin *trans*, "across") occurs when two groups lie across the double bond. Many reactions in living organisms involve the shapes of molecules. The chemistry of vision involves light converting the cis isomer of the retinal molecule (the vision molecule) to its trans isomer. The detection of odors is thought to result from molecules of certain shapes fitting closely on the receptor sites of olfactory nerve endings. Enzyme action depends upon molecules of certain shapes fitting into pockets of the enzyme molecule. No other chemical elements form as many shapes as carbon.

Functional Groups. Additional variety results from the fact that the

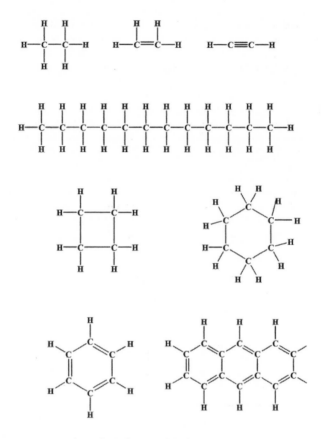

Fig. 5.9. Some compounds with carbon-carbon bonds

energy involved in forming carbon-carbon bonds is not much different from forming carbon-hydrogen or carbon-oxygen bonds. By attaching hydrogen, nitrogen, or oxygen groups to the carbon-carbon backbones, many different biological molecules can easily be formed. These groups attached to the carbon-carbon backbone are called functional groups (fig. 5.11). The chemistry of an organic molecule, regardless of its size, is largely determined by its functional group. For example, all molecules have the properties of an alcohol when the OH fragment is bonded to carbon. Thus, whether the OH is bonded to one carbon or to a ten-carbon chain or to a five-carbon ring, they are all alcohols. The alcohol group is an important functional group in carbohydrates. The ester group is important in lipids (fats and oils), while the amide, amine, and carboxylic acid groups are important in proteins.

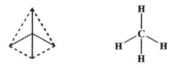

A. The tetrahedral arrangement around the carbon atom.

B. Zig-zag geometry

Fig. 5.10. *Three-dimensional geometrics of carbon compounds*

Energy-rich Compounds. Most organic compounds are rich in hydrogen. A chemist would say they are "reduced." They have a lot of potential energy available for reacting with oxygen. In contrast, most inorganic carbon compounds such as carbon dioxide and carbonates are oxygen rich or oxidized. They do not have the potential for further reaction with oxygen.

Although organic molecules have the potential to react with oxygen, they do not spontaneously react with the atmosphere. If they did spontaneously react, then life could not have been based on carbon, since the needed compounds would have already reacted with oxygen. A spark is needed to cause natural gas or gasoline to react with oxygen. Living organisms moderate this reaction by the use of enzymes.

Carbon Dioxide

Carbon dioxide is a simple gas molecule composed of two oxygen atoms double-bonded to a carbon atom: O=C=O. The ultimate source of carbon in living organisms is carbon dioxide. Through photosynthesis, plants remove

Hydrocarbon

Ketone

Alcohol

Carboxylic acid

Amine

Ester

Ether

Amide

Aldehyde

Fig. 5.11. Functional Groups

carbon dioxide from the air and convert carbon dioxide into the chemicals of life. By eating plants, animals transfer the carbon to their bodies.

Carbon dioxide has several properties that make it an important molecule for life. At the temperatures associated with living organisms, carbon dioxide is found in nearly the same concentration in air as in water. Among the gases, this is a unique property for carbon dioxide. Being in nearly the same concentration allows carbon dioxide easily to exchange between air and water or between living organisms and their surroundings.

When animals process food during their metabolic process, carbon dioxide and water are the two waste products. One could say that animals get energy by converting carbon compounds to carbon dioxide. An average person produces about a kilogram (2.2 pounds) of carbon dioxide each day. This amount of waste would be very difficult to remove if carbon dioxide were not a gas. Gases cross the cell membrane by diffusion, which does not require energy since the gas spontaneously flows from high pressure to low pressure. In contrast, liquids and solids have to be pumped across the membrane.

Once the carbon dioxide gas diffuses through the cell membrane into the bloodstream, the carbon dioxide is hydrated to form carbonic acid, H_2CO_3. Carbonic acid is a weak acid and partially disassociates into the bicarbonate (HCO_3^-) ion. A mixture between a weak acid and the salt of a weak acid (the bicarbonate) forms a buffer. A buffer maintains the acidity or basicity of a solution by neutralizing any acid or base added to the solution. Or the buffer maintains a constant pH for the solution. The normal pH of blood is 7.4. Blood pH below 7.4 is called acidosis, with the blood pH above 7.4 being called alkalosis. If the pH of the blood should rise above 7.8 or fall below 7.0, the result can be fatal. The body regulates the amount of carbon dioxide in the blood and hence the pH by regulating the rate of breathing.

Carbon dioxide also has an important role in regulating the Earth's temperature. When sunlight strikes the surface of the Earth, some of the light energy is absorbed, while the rest of the energy is reflected back into the atmosphere. Carbon dioxide absorbs some of this energy, thereby moderating the Earth's temperature. Without this greenhouse effect of carbon dioxide, the average temperature of the Earth would be similar to that of the moon: an average of minus 22 degrees Centigrade or minus 6 degrees Fahrenheit, rather than the Earth's 14 degrees Centigrade or 57 degrees Fahrenheit. This is the good greenhouse effect. Recently, an international group of scientists through the Intergovernmental Panel on Climate Change concluded that industrialized societies are causing an enhanced greenhouse effect (the bad one), or global warming.[9] A carbon dioxide level above that produced by living organisms could raise the Earth's average temperature high enough to disrupt the Earth's ecosystems.

Why Not Silicon?

I remember as a child watching a B-grade movie about scientists creating life based on silicon. At first, life based on silicon seems reasonable, since carbon and silicon are in the same family in the periodic table. Thus, why not silicon?

Silicon does lie below carbon in the periodic table, but the properties of silicon differ greatly from carbon. Carbon is a nonmetal, while silicon is a metalloid that lies on the boundary between nonmetals and metals. Thus, the chemistry of silicon is different from that of carbon. Unlike carbon, in which carbon-carbon, carbon-hydrogen, and carbon-oxygen bonds have about the same energy, silicon-silicon bonds are easier to form than silicon-hydrogen or silicon-oxygen. Thus, the great variety of compounds seen for carbon is not seen for silicon.

As we just discussed, carbon dioxide, being a simple gaseous molecule, is critical for life processes. Silicon dioxide is a polymeric solid called quartz. Silicon does not form double bonds as carbon does in carbon dioxide. The structure for silicon dioxide is an extended structure with single bonds between the silicon and oxygen atoms. Thus, it would be much harder for a living organism to excrete a kilogram of solid quartz than a kilogram of gaseous carbon dioxide. For this reason, many chemists and biologists do not think that silicon could be the element around which a living organism could be formed.

Observations. Because its compounds are everywhere, it is easy to overlook the fact that carbon is a unique element. The carbon atom's ability to bond easily to itself and to other elements results in structures found in oil, trees, dogs and cats, plastics, and people. By removing carbon from nature, we would not only lose most of the variety in the chemical compounds in the universe; of more importance, we would lose life. The unique chemistry of carbon suggests design.

WATER

"Ocean, *n.*: A body of water occupying about two-thirds
of a world made for man—who has no gills."
–A. BIERCE

Before we leave chemistry, let us examine one very common but unusual molecule: water. As Coleridge wrote, we have "water, water, everywhere,"[10] in rain, snow, rivers, oceans, lakes, underground streams, swimming pools, plants, animals, and people. Water is the most abundant compound on the Earth. Yet, this common compound is very strange. The following properties of water, which we experience every day, make water a unique substance:

Water is a liquid at room temperature.

Solid water (ice) floats.

Water has a high heat capacity.

Water has the highest heat of vaporization of all known substances.

Part A. Molecular Weights & Boiling Points		
Molecule	Molecular Weight	Boiling Point
CH_4	16.04	-161.5
SiH_4	32.09	-111.8
GeH_4	76.63	-90.0
SnH_4	122.73	-52.0

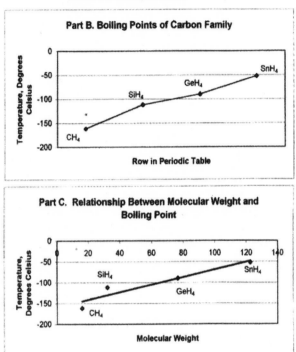

Fig. 5.12. Hydrogen compounds of the carbon family

Water has a large surface tension.

Water is an excellent solvent.

Boiling Point of Water. If one considers the hydrogen compounds of the first member of the carbon, nitrogen, oxygen, and halogen families, all of these hydrogen compounds (CH4, NH3, and HF) are toxic and/or corrosive gases except for water (H2O), which is a nontoxic, noncorrosive liquid. The properties of water are anomalies, since its properties do not fit the expected periodic trends. For most families of compounds, the observed

Fig. 5.13. Boiling points of various hydrogen compounds

periodic trend is that as the molecular weight of a compound increases, its boiling point also increases. The hydrogen compounds made from the members of the carbon family (carbon, silicon, germanium, and tin) are an example of this periodic trend (fig. 5.12). Part B of the figure presents the periodic distribution of boiling points; all are gases at room temperature. Figure 5.12, Part C, presents the relationship between the molecular weight of a compound and its boiling point. The periodic trend observed is that as the molecular weight increases, the boiling point increases.

Figure 5.13 extends the data on the hydrogen compounds to the nitrogen family (nitrogen, phosphorus, arsenic, and antimony), the oxygen family (oxygen, sulfur, selenium, and tellurium), and the halogens (fluorine, chlorine, bromine, and iodine). Ignoring the first members of each family, the clear periodic trend is that the boiling points all increase with increasing molecular weights. Three of the first members (ammonia, hydrogen fluoride, and water) show anomalous behavior, with water having the greatest anomaly. If the oxygen family behaved like the carbon family, the expected boiling point of water would be near −100 degrees Centigrade, not the observed +100 degrees Centigrade!

The unique properties of water result from its molecular structure. The shape of the water molecule is similar to an isosceles triangle (fig. 5.14), with the distance between the oxygen and hydrogen nuclei being 9.65 nanometers and the H-O-H angle being 104.5 degrees. The sharing of electrons between the oxygen and the hydrogen atoms holds the water molecule

Bond length = 9.65 nanometers

H—O—H

Bond angle = 104.5 degrees

Fig. 5.14. Isosceles triangular shape of water

H—O—H

H
|
O
:
H
|
O
H—O ··· H
|
H—O—H

Fig. 5.15. Three-dimensional structure of water. Hydrogen bonding between water molecules results in a tetrahedral structure. Solid lines denote covalent bonds. Dashed lines denote hydrogen bonds.

together. As we discussed previously, the oxygen atom has a greater attraction for the shared electrons than do the hydrogen atoms. Thus, the electron density shifts from the hydrogen atoms and builds up around the oxygen atom, making water a polar molecule. The hydrogen atoms of one water molecule are now electrostatically attracted to the oxygen atom of another molecule. This attraction forms a strong bond between the molecules, which is called the hydrogen bond. In water, the hydrogen bonding extends from molecule to molecule until a three-dimensional polymer with a tetrahedral structure is formed (fig. 5.15). The energy required to break all these hydrogen bonds is great; thus, water boils at the very high, anomalous temperature of 100 degrees Centigrade.

Fig. 5.16. Structure of ice.
A fragment of one layer of the ice
structure is shown. Dashed lines
represent hydrogen bonding.

Ice Floats. The hydrogen bond–formed three-dimensional structure is very rigid in ice. As shown in figure 5.16, this is a very open structure, because each molecule in the structure has only four neighbors. Many solids are more compact, with arrangements where each molecule has up to twelve neighbors.[11] Upon the melting of ice, about 15 percent of the hydrogen bonds are broken; the percent broken is low because of the strong tendency of the water molecule to hydrogen bond. The breaking of these hydrogen bonds disrupts the pure tetrahedral structure. In the liquid state, some water molecules would have more than four neighbors, making liquid water more compact and less open than solid water. Since liquid water is more compact (takes up less volume) than solid water, ice is less dense and ice floats.

Ice floats and aquatic life survives the winters. As water freezes, ice only forms on the surface of the river or lake, leaving liquid water below it for marine life to exist. The surface ice insulates the water and the aquatic life below. If ice were denser than liquid water, the ice would sink upon freezing and accumulate on the bottom. During the summer, the ice on the bottom would not melt. Year by year, more and more ice would accumulate until all aquatic life would be eliminated. Thus, floating ice is a lot more important than as an addition to one's tea.

High Heat Capacity of Water. The heat capacity (specific heat) is the amount of heat required to raise the temperature of one gram of a substance 1 degree Celsius. The greater the heat capacity, the longer it takes substance to warm up. Water has a large heat capacity and thus heats up very slowly, which leads to the expression "a watched pot never boils." The heat capacity of water is about ten times larger than that of copper or iron (fig. 5.17) and about twice as large as simple organic liquids. The absorption of heat by water causes the vibration and breakage of its hydrogen bonds. Thus, the extensive hydrogen bonding in the three-dimensional structure of water results in a large heat capacity.

The oceans cover about 72 percent of the Earth's surface with 97.2 percent of the world's water. About 2.1 percent of the water is in ice caps and glaciers. Fresh water in lakes, rivers, and ground water amounts to only 0.6 percent, with the remaining 0.1 percent in the form of brine wells and brack-

SUBSTANCE	HEAT CAPACITY
Water	4.18
Ethyl alcohol	2.43
Aluminum	0.901
Iron	0.449
Copper	0.384

The heat capacities are measured at 25°
and are in units of joules per gram-degree Celsius.

Fig. 5.17. Heat capacity of some substances

ish waters. All of this water moderates the climate of the Earth. During the daylight hours, these large bodies of water absorb and store heat from the sun. At night, the waters slowly release the heat. These processes prevent extreme temperature variations.

High Heat of Vaporization for Water. The heat of vaporization is the quantity of heat necessary to change one gram of liquid water to vapor without a temperature change. It is a measure of how easily a liquid will evaporate. Water has the highest heat of vaporization of any known substance (fig. 5.18). This high heat of vaporization makes water a great coolant through the process of evaporation. As can be seen in figure 5.18, the heat of vaporization of water is almost five times higher than the two common rubbing alcohols, ethyl and isopropyl. Living creatures use the evaporation of water as a cooling mechanism.

LIQUID	HEAT OF VAPORIZATION (CALORIES PER GRAM)
Water	540
Ethyl alcohol	204
Isopropyl alcohol	159
Acetone	125
Ethyl acetate	102
Ethyl ether	89.3
Chloroform	59

Fig. 5.18. Heats of vaporization of various liquids

The large heat of vaporization of water also affects the Earth's weather. The hydrologic cycle involves the movement of water from the oceans to freshwater sources and from the freshwater sources back to the ocean. The cycle begins with the evaporation of surface waters, which absorbs about 30 percent of the solar energy reaching the Earth. The energy is released as this water condenses, resulting in precipitation, sometimes in the form of thunderstorms. This precipitation replenishes freshwater sources.

Large Surface Tension of Water. Surface tension is the resistance of a liquid to spreading out and increasing its surface area. Surface tension allows a water strider to move across water and causes water to bead on a waxy surface. Because of water's strong intermolecular hydrogen bonds, it has a very large surface tension, even larger than glycerin and ethyl alcohol. The large surface tension of water allows plants and trees to use capillary action to carry water and nutrients to their leaves.

Water as an Excellent Solvent. Because water is both a polar molecule and a hydrogen bonding molecule, water has unusual solvent properties. It is able to dissolve both ionic substances, such as salts, as well as polar compounds, such as sugars. Water has been called the "universal solvent." Because of its solvent properties, water is the premier biological solvent, allowing the transportation of carbohydrates, fats, proteins, and nucleic acids throughout an organism. Also, since water contains both the H+ of an acid and the OH− of a base, water is an excellent solvent for both acids and bases.

Water is not the "universal solvent," however, because it does not dissolve nonpolar compounds. Oil and water do not mix because oil is nonpolar and

Fig. 5.19. A lipid. A. Chemical structure of a typical lipid. B. Symbolic representation of lipid. C. Lipid bilayer found in cell membranes.

water is polar. Many biological molecules, such as enzymes, contain parts of their structure that are polar and other parts that are nonpolar. When an enzyme is placed in water, the enzyme molecule twists and turns so that its polar parts (hydrophilic parts) are on the outside of the molecule and its nonpolar parts (hydrophobic parts) are on the inside, away from the polar water molecules. The resulting shape of the enzyme enables the molecule to catalyze biochemical reactions in the cell. Cell walls and cell membranes are also formed by similar hydrophilic and hydrophobic interactions. A lipid is another type of biological molecule that contains hydrophilic and hydrophobic components. One end of the lipid is polar and is called the head, while the rest of the molecule is nonpolar and is called the tail (fig. 5.19). The main structure of membranes is a lipid bilayer of two rows of lipid arranged tail to tail, with the heads on the outside interacting with the water within and without the cell.

Observations. Because water is so common, we easily miss its uniqueness. Using the trends of chemistry, we would expect water to be a gas at room temperature or for ice to sink in our iced tea. Either one of these properties would be enough to make the Earth very hostile to life. The high heat capacity and heat of vaporization of water further moderate the climate of the Earth. Water is a unique molecule whose existence is a mark of design to some.

WHERE'S THE BEEF?

"Design is not so much a set of facts as it is a way of reasoning."
–NANCY PEARCEY

Mathematics and Physics

Key Concepts. Does mathematics really describe nature? Several responses to the question have been proposed. The conventionalist[12] would state that mathematical equations are provisional models of reality. They give us a partial truth. The model (type of mathematics) changes as one's knowledge of nature increases. The model is just curve fitting, modifying mathematics until it fits reality. According to the conventionalist view, Ptolemy (c. AD 100–165) started with a geometric model of the circle to model the orbit of Mars. When that did not work, he kept adding circles upon circles until he reproduced the orbit of Mars. The conventionalist would say that Newton did the same thing. Newton started by solving the differential equation involving Mars and the sun. The elliptical orbit predicted does not exactly fit the orbit of Mars. Adding other masses such as Jupiter will more closely reproduce the orbit of Mars. The conventionalist would say, "We are still curve fitting, but are doing it on the basis of a more versatile vocabulary of the solutions of differential equations rather than on a vocabulary of 'ready made' simple curves such as circles."[13]

A second response is the Platonic view. This view believes that mathematical objects exist independent of our knowledge of them. When one discovers mathematical concepts, one is discovering the "blueprint" of nature. The mathematical concepts are more than just mental constructs. The Platonist would say that the conventionalists have not really answered why mathematics is so unreasonably effective.[14]

One amazing thing is why something as abstract as a number can be broadly applied to physical objects. As the mathematician Richard W. Hamming wrote:

> Is it not remarkable that 6 sheep plus 7 sheep make 13 sheep; that 6 stones plus 7 stones make 13 stones? Is it not a miracle that the universe is so constructed that such a simple abstraction as a number is

possible? To me this is one of the strongest examples of the unreasonable effectiveness of mathematics.[15]

The unreasonable effectiveness of mathematics is also reflected in the fact that "what we predict from the manipulation of mathematical symbols is realized in the real world."[16] In 1873, James Clerk Maxwell (1831–1879) published the fully developed form of his equations, which described the behavior of visible light. Maxwell's equations predicted that visible light had "brothers and sisters" in the electromagnetic spectrum. This prediction was confirmed by Heinrich Rudolph Hertz (1857–1894) in 1887, when he discovered radio waves. Soon, microwaves, infrared, ultraviolet, x-rays, and gamma rays were discovered to be part of the electromagnetic spectrum. Manipulations of mathematical equations led to a greater understanding of nature.

An even more amazing example of the unreasonable effectiveness of mathematics concerns types of mathematics that developed abstractly, without any reference to nature. Yet, many of these mathematical types were later shown to describe nature better than previous mathematical concepts. One example is non-Euclidean geometry, which was developed independently early in the nineteenth century by Carl Friedrich Gauss (1777–1855), Nikolay Ivanovich Lobachevsky (1793–1856), and János Bolyai (1802–1860). Euclidean geometry is the geometry usually taught in introductory high school geometry classes. Euclidean geometry seems to fit common sense. Euclidean geometry allows only one line to be drawn parallel to a given line through a given point not on the line. Non-Euclidean geometry allows more than one line to be drawn parallel to a given line through a given point not on the line. At first, non-Euclidean geometry was considered at best useless, at worse, monstrous. Einstein later showed that non-Euclidean geometry gives a more precise description of astronomical space than Euclidean geometry.

Another example of "bizarre" mathematics is fractal geometry, developed by Benoit B. Mandelbrot (1924–). A fractal is an irregular geometric figure with the property that when any given part of the figure is enlarged or reduced, a similar shape is maintained. Zooming in for a closer view of a non-fractal object tends to smooth out its irregularities. As in the case of non-Euclidean geometry, fractals at first were considered bizarre and useless. Mandelbrot later suggested that coastlines, clouds, mountains, and trees are fractal in shape. A cloud keeps its detailed shape whether viewed from the ground or from an airplane. A rock looks like the mountain from which it came. On an atlas, the eastern coastline of the United States looks like a fairly smooth line with a length of two to three thousand miles. On a more detailed map of just the United States, the coastline has bays and inlets; the coastline is a more complex line with a length of four to five thousand miles. At the greater magnification of a person walking along the coastline, the path becomes very ragged, with a length of over fifteen thousand miles. The bizarre fractal geometry seems to describe some parts of nature better than the smooth curves of Euclidean geometry.

Whether one sees design in the "unreasonable effectiveness of mathematics" depends upon one's philosophy, one's worldview, or one's frame of reference. As the quote from Nancy Pearcey states, whether one sees design does not depend upon the "facts" but upon how one reasons about those facts. Both the conventionalist and the Platonist see how mathematics is applied to physics problems. Their worldviews determine whether they see a model or design.

Chemistry

Key Concepts. Consider a handful of organizable building blocks, the unique chemistry of carbon, and the extraordinary properties of water. A materialist would explain these phenomena in terms of the interaction of matter and forces. He or she would say that it is not surprising that there are so few elements. Since the atomic nucleus is a very small space, electromagnetic repulsion between increasing numbers of protons will eventually overpower the attractive effects of the strong nuclear force and tear the nucleus apart. He or she would also attempt to use electromagnetic interactions to explain the chemistry of carbon and the properties of water.

It is true that many aspects of chemistry can be explained in terms of the forces of physics. Yet, there is much about chemistry that has not been calculated by the use of the forces of physics. Happily, chemists still need to go into the laboratory to discover what happens when two substances are mixed. Even if the dark day were to come when all chemistry could be reduced to a series of calculations, the possibility of design would not be removed. The argument for design would just be moved back to the laws of nature, as discussed in chapter four.

As Nancy Pearcey stated, whether one sees design depends upon one's reasoning or worldview. Chemistry does reveal an astonishing set of facts that do have the appearance of design. Rather than getting lost arguing this or that point, however, one should look at the big picture. The big picture reveals a universal science where the one hundred or so elements form the basis of matter throughout the universe. The chemistry of the element carbon, which makes carbon such a unique element, provides carbon with the properties required for life. The remarkable properties of water allow water to provide a wonderful external environment for life as well as a wonderful internal medium for life. Likewise, carbon dioxide has the right properties for removing carbon-based waste from living organisms.

6. The Complexity of Life

Jimmy H. Davis

"The marks of design are too strong to be gotten over."
—William Paley

"Biology is the study of complicated things that give
the appearance of having been designed with a purpose."
—Richard Dawkins

INITIALLY, THE COMPLEXITY and interdependence of living organisms was used as evidence for design. As Dawkins' quote shows, to many people, Darwinian evolution implies that what others thought was design was really the result of the adaptation of organisms to their environment by natural processes. In this chapter, we will consider the difficult question of whether living organisms show evidences of design.

Web of Life

Here we will review certain areas of biology that appear to be designed. We will look at the relationships between organisms, review the anatomy that undergirds the organism, and examine the biochemistry that powers the organism.

Interdependence of Living Organisms

When natural philosophers or naturalists (later called scientists and biologists) began studying living organisms, they noticed that many organisms were dependent on each other for existence. They seemed to be made for each other. They had the correct shape or color for the mutual benefit of the other. From the thousands of cases that we could consider, we will examine pollination, species that exchange nutrients, camouflage, mimicry, and beaks of birds.

Pollination. Flowering plants depend on external agents to transfer pollen from the male part of the flower of one plant to the female part of the flower of another plant. Bees, hummingbirds, moths, wasps, and flies are common pollinating agents. Scientists discovered that the color, shape, and odor of the flowers coordinated well with the physiology of the pollinating agent. Bees can see ultraviolet, blue, and yellow parts of the spectrum. Bees are attracted by sweet, aromatic, or minty odors. They alight on a petal before exploring the flower; they do not hover like hummingbirds. Bees are active during the day. Scientists discovered that flowers that bees pollinate have "colors" in the ultraviolet, blue, and yellow range; they have petals that the bees can alight on before moving on to the nectar and pollen; they have a sweet, aromatic, or minty odor; and they are open during the day.

Fig. 6.1. Structures of columbine flowers correlated with anatomy of pollinators. A. **Aguilegia** *ecalcarata, pollinated by bees. B.* **Formosa,** *pollinated by hummingbirds. The length and curvature of the bees' tongue and the curvature of the nectar tubes of the flower. Adapted from V. Grant, "The Fertilization of Flowers,"* Scientific American, June 1951.

Hummingbirds, in contrast to bees, see red well but blue poorly; they have a poor sense of smell and they like to hover. Other flowers are red, have almost no odor, and do not have landing platforms. Hummingbirds pollinate these flowers. Figure 6.1 illustrates how the shape of the popular garden plant, the columbine, varies from pollinator to pollinator. In contrast to hummingbirds and bees, moths are active at night. The flowers that moths pollinate open at dusk, are mostly white, and have strong odors to guide the moths.

Another interesting relationship between the flowers pollinated and the pollinators concerns the shape of the nectar tubes of the flowers and the shape of the tongues or bills of the pollinators. There is a good correlation between the curvature and length of the nectar tube of the flower and the curvature and length of the tongue of the bees and moths or curvature and length of the bills of the hummingbirds (fig. 6.1). The fit is remarkable.

Other flowers are pollinated by short-tongued flies. These flies feed on carrion, dung, and blood. They are attracted by vile rather than sweet odors. They depend on detecting vile odors more than vision to find food. Thus, the flowers that these flies pollinate are dull colored and vile smelling. These flowers are also shaped so that the fly is temporarily trapped. This entrapment ensures that the fly becomes covered by pollen.

In the above cases, the relationships are between a general class of pollinator and a general class of flower. In some cases, the relationship is very specific and extreme. One specific relationship is between the flower, Scotch broom (*Cytisus scoparius*), and certain bumblebees. The stamens spring up and dust the underside of the bee with pollen only when the right type of bumblebee enters the Scotch broom flower. An extreme example is the mirror orchid, *Ophrys speculum*. The shape and color of the flower of this orchid resembles the shape and color of the female of one wasp species. When the male wasp attempts to copulate with the orchid, he is covered with pollen, which he then spreads from flower to flower.

Exchange of nutrients. Termites eat wood. Yet termites could not digest the wood if it were not for the protozoa that live in their intestinal tract. Yet, the protozoa do not digest the wood; bacteria living in the protozoa digest the wood. Residing in the termites provides a safe home and steady food supply for the protozoa and the bacteria. The latter provides the termites carbohydrates from the digestion of the wood. Cows eat grass. Yet, cows cannot digest the cellulose in the grass. Microorganisms that live in the cow's digestive tract digest the cellulose. Being in the cow's digestive tract provides the bacteria with a steady source of food, while the bacteria provide the cows with carbohydrates from the cellulose. Humans have a similar relationship with bacteria in their intestines that synthesize vitamin B12. The bacteria are provided with a steady source of food and they provide humans with a vitamin that humans cannot synthesize.

In the far northern part of North America, Europe, and Asia lies the tundra. In this extreme climate, lichens are found. Lichens demonstrate a symbiotic relationship between a fungus and a green alga (cyanobacterium). The body of a lichen is composed of three layers: a lower layer of fungus and a top layer of fungus that shield the photosynthetic cells of the alga in the middle. Their association enables them to live in the extreme conditions of the tundra where neither could survive alone. The fungus apparently benefits from the photosynthetic activity of the alga. The alga apparently benefits from the water-retaining properties of the fungal layers.

Camouflage. Many animals, because of their color and/or shape, blend into their surroundings so well that they are nearly undetectable. Animals that fly or swim are dark on top (dorsal) and lighter in color on their undersides (ventral). Thus, from below, these animals blend into the sky or surface waters and, from above, they blend into the darker earth or stream bottom. Other animals, such as lizards (chameleons), frogs, and fish, can change color to match their backgrounds. Flounder are uniform in color against a uniform-colored sea floor but become spotted against a spotted background. Some animals change color with the seasons. The ptarmigan, arctic fox, and snowshoe hare are brown in summer but white in winter. The pupae of certain butterflies have two color forms. If the pupae are developing in green vegetation, the pupae will be green and resemble leaves. If the pupae are developing against a brown background, the pupae will be brown and resemble rotting wood. Certain insects (*Phyllium pulchrifolium*, beautiful moving leaf) resemble the leaves upon which they rest. This resemblance is so thorough that the insect has the vein pattern of a true leaf and includes coloration that resembles insect-infected holes in real leaves.

Mimicry. Some harmless animals (the mimic) resemble more dangerous or poisonous animals (the model). This resemblance results in protection from predators or in some other benefit to the mimic. In the southeastern United States, the nonpoisonous scarlet king snake, *Lampropeltis triangulum*, resembles the very poisonous coral snake, *Micrurus fulvius*. Bees and wasps are brightly colored and are known for their painful stingers. Flower flies, which do not have stingers, have black and yellow markings similar to bees or wasps and are even found on flowers eating nectar. The pipevine swallowtail is a poisonous butterfly avoided by birds. Its color pattern is mimicked by the females of the black swallowtail, the tiger swallowtail, and the Bianca fritillary, but the males of these species do not mimic the color pattern of the pipevine swallowtail. Both sexes of the red-spotted purple butterfly, which are in the same range as the pipevine swallowtail, mimic the pipevine swallowtail's color pattern. Snapping turtles and anglerfish show another type of mimicry. The tongue of the snapping turtle resembles a worm. Anglerfish have lures that resemble worms. In both cases, it is thought that this mimicry of worms lures fish within reach.

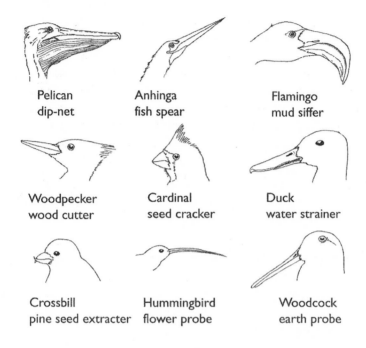

Fig. 6.2. Bird beaks associated with different kinds of feeding

Beaks of Birds. When naturalists studied birds, they noticed that there were many different types of bird beaks. They also observed that each type of beak was of the right shape for the food-gathering habits of the bird. Figure 6.2 displays some typical bird beaks. Some birds have beaks suitable for cracking seeds and nuts. The crossbill feeds on the seeds of conifer cones. Each species and subspecies of crossbill has beaks shaped for a particular size and shape of conifer cone. The hawfinch feeds on tough, large seeds of the wild cheery and damson. Its massive bill can exert a pressure of about two hundred pounds per square inch (14 kg per square cm). Other birds have beaks suitable for fishing or feeding in water. The pelican has a long bill with a pouch suspended from the bill and throat. This arrangement acts like a net to scoop up fish. Ducks and flamingos have bills lined with bony notches for straining plant and animal matter from the water. Some birds have beaks suitable for hunting insects. The cactus wren has a long, curved beak for catching insects. Woodpeckers have sharp, straight, chisel-shaped beaks with long, extensile tongues. They use their sharp beaks to chisel into the wood and work the insects out with their long tongues. Other birds have beaks suitable for probing flowers. We have already discussed the hummingbird. The shape and curvature of the hummingbird's slender bill corresponds to the shape and curvature of the flower favored by each species of hummingbird. Some birds have beaks suitable for probing mud or sand. The spoonbill has a long, broad beak to shovel through mud in search of food. The sandpiper is a common shore bird that catches small fish and invertebrates as it probes the sandy or muddy shore with its long bill. The heron has a long, sharp, pointed bill. The heron hunts by waiting in shallow water or on land to spear prey with its long bill.

Observations. The interdependence of living organisms gives a strong appearance of design. The correlation between the eyesight of pollinators and the color of flowers is truly amazing. Also astonishing is the fit between the shapes of flowers and the tongues and bills of the pollinators. How much design went into termites depending upon protozoa that depend upon bacteria? The camouflage and mimicry of animals again give the appearance of design. By looking at the relationships of organisms today, one does not know how much they have changed over time and how any changes may have affected the relationships.

Comparative Anatomy

When scientists examine the insides of the plants and animals, they find structures and patterns that just seem made for the particular plant or animal. We will examine two cases: homologous structures and the bodies of birds.

Homologous Structures. A comparison of the anatomies of a variety of vertebrates reveals a common architecture. The forelimbs of vertebrates are used for running (horse), swimming (whale), climbing (cat and human), and flying (bird). In spite of all these different functions, all these forelimbs contain the same set of bones. Figure 6.3 shows that all these forelimb bones are organized in a similar manner. Since these forelimbs contain the same relative pattern, they are called homologous structures. Another example of homologous structures is the similarity between the facial muscles of humans and monkeys (fig. 6.4). Because the human has more facial muscles, a human can make more facial expressions than a monkey can.

Bodies of Birds. Birds have bodies that appear to be made for flight. The effihuman cat horse whale bird

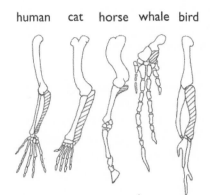

Fig. 6.3. Homologous structures. The bones of the vertebrate forelimbs display a similar pttern. Adapted from Sylvia Mader, Inquiry into Life, *8th ed. (Dubuque, Ia.: Wm. C. Brown Publishers, 1997).*

ciency of flight depends upon how light the body is. One way birds have a lighter framework is through the construction of their bones. Many bones are hollow instead of being filled with marrow, and these bones are connected to a system of air sacs. The bones of the skull and pelvic girdle are fused for lightness and strength. The wing needs to provide strong support for the large flight feather; the fusing of the digital and wrist bones of the forelimb provide this support (fig. 6.3). Birds need powerful muscles to power the flight stroke. Powerful muscles need a firm anchor. Birds' large, overdeveloped breastbones provide this anchor. In flightless birds, the breastbone is reduced in size. Large amounts of energy are consumed in flight. Thus, the hearts of birds are large and well developed. The complexities of flight require keen eyesight. Thus, it is not surprising that the eyesight of birds is several times better than man's. The complexities of flight also require complex muscle coordination; the cerebellum, the part of the brain that controls muscle coordination, is large in birds.

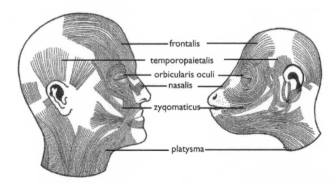

Fig. 6.4. Similarities between facial muscles of humans and monkeys

Observations. When one examines the anatomy of organisms, design again seems to be present. Living organisms seem to be built along similar patterns whether one is talking about forelimbs or muscles. The bodies of birds are amazing machines that appear to be made for flight.

Biochemistry

When scientists began exploring below the anatomical level, they discovered that all living organisms contain similar chemical compounds and reactions. Biochemistry is the branch of chemistry that deals with these chemical compounds and reactions.

		The Cell		
Organelles		Nucleus Mitochondria Chloroplasts Endoplasmic reticulum		
Supramolecular assemblies *Particle mass* 10^6 - 10^9		Lipoproteins Ribosome		
Macromolecules *Mol mass* 10^3 - 10^9	Carbohydrates (polysaccharides)	Lipids	Proteins	Nucleic acids
Building blocks *Mol mass* 100 – 350	Simple sugars	Fatty Acids	Amino Glycerol	Nucleotides acids
Intermediates Mol mass 50 – 250	Phospho- pyruvate	Acetate Malonate	∞-Keto acids	Ribose Carbamyl phosphate
Precursors from *the environment* *Mol mass* 18 -44		CO_2 H_2O N_2		

Figure 6.5. Hierarchy of molecular organization of life. Adapted from Albert L. Lehninger, Biochemistry, *1st ed. (New York: Worth Publishers, 1970).*

Cellular Hierarchy. Figure 6.5 shows the hierarchical arrangement of the chemicals found in living organisms. Simple inorganic molecules (carbon dioxide, water, and nitrogen) are taken in by living organisms and converted through the intermediate compounds to building-block molecules. The building-block molecules are covalently linked together to form the macromolecules. Simple sugars combine to form carbohydrates (sucrose, starch, glycogen, and cellulose). Amino acids link together to make proteins (muscles, enzymes, and connective tissue). Fatty acids combine with glycerol to form lipids (fats and oils). Nucleotides combine to form nucleic acids (DNA and RNA). These macromolecules form the four large classes of compounds found in living organisms: carbohydrates, lipids, proteins, and nucleic acids.

Different macromolecules associate together to form supramolecular complexes, the next level of organization. For example, lipids and proteins associate together to form lipoproteins. Two lipoproteins are high-density lipoproteins (HDL) and low-density lipoproteins (LDL). Coronary heart disease is associated with elevated levels of LDL while HDL seems to reduce a person's risk of developing coronary heart disease. Another supramolecular complex involves the ribosomes, which are associations of proteins and nucleic acids. The ribosome serves as the site for protein synthesis in the cell.

The next level of organization is the assembly of the supramolecules into organelles. The organelles are membrane-enclosed structures within a cell. Examples of organelles include nuclei (contain chromosomes that control the function of the cell), mitochondria (produce energy for the cell through cellular respiration), chloroplasts (contain chlorophyll and are where photosynthesis occurs in plants), and endoplasmic reticulum (system of interconnected tubules and sacs that function in the transport of materials in the cell).

Finally, all these hierarchical components are organized into a cell. The cell is the smallest unit capable of carrying out the functions of life. Some cells are complete organisms, such as a protozoa. Other cells, such as muscle cells, are specialized parts of multicellular organisms. The smallest cells (mycoplasmas) are about 0.1 micrometer in diameter. The largest cells (ostrich egg yolk) are about 8 centimeters (3 inches) in diameter. All cells are surrounded by a membrane. The inside of the cell is a water-rich environment (cytoplasm) containing genetic material (DNA) that contains the instructions for the functioning of the cell.

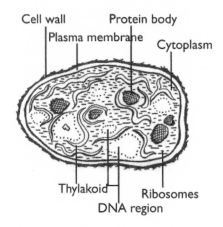

Cell wall   Protein body
Plasma membrane
                        Cytoplasm

Thylakoid
              Ribosomes
DNA region

Fig. 6.6. Prokaryote cell. These cells lack a nucleus. The DNA is in direct contact with the cytoplasm.

Cells come in two types: prokaryotes and eukaryotes. Examples of prokaryotes are unicellular bacteria and cyanobacteria. The prokaryote cell lacks a nucleus. The DNA is in direct contact with the cytoplasm (fig. 6.6). Eukaryotic cells are found in plants (fig. 6.7) and animals (fig. 6.8). In eukaryotic cells, the DNA is separated from the cytoplasm by a membrane. Eukaryotic cells also contain the membranous organelles. Generally, plant cells differ from animal cells in that plant cells have a cell wall, chloroplasts, and a large vacuole.

Macromolecules. As discussed previously, the major cellular components are made of the four major classes of macromolecules (carbohydrates, lipids, proteins, and nucleic acids). The distribution of the macromolecules in the *Escherichia coli* cell are shown in figure 6.9. If we exclude the exoskeleton and storage materials, the four classes of macromolecules are found in these proportions in all types of cells. As can be seen in figure 6.9, proteins are the most abundant macromolecule.

Not only do the macromolecules occur in the same proportions, but they also have the same functions in all cells. Carbohydrates occur as monosaccharides such as glucose and fructose, dissaccharides such as sucrose and lactose, and polysaccharides such as starch and glycogen (energy storage molecules) or cellulose (structural elements). Lipids are the major components of membranes and for energy storage (fat). Proteins serve as catalysts (enzymes), communication (hormones), and structural elements (muscles, collagen, and keratin). Nucleic acids store and transmit genetic information.

One difference between the macromolecules is that the nucleic acids and proteins are informational due to their structure while polysaccharides and lipids are not (fig. 6.10). Each nucleotide contains one of four different bases, symbolized by the letters A, T, G, and C. The sequence of these bases in the nucleic acid encodes the hereditary information contained in DNA.

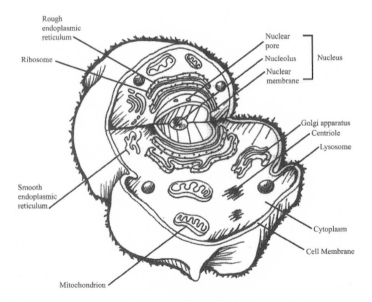

Fig. 6.7. Plant cell. This type of cell is surrounded by a rigid cell wall. The cell contains a nucleus as well as other membrane-surrounded organelles.

Fig. 6.8. Animal cell. This type of cell is surrounded by a flexible cell membrane. The cell contains a nucleus as well as other membrane-surrounded organelles.

Substance	Percent total weight
Water	70
Protein	15
Nucleic acids	
DNA	1
RNA	7
Carbohydrates	3
Lipids	2
Building-block molecules and intermediates	2
Inorganic ions	1

Fig. 6.9. Macromolecules in E. coli cells. Adapted from Albert L. Lehninger, Biochemistry, *1st ed. (New York: Worth Publishers, 1970), 20.*

Likewise, each protein contains information in its sequence of amino acids. In contrast, polysaccharides do not contain information in their sequences. The polysaccharide starch is just a repeating sequence of the building block glucose. Lipids are also noninformational, since they involve the repeating of CH_2 units.

Observations. It is amazing that the same chemistry is found in all living organisms. Does this fact reflect the constructing of all living organisms on a common chemical design? What an astonishing fact that organisms contain the same genetic code. Even more amazing, the cells of all organisms from the smallest one-cell bacterium to the largest multicellular whale contain information. Was this information designed into the cells?

Designer Genes: Flow of Information in the Cell

For centuries, one of the great mysteries of life was how characteristics of parents were transmitted to their offspring. Where in the organism was the hereditary information stored? How was it encoded? Was it localized in one part of the cell? Did this information also control the day-to-day activities of the organism?

Informational

    Nucleic Acid (DNA)
    -A-C-G-T-G-A-A-C-G-T-T-A-

    Protein
    -Phe-Arg-Arg-Ala-Lys-Trp-Lys-Met-

Noninformational

    Polysaccharide
    -Glu-Glu-Glu-Glu-Glu-Glu-Glu-Glu-Glu-

    Lipid
    $-CH_2-CH_2-CH_2-CH_2-CH_2-CH_2-CH_2-CH_2-$

The letters A, C, G, and T symbolize the four bases in DNA. Three-letter abbreviations (Ala, Arg, Lys, Met, Trp) are used to symbolize the amino acids that make up a protein. In the polysaccharide, glucose is symbolized by Glu. The CH_2 are the repeating units in the fatty acid part of the lipid.

Fig. 6.10. Informational and noninformational macromolecules

The first step in answering these questions was taken by the Austrian/ Czech Republican monk Gregor Mendel (1822–1884), who spent seven years studying garden peas. He discovered the rules of heredity and published his findings in 1866. His work was forgotten for thirty-four years until it was rediscovered in 1900. While Mendel's work was being overlooked, scientists in the 1870s developed microscopic staining techniques. By staining the nucleus of the cell, scientists discovered that it was full of tiny threads. These threads were labeled chromosomes or "colored bodies," from the Greek words *chromo* (color) and *soma* (body). The German biologist August Weismann (1834–1914) conjectured in the 1880s that chromatin, the component chromosomes are made of, was probably responsible for heredity. In 1874, the Swiss biochemist Johann Friedrich Miescher (1844–1895) analyzed the non-protein material in the nucleus and determined that its chemical identity was an acid, which he named nucleic acid. Today, this acid is called deoxyribonucleic acid or DNA. By 1909, the name "gene" had been coined to describe parts of the chromosome that carry traits. In 1941, the American geneticist George Beadle (1903–1989) and the American biochemist Edward L. Tatum (1909–1975) showed that one gene is responsible for synthesizing one enzyme, which catalyzes a particular reaction. For this work, Beadle and Tatum received the Nobel Prize in 1958. Since the chromosome contains protein as well as nucleic acid, scientists were trying to determine if this protein stored hereditary information. In 1944, the Canadian bacteriologist Oswald Avery (1877–1955) showed that DNA alone was responsible for the hereditary traits. His work influenced the English biologist Francis Crick (1916–2004) and the American biologist James Watson (1928–) to investigate the structure of DNA. In 1953, Watson and Crick reported that DNA consisted of a double helix (spiral staircase). For their work, they received the Nobel Prize in 1962. The genetic code was shown to be a triplet combination of the DNA bases. For this work, American biochemists Marshall Warren Nirenberg (1927–) and Robert Holley (1922–1993) and the Indian-American geneticist Har Gobind Khorana (1922–) shared the 1968 Nobel Prize. Scientists also realized that another nucleic acid, ribonucleic acid or RNA, was involved in carrying the genetic information from inside the nucleus to protein synthesis sites outside the nucleus.

Deoxyribonucleic Acid

The DNA in a human cell is at least two meters (6.6 feet)[1] long. Yet this DNA is stored in a nucleus only about five micrometers in diameter. How is this possible? The human chromosome is about 25 percent DNA and 75 percent protein. This protein is involved in packing the DNA; it forms a scaffold around which the DNA coils. The protein-DNA package continues to coil until a chromosome forms. During cell division, the extremely compact chromosomes are duplicated into two daughter chromosomes. By the end of mitosis (the process of cell division), the daughter chromosomes have separated and a copy of each chromosome ends up in the two daughter cells. In this way, the hereditary information is duplicated and passed on to the new cells. Does the structure of DNA help us understand how the hereditary information is copied? Yes. In their original publication, Watson and Crick stated, "It has not escaped our notice that the specific pairing we have postulated immediately suggests a possible copying mechanism for the genetic material."[2] Let us review the structure of DNA and examine how this structure explains the reproduction of hereditary information.

DNA is a polymer made by stringing together nucleotide molecules. The nucleotides from which deoxyribonucleic acid is formed consist of three parts—a phosphate group, a pentose sugar (deoxyribose), and a nitrogen base (fig. 6.11). There are four possible nitrogen bases. Two of the bases are

Fig. 6.11. Representative nucleotides

pyrimidines containing one ring, and two are purines containing two rings. The names of the bases are: pyrimidines (thymine or T, and cytosine or C); and purines (adenine or A, and guanine or G). Nucleotides combine to form the DNA polymer. The backbone of the polymer consists of the sequence: phosphate-sugar-phosphate-sugar. The nitrogen bases extend from the side of the backbone (fig. 6.12). Using the numbering system in figure 6.11, scientists designate one end of a DNA strand as 5' and the other end as 3'. The term "primary structure" is used to describe the sequence of bases along the backbone of a DNA strand. The sequence of the bases is read from the 5' end to the 3' end. Thus, the sequence of bases AGCT is not equivalent to the sequence TCGA. Since the base sequence in a strand can be in any order, tremendous variability results. In a chromosome with about 140 million base pairs, $4^{140,000,000}$ possible combinations are possible. No wonder each living organism is unique.

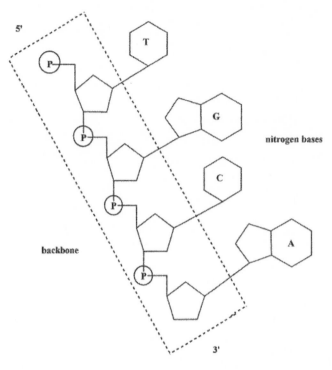

Fig. 6.12. DNA backbone. Each strand has a backbone composed of phosphate-sugar sequences. The sequence of bases is read from the 5' end to the 3' end. In this example, the sequence is read as TGCA rather than ACGT.

The term "secondary structure" is used to describe the three-dimensional pattern for the DNA molecule. The secondary structure of DNA consists of two strands that twist about each other to form a double helix (fig. 6.13). In the DNA double helix, the two strands run in opposite directions. At each end of the double helix, there is one 5' end and one 3' end. In the double helix, the strand backbones are on the outside, with the bases pointing toward the inside. The two strands are held together by hydrogen bonding between bases on the two strands. The base A on one strand always pairs with the base T on the other strand, while the base C always pairs with the base G. These base pair combinations are known as complementary bases.

Each organism has a unique number of chromosomes. Tomatoes have twelve pairs of chromosomes; dogs have thirty-eight pairs; and humans, twenty-three pairs. Genes are the units of heredity. They are carried by the

Unwinding proteins

Old 3'

New 5'

DNA polymei

DNA nι

Old 5'

Left: Fig. 6.13. The DNA double helix. Base A always pairs with base T. Base C always pairs with base G.

Above: Fig. 6.14. Duplication of DNA. The unwinding proteins unzip the double helix.

chromosomes and are arranged in a line along the chromosome. Each gene is a segment of DNA that codes for one protein molecule. Each gene is a section of the DNA molecule in the chromosome. The gene is the specific sequence of the four bases (A, C, G, and T) along this section of DNA and can contain from about one to two thousand bases. Thus, transmission of genetic information involves copying the DNA strands in the chromosomes. How is a DNA strand copied?

The DNA double helix arrangement provides a template for the copying process. The old strand acts as a mold (template) for the new (daughter) strand formed. The duplication of the DNA molecule is called replication. The first step in replication is the unwinding of the double helix. The unwinding can start at either end or in the middle. Special enzymes (unwinding proteins) attach themselves to one of the DNA strands, cause the hydrogen bonds between the bases to break, and bring about the unzipping of the double helix (fig. 6.14). The next step in replication is the pairing of the complementary bases. The necessary nucleotides are in the fluid surrounding the unzipping DNA. Once a free base T comes in contact with a base A on the parental strand, they stick together through hydrogen bonding. The final step in replication is joining the complementary bases to form the daughter strand. The enzyme DNA polymerase joins the complementary nucleotides into the backbone of the daughter strand. Interestingly, the polymerases work only from 5' to 3'. The two complementary strands are connected in different ways. The new 5' to 3' strand is continuously synthesized by the polymerase. For the new 3' to 5' strand, the polymerase can synthesize only short fragments of about a thousand nucleotides. Another enzyme, DNA ligase, eventually joins these fragments together to complete the 3' to 5' complementary strand. The complementary strand synthesized continuously is called the "leading strand." The complementary strand made from fragments is called the "lagging strand."

Replication is a semiconservative process in that two of the four strands are new. The information that was contained in the original DNA is now contained in each of the duplicates. When the cell divides, this information will end up in each daughter cell.

RNA: A Second Type of Nucleic Acid

In eukaryotes, DNA is located in the nucleus. Yet, protein synthesis takes place outside the nucleus. What transfers the information encoded in DNA out into the cell? Before we can discuss this, we need to discuss another type of nucleic acid found in cells. RNA, or ribonucleic acid, is found both in the nucleus and in cytoplasm. Like DNA, RNA is a polymer made from nucleotides. Unlike DNA, RNA is a single strand, uses the pentose sugar ribose rather than deoxyribose, and contains the pyrimidine base uracil (U) rather than the base thymine (T). There are three types of RNA. Messenger RNA (mRNA) contains a strand of bases that are complementary of a section of DNA. This type of RNA carries the genetic information from the nucleus into the cytoplasm. Messenger RNA has a short life span; it is synthesized as needed and then degraded. Transfer RNA (tRNA) is a small nucleic acid that carries amino acids to the protein synthesis site. There is a different tRNA for each of the twenty amino acids. The third type of RNA is ribosomal RNA (rRNA). Protein synthesis occurs in the ribosome. The ribosome is a supramolecular assembly that is about 65 percent rRNA and 35 percent protein. A ribosome is composed of two parts. The larger part has an affinity for tRNA; the smaller part has an attraction for mRNA. In animal cells, ribosomes are bound to endoplasmic recticulum organelle. Figure 6.15 contains information about the three types of RNA.

Type	Percent	Approx. Number of Bases
Messenger RNA (mRNA)	5	1200
Transfer RNA (tRNA)	15	70-90
Ribosomal RNA (rRNA)	80	1800

Fig. 6.15. Types of RNA

THE GENETIC CODE

UUU Phe	UCU Ser	UAU Tyr	UGU Cys
UUC Phe	UCC Ser	UAC Tyr	UGC Cys
UUA Leu	UCA Ser	UAA END	GUA END
UUG Leu	UCG Ser	UAG END	UGG Trp
CUU Leu	CCU Pro	CAU His	CGU Arg
CUC Leu	CCC Pro	CAC His	CGC Arg
CUA Leu	CCA Pro	CAA Gln	CGA Arg
CUG Leu	CCG Pro	CAG Gln	CGG Arg
AUU Ile	ACU Thr	AAU Asn	AGU Ser
AUC Ile	ACC Thr	AAC Asn	AGC Ser
AUA Ile	ACA Thr	AAA Lys	AGA Arg
AUG Met & START	ACG Thr	AAG Lys	AGG Arg
GUU Val	GCU Ala	GAU Asp	GGU Gly
GUC Val	GCC Ala	GAC Asp	GGC Gly
GUA Val	GCA Ala	GAA Glu	GGA Gly
GUG Val	GCG Ala	GAG Glu	GGG Gly

Fig. 6.16. The Genetic Code. In each box, the left-most triplet (for example UUU) refers to a set of bases on the mRNA molecule. The right-most triplet (for example, Phe) is a three-letter abbreviation for an amino acid. The word START signals the beginning of the gene sequence. The word END refers to the ending of the gene sequence. As can be seen, many amino acids are coded for by more than one base triplet.

Protein Synthesis—Flow of Information

To express an inheritable trait, the information contained in DNA must be expressed as the correct sequence of amino acids in a protein. Since the information (the DNA) is inside the nucleus and the protein synthesis occurs outside the nucleus, a way has to exist for transferring the information outside the nucleus. The way living organisms carry out this process is to transfer the information contained in a DNA molecule to RNA molecules. The information carried by the RNA molecules is then used by cell organelles to synthesize proteins. A summary of the process is

DNA $\xrightarrow{\text{transcription}}$ mRNA $\xrightarrow{\text{translation}}$ protein

Transcription describes the process of transferring information from DNA to messenger RNA. How is the information written in DNA and RNA? As we mentioned in the previous historic sketch, the information is written in a triplet combination of the DNA bases. For each gene, there is a triplet combination that signals the start of the gene, followed by the triplet codes for each amino acid in the protein, followed by a triplet combination that signals the end of the gene. The genetic code is listed in figure 6.16.

Fig. 6.17. Synthesis of mRNA from DNA

Transcription begins with a segment of the DNA molecules unwinding at the point where the gene is located (fig. 6.17). The *ribonucleotides* needed to synthesize the mRNA assemble along the unwound DNA strand. They assemble in a complementary fashion. Opposite each G on the DNA there will be a C on the mRNA; the other base pairs are C with G, A with U, and T with A. The enzyme *RNA polymerase* joins the complementary ribonucleotides into the backbone of the mRNA.[3] Interestingly, the code between the start sequence and the end sequence contains segments that seemingly do not code for anything. The base triplets that code for an amino acid are called "exons" and the noncoding triplets are called "introns." The mRNA transcribed from the DNA contains both exons and introns. Somehow, enzymes know how to cut out the introns and splice together the exons before the mRNA is used to synthesize a protein. If the introns were left in the mRNA, the synthesized protein would not function properly. The modified mRNA moves out of the cell into the cytoplasm.

Translation is the process by which the information contained in the mRNA is used to assemble the protein. This process is called translation because it involves translating the language of the nucleotide triplets into the language of individual amino acids. The translator is the transfer RNA molecule. A simplified cloverleaf structure of tRNA appears in figure 6.18. The molecule is a single chain, but base pairing allows the molecule to fold back on itself.

Translation or protein synthesis involves four steps: activation, initiation, elongation, and termination. *Activation* involves attaching an amino acid to a tRNA molecule. Once an amino acid is activated with energy from *ATP* (the body's energy storage molecule), the enzyme *tRNA synthetase* binds the amino acid to the tRNA molecule (fig. 6.18). Since there is one tRNA for each amino acid, somehow the synthetase enzyme recognizes which amino acid should join to which tRNA molecule.

Initiation involves all three types of RNA (messenger, transfer, and ribosomal). Protein synthesis occurs in the supramolecular assemblies called ribosomes. The ribosome contains two subunits. The smaller ribosomal unit is made of one rRNA molecule and several proteins, and the larger ribosomal subunit is made of two rRNA molecules and several proteins. Among these proteins is the enzyme that will join the amino acids together to form the protein. During initiation, the mRNA, carrying information needed to synthesize one protein, binds to the smaller ribosomal subunit (fig. 6.19). The first tRNA molecule binds to the first ribonucleotide triplet (*codon*) of the mRNA. The area of the tRNA molecule shown in figure 6.18 (labeled *anticodon*) binds in a complementary fashion to the codon of the mRNA.[4] Once the tRNA molecule has bound to the mRNA, the larger ribosomal subunit combines with the smaller ribosomal subunit. The larger subunit has two binding sites. The site on the left of figure 6.19 is called the "P site," because this is where the growing protein molecule will be attached. The

Fig. 6.18. Simplified cloverleaf
structure of tRNA

Anticodon base triplet

other site is called the *A site*, because this is where the tRNA will bring the next amino acid.

Elongation involves connecting the amino acids to form a protein. The next tRNA binds to the vacant P site (fig. 6.20). The enzyme *transferase* links the two amino acids together. The ribosome moves along the mRNA, releasing the first tRNA. Another tRNA will bind to the resulting vacant A site. This amino acid will be joined to the other two. The ribosome moves along the mRNA, continuing the process until the last amino acid is attached.

Termination occurs when the end condon is reached. *Releasing factors* cut the protein from the last tRNA. The mRNA is released. The two subunits of the ribosome come apart.

Using the information from one mRNA, five to eight ribosomes will usually be simultaneously synthesizing five to eight copies of the same protein. In mammals, it takes about three minutes to join three hundred amino acids. Insulin is a small protein containing 51 amino acids; on the other hand, a large protein like hemoglobin contains a total of 574 amino acids.

Fig. 6.19. Initiation of protein synthesis. A. The mRNA molecule binds to the smaller ribosomal subunit. B. tRNA binds to mRNA. C. The larger ribosomal subunit binds to the complex. Adapted from Bettleheim and March, General, Organic, and Biochemistry *(Fort Worth: Saunders College, 1998).*

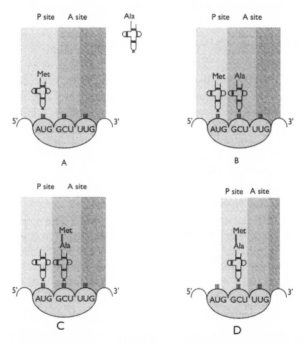

Fig. 6.20. Elongation phases of protein synthesis. A. Second tRNA approaches empty A site. B. The tRNA binds to the A site. C. The two amino acids are connected. D. The ribosome moves along the mRNA releasing the first tRNA and generating a vacant A site. Adapted from Bettleheim and March, General, Organic, and Biochemistry *(Fort Worth: Saunders College, 1998).*

Proteins are used for structure (collagen in bone), contraction (muscles), catalysts (enzymes), hormones (insulin), antibodies (gamma globulin), and transport (hemoglobin). Proteins have four different structures: primary, secondary, tertiary, and quaternary. The *primary structure* is the sequence of the amino acids that results from the translation process. A protein must be linked in the right sequence for a protein to function properly. For example, hemoglobin contains 574 amino acids. Sickle-cell hemoglobin differs from normal hemoglobin in only two of these 574 amino acids. The *secondary structure* of a protein results from the chemical interactions between amino acids in the chain, which creates a three-dimensional structure. One such structure is the alpha helix, a three-dimensional structure in the form of a right-handed screw. A *tertiary structure* results from further chemical interactions with the secondary structure components. This tertiary structure gives the protein a lock-and-key relationship to other molecules. By having a certain tertiary structure, the protein acts like a lock that only certain molecules can fit into like a key. Without the correct tertiary structure, the protein cannot catalyze specific chemical reactions. A *quaternary structure* results if the protein is composed on two or more chains of amino acids. Each chain has its own primary, secondary, and tertiary structure. In the quaternary structure, the chains are held together by chemical attractions. Both insulin (2 chains) and hemoglobin (4 chains) have quaternary structures. The change of two amino acids in sickle-cell hemoglobin affects all structural levels. To degrade or *denature* a protein is to change one or more of these structural levels.

The Human Genome Project

A *genome* is the complete DNA sequence of any organism. An average human has twenty-three pairs of chromosomes with approximately 20,000 to 25,000 genes.[5] Each chromosome consists of a single DNA molecule. The DNA of an average human contains approximately 3 billion base pairs. The Human Genome Project, a joint project of the U.S. Department of Energy and the National Institutes of Health, began in 1990 with a thirteen-year goal of determining the location of the genes in the forty-six human chromosomes as well as the sequencing of all the DNA base pairs. In addition to U.S. support, the project involves international support from the United Kingdom, France, Germany, Japan, and China. The goals of the project included identifying the genes in human DNA, determining the sequences of the approximately 3 billion bases in human DNA, providing this information to the public, and addressing the ethical, legal, and social issues raised by the project. In 1998, a private U.S. company, Celera Genomics Corporation, began a private-sector attempt to map the human genome in three years. In December 1999, researchers involved in the Human Genome Project announced the complete sequencing of the first human chromosome; chromosome 22 was found to contain 33.5 million bases. A total of 545 genes, ranging in length from 1,000 to 583,000 bases of DNA, were detected. These efforts reveal that chromosome 22 is implicated in the workings of the immune system, schizophrenia, birth defects, congenital heart disease, mental retardation, and cancers such as leukemia. On June 26, 2000, President Clinton, with British Prime Minister Tony Blair, announced that the Human Genome Project and Celera Genomics Corporation had completed an initial sequencing of the human genome. They reported that 97 percent of the bases had been decoded; the other 3 percent were considered unable to be sequenced and irrelevant. Continuing to refine their data, the project presented a final draft of all the human chromosomes in May 2006. Potential benefits of sequencing the human genome include:

molecular medicine: improved diagnosis of disease, earlier detection of genetic predispositions to disease, better drug design, gene therapy;

microbial genomics: biofuels, environmental monitoring of pollutants, safe toxic waste cleanup;

risk assessment: caused by radiation exposure, caused by mutagenic chemicals, caused by cancer-causing toxins;

DNA identification: identify suspects, exonerate persons wrongly accused, identify endangered species;

agriculture: produce disease- or insect- or drought-resistant crops, produce healthier crops and animals, produce more nutritious crops.

Potential concerns arising from the sequencing of the human genome include:

privacy: preventing your genome information from being used in employment decisions;

genetic determinism: preventing society from assuming if one has a certain gene, one will automatically have a certain set of traits;

patenting: preventing patented genetic information from delaying the benefits discussed above;

genetic modification: preventing a rush to improve on the genetic text to obtain the "perfect" offspring.

In addition to the humans, the genomes of around two hundred organisms have been sequenced, including mouse, fruit fly, a malaria-carrying mosquito, and rice. The U.S. government's current genome project will use this genomic data to develop technologies for energy and environmental applications, such as generating clean energy, cleaning up toxic waste, and removing carbon from the atmosphere.

Observations. The flow of information from the DNA to the RNA to the protein is even more complicated than described in this section. Many supporting enzymes have been left out for narrative clarity. The major challenge for those denying design is the origin of the information contained in the DNA. Did all the parts of this complicated system have to be present for it to begin working, or could it be built up gradually from its parts? A challenging question is: If enzymes (proteins) are required to make messenger RNA from DNA, where did the enzyme come from before the first mRNA was synthesized? All the parts seem designed to work together as a unit.

WHERE'S THE BEEF? ADAPTATION NOT DESIGN

"Biologists must constantly keep in mind that what they see was not designed, but rather evolved."
—FRANCIS CRICK

In the description of the interactions of biological organisms in the first part of this chapter, it was very difficult not to include the word "adaptation." When one opens a biology text of any level, one reads that everything is adapted to its environment. If design is mentioned, it is to state that what appears to be design is really adaptation. A modern biology text would say that hummingbirds and columbine flowers were not designed so that the bill and nectar tube fit, but environmental changes selected those hummingbirds and columbines most adapted to survive, resulting in the observed fit.

Why does modern biology deal with adaptation rather than design? The watershed event was the publication of *The Origin of Species* by Charles Darwin. Although a thorough discussion of Darwin's theory of evolution by natural selection is beyond the purpose of this text,[6] the modern formulation of Darwin's theory contains the following points. The physical characteristics of each member of a species vary due to genetic variations. As the members of a species daily compete for limited resources, some will have characteristics that will make them more competitive. Those members better suited to the environment will more likely produce more offspring. Thus, they are selected by the environment to survive and reproduce. Through the generations, natural selection causes certain organisms to become adapted to the environment. Darwin replaced design with adaptation: "The sum total of the accidents of life acting upon the sum total of the accidents of variation thus provided a completely mechanical and material system by which to account for the changes in living forms."[7]

If we consider again the organisms discussed in the "Interdependence of Living Organisms" section of this chapter, modern biologists would say that natural selection over a long period of time resulted in the amazing fit between pollinators and flowers, the symbiotic relationships discussed, the amazing way organisms camouflage themselves, clever mimicry, and each bird having a beak matched to its food source. Darwin also pointed out that in some cases, there are surprising matches between the bird and its food source:

> How strange it is that a bird, under the form of a woodpecker, should prey on insects on the ground; that upland geese which rarely or never swim, should possess webbed feet; that a thrush-like bird should dive and feed on sub-aquatic insects; . . . and so in endless other cases. But on the view of each species constantly trying to increase in number, with natural selection always ready to adapt the slowly varying descendants of each to any unoccupied or ill-occupied place in nature, these facts cease to be strange, or might even have been anticipated.[8]

Concerning the comparative anatomy examples, Darwinists would say that these examples are explained "on the theory of descent with slow and slight successive modifications."[9] In regard to homologous structures, Darwin stated, ". . . we may further venture to believe that the several bones in the limbs of the monkey, horse, and bat were originally developed, on the principle of utility, probably through the reduction of more numerous bones in the fin of some ancient fish-like progenitor of the whole class."[10]

PAIRS OF ORGANISMS	PERCENT DIFFERENCE IN DNA BASE SEQUENCES	PAIRS OF ORGANISMS	AMINO ACID DIFFERENCES IN HEMOGLOBIN
Human/chimpanzee	2.5	Human/gorilla	1
Human/gibbon	5.1	Human/rhesus monkey	8
Human/old world monkey	9.0	Human/mouse	27
Human/new world monkey	15.8	Human/chicken	45
Human/lemur	42.0	Human/frog	67
mouse/rat	30.0	Human/lamprey	125

Fig. 6.21. Differences in DNA base and protein amino acid sequences

In regard to biochemistry, the modern biologist emphasizes the fact that all living organisms share a common biochemistry or, as Darwin said, "Nevertheless, all living things have much in common, in their chemical composition, their cellular structure, their laws of growth, and their liability to injurious influences."[11] Modern biologists use the degree of difference between DNA base sequences or amino acid sequences to indicate the degree of relatedness between organisms (fig. 6.21). Currently, an exciting research area regarding the beginning of life is trying to determine which came first—DNA, RNA, or proteins. At present, there is no consensus concerning these questions, which amounts to a more sophisticated variation of "What came first, the chicken or the egg?" Since components of DNA and proteins cannot spontaneously join in water, one proposal involves the formation of RNA first. Ribonucleotides can join together in water to form RNA. Also, certain RNA can act as enzymes. In this proposal, RNA would be the first self-replicating information-storage molecule. Because of its structure, this RNA molecule would be capable of evolving by natural selection. This RNA would catalyze the formation of proteins. Later, the more complex DNA molecule would be synthesized. Much work still needs to be done, however, to answer all the questions that arise.

WHERE'S THE BEEF? ADAPTATION AND DESIGN

"The result of these cumulative efforts to investigate the cell —to investigate life at the molecular level—is a loud, clear, piercing cry of '*design!*'"
—MICHAEL J. BEHE

Even before the publication of *The Origin of Species*, scientists were trying to determine whether one species could change into another species. One scientist who dealt with this question was the Swedish naturalist Carolus Linnaeus (1707–1778). Linnaeus developed the binomial system for classifying and organizing plants and animals. His system is called binomial nomenclature, because it assigned a unique two-word Latin name to each organism. The first word refers to the genus to which the organism belongs, while the second word refers to the species. For example, the dog has the scientific name, *Canis familiaris*; *Canis* (dog) is its genus name and *familiaris* (of the family) is its species name. The complete classification system is kingdom, phylum, class, order, family, genus, and species. Linnaeus' inspiration for a classification system was his belief in design and in God's original creation of "fixed kinds" as stated in the first chapter of Genesis. His faith in God the Creator convinced him that there would be common characteristics within similar types of organisms that would allow him to classify them. In addition, this belief spurred Linnaeus to search to see how the concept of "fixed kinds" fit into his classification scheme. At first, based on his observation of limited numbers of species in Scandinavia, he thought that species referred to the Genesis "kinds." As he was exposed to more organisms from other areas, he became convinced that species can change and that the genus level corresponded to the "fixed kinds." Finally, he revised his thinking to propose that the order level corresponded to the "fixed kinds." Currently, the American Scientific Affiliation (ASA), an organization of Evangelical scientists, proposes that the fossil record supports species changing into other species. They propose that body types (phyla) were finalized in the Cambrian period and that all changes occur in either the class, order, family, genus, or species categories.[12] In contrast to the ASA proposal, current evolutionary theory proposes gradual descent from a common ancestor, with changes involving all the classification categories from kingdom to species. Figure 6.22 contrasts the two views.

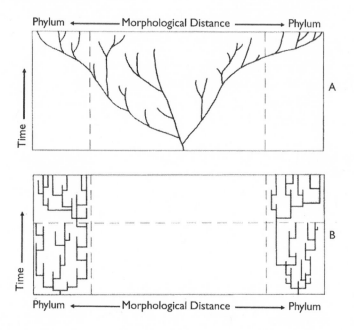

Fig. 6.22. Two views of how new organisms arise. A. Gradualism assumes all animals began with a common ancestor. Gradual changes lead to new orders, classes, and phyla. B. Since the Cambrian Period (about 570 million years ago), the fossil record shows changes within phyla but no change between phyla. After a major extinction (dashed line), rapid variation within the phyla occur. Adapted from the American Scientific Affiliation, Teaching Science in a Climate of Controversy, *1986.*

Almost everyone recognizes that organisms undergo adaptation. A dramatic example was the recent change in beaks of the Galapagos Islands finches, divided into thirteen species and placed in three genera. Darwin proposed that the Galapagos finches descended from mainland finches that migrated to the islands (fig. 6.23). Peter and Rosemary Grant have studied the finches since 1973. The Grants found that the finches' beak types varied with the climate. During a dry spell, when large, hard-shelled seeds are the only available food, finches with large, strong beaks reproduce more successfully. During the wet season, small, easily opened seeds become more available, and smaller-beaked finches reproduce more successfully.[13] The finches indicate that some organisms can adapt rapidly to changing environmental conditions.

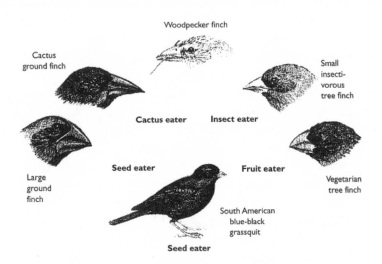

Fig. 6.23. Finches of the Galapagos Islands. These birds were important to Charles Darwin in developing the theory of evolution. The island finches closely resemble the South American grassquit.

There are two major areas where some scientists think purpose and design are reflected in biology. The two areas are *biological complexity* and *information systems*. These scientists propose that these areas cannot be totally explained by material and mechanical processes. They state that these areas indicate design.

Biological Complexity

An argument for design involves the idea of biological complexity, which is that the origin of life and the ensuing complexity in the history of life cannot be explained totally by natural causes alone. One version of this argument is that of the American biochemist and intelligent design movement member Michael J. Behe, with his concept of irreducible complexity as discussed in detail in chapter seven. Behe proposed that certain biochemical structures are too complex to arise from successive modification of preexisting components but must have been designed; otherwise, they could not function unless all parts were present. He further proposed that not all complex biological structures are designed; he proposed that some, like hemoglobin, arose by natural processes, while others, such as blood clotting, were designed. Among those proposing biological complexity/irreducible complexity as an argument for design, the underlying assumption is that if one can show that the particular biological system could have developed by natural processes, such as the hemoglobin example, then there was not any design. Yet, as we saw in chapter four, design arguments are also based on the fine-tuning of the universe. In the fine-tuning of the universe design argument, the underlying natural forces and laws result in the development of a universe that was fine-tuned to self-assemble atoms, molecules, stars, galaxies, and planets. But for those in the intelligent design movement, it is not an example of design if this same fine-tuning is extended to the self-assembly of biological life and biological complexity as shown in figure 6.5. Should this self-assembly be evidence for design? In the parlance of current groupings, this type of fine-tuning would be more of a theistic evolution argument rather than an intelligent design argument.

Whether one is focusing on biological complexity as fine-tuning or as irreducible complexity, we have observed many complex biological systems in this chapter. For example, when one considers the process of protein synthesis, one sees a very complex process that operates like a factory. In the central office (the nucleus) are the plans (DNA) for making all the factory's products (proteins). The plans for one product are copied (mRNA) and modified (introns removed) and carried out to the factory floor. The plans are fed into the computer (ribosome) that controls the machine (ribosome) that makes the protein. Meanwhile, forklifts (tRNA) are returning from the supply room with the parts (amino acids). The barcode (anticodon) on each part is read to ensure that the protein is assembled in the correct order. The shop floor is so designed that an assembly line can be set up with several machines (ribosomes) simultaneously reading the plans (mRNA). This way, several copies of the protein can be made at one time. Once the protein is assembled, it is taken into the shape room, where it is allowed to take on its final three-dimensional shape (secondary, tertiary, and quarternary structures).

Many scientists say that injecting design (or, as they would say, "faith") into the information-gathering, knowledge-formation process results in a dead end. They say once God is invoked, further exploration is ruled out.

An example of this thought process is represented by Robert Pennock in the *Tower of Babel*. In discussing Behe's book, Pennock writes,

> The most that Behe has done there is to point to a number of interesting research problems. One wonders why he, as a biochemist, does not begin the research himself. . . . Of course, Behe has no motivation to pursue the research himself, since he thinks he already knows the answer: biochemical complexity was produced by the intentional action of an intelligent designer. With intelligent-design theory, Behe has found a way to save himself a lot of work.[14]

Pennock is confusing how to carry out an experiment with how to interpret an experiment. The worldview of the experimenter will influence what questions are asked and how the experimental results are interpreted.[15] The example of Linnanus reveals that his use of design made many positive contributions to the accumulation of knowledge. Design did not stifle the acquisition of knowledge but provided the insight needed to advance understanding at many key points.

WHO PROVIDED THE INFORMATION?

Where did the information contained in the DNA molecule come from? On the one hand, the DNA molecule confirms the materialist view of nature because all the cell's functions depend upon the physics and chemistry of DNA. The components of DNA obey the same chemistry as all other molecules. There is no new chemistry involved in the phosphate groups reacting with the sugars to form the backbone of DNA. The usual chemistry is involved with the bases bonding to the backbone or from one strand to the other strand. As we discussed previously, the materialists spend their effort trying to determine how DNA or RNA could arise from just the interaction between matter and force. The materialist approach overlooks the question of how information became incorporated into the DNA molecule.

Materialists hoped that the structure of DNA would solve the information question. As a review of figure 6.12 reveals, in a strand, there are no chemical bonds between the bases. Thus, there are no chemical rules to determine the order in which the bases will be attached to the backbone. The base T can be followed by G or C or A or another T. Another approach is to look outside the DNA molecule. Maybe DNA or RNA formed on a mineral crystal. Crystals are self-ordering. Maybe the crystal's order formed the template for the synthesis of the nucleic acid. Crystals are highly ordered. In table salt (sodium chloride), each sodium ion is followed by a chloride ion that is followed by a sodium ion that is followed by a chloride ion, and so forth. Because the structure of a crystal is so repetitive, a crystal has low information content. If a nucleic acid were constructed like a crystal, then it could have a pattern like GAGAGAGA. This crystal-like pattern for a nucleic acid would not contain all the variety found in biological nucleic acids.

A different approach to the information content of DNA is provided by the chemist-philosopher Michael Polanyi.[16] Polanyi accepted the fact that materialists define life like a machine (forces and matter). Then, he asked what makes something a machine. Is it the material from which the machine is composed, or is it the function of the machine? Consider a pile of iron filings and a pair of scissors. There is no difference in the two at the atomic level. Where they differ is in their function. (A similar argument by Paley is discussed in chapter three.) Polanyi is saying that for any machine (nonbiological or biological), we have to look beyond the physical-chemical components to the organizational function or purpose.

Using Polanyi's reasoning, what is the function of the DNA molecule? DNA provides the instructions for the growth and reproduction of a cell.[17] Instructions or information is independent of the medium. The information in this book is written in ink. Someone could copy the contents in pencil, crayon, or face paint. Likewise, the information in DNA can be written in nucleotide bases. Once a section of DNA is sequenced, its information is stored in a computer and can be transferred by a scientist to a colleague in a note written in ink. The colleague can then use the ink message to synthesize a copy of the DNA using nucleotide bases. The message (information) does not depend on the medium. One has to look outside the medium to discover the origin of the information.

We have stated that DNA contains information, but what makes a string of letters (bases) convey a message? In human languages, there are arbitrary rules that make one string of letters a message and another string meaningless. In English, the string of letters *b-o-y* has meaning but the string *y-o-b* does not. In Spanish, to give the equivalent English meaning, one needs the sequence *e-l c-h-i-c-o*. These are arbitrary letter combinations. There is nothing inherent in the letters that give meaning to these combinations. The same combination has drastically different meanings in different languages. The sequence *g-i-f-t* brings you a "present" in English but a "poison" in German!

What conferred meaning to the sequence of bases in the DNA molecule? What established the linguistic rules that "endow what otherwise would indeed be ordinary molecules with symbolic properties?"[18] From our everyday experience, intelligence is required to confer meaning to a sequence of letters. Intelligence implies design. Many scientists dismiss appeal to design as nonscientific. Some say that design is just the old "god-of-the-gaps" argument. Yet, design in terms of information is not based on a gap in our knowledge but on the growth in our knowledge.

Is design good science or even science? Many believe that there is an obvious boundary separating science from pseudoscience. Although concepts such as observability, testability, repeatability, and falsifiability have been proposed, there is no universally accepted boundary. In fact, boundaries are philosophically tainted. The philosopher of biology David Hull states, "They tend to be suspiciously self-serving, designed to put one's opponents at a disadvantage while shoring up one's own position."[19]

What about the argument that science is guided by the principle of uniformity, or that existing processes can explain past processes? Scientists are comfortable invoking natural processes. Scientists observe that water erosion on Earth results in long, narrow trenches. When similar trenches are observed on waterless Mars, scientists propose that water in the past caused erosion on Mars. Most current scientists would say that it would not be appropriate to invoke intelligent cause. Yet, the skeptic Hume of chapter three wrote, "The same rule holds, whether the cause assigned be brute unconscious matter, or a rational intelligent being."[20] Thus, the principle of uniformity should be neutral in regard to the kind of cause. In our everyday experience, the only sources of information are intelligence. Around us, we see intelligent agents creating newspapers, books, musical scores, computer programs, plans for buildings, and so forth. The principle of uniformity suggests that intelligence was involved in the origin of DNA. Currently, this seems like the strongest evidence for design.

7. The Intelligent Design Project

Jimmy H. Davis and Harry Lee Poe

I N THE LAST DECADE of the twentieth century, a loosely knit group of scientists, philosophers, and theologians came together around the idea that the universe and everything in it arose from some intentional design by an intelligent agent. Hardly a soul in the academic community had taken the notion of design seriously for more than a hundred years, when suddenly a multidisciplinary intellectual movement emerged around the concept of the design of life and everything else.

The Origins of the Intelligent Design (ID) Movement

The publication of *Darwin on Trial* by University of California at Berkeley legal scholar Phillip Johnson in 1991 made Johnson a leading figure in the intelligent design movement.[1] Rather than focusing on science issues, Johnson advocated an attack on the materialist philosophy that had come to dominate biological science.[2] Although Johnson used the phrase "intelligent design" in his book, he never defined it. Later, intelligent design would be defined by William Dembski as

> the hypothesis that in order to explain life it is necessary to suppose the action of an unevolved intelligence. One simply cannot explain organisms, those living and long gone, by reference to normal natural causes or material mechanisms. . . . The claim is simply that there must be something more than ordinary natural causes or material mechanisms, and moreover, that something must be intelligent and capable of bringing about organisms.[3]

The scholars working on the intelligent design project soon had an intellectual home in the Discovery Institute, a Seattle-based think tank.[4] Michael Behe, Dembski, Paul Nelson, Nancy Pearcey, and Jonathan Wells received appointments as fellows of the Discovery Institute's Center for Science and Culture, with Phillip Johnson as advisor and Stephen Meyer as director of the Center.[5] Discovery Institute fellows "submit their analyses and proposals for dialogue through seminars, conferences, and debates; they produce reports, articles, books, Congressional testimony, films and an interactive Internet website that helps spread the knowledge of the Institute's ideas."[6]

From the beginning, the intelligent design movement had two major challenges. It had to convince the scientific community and the public that it had a viable scientific method and not just another set of antievolution arguments. ID also had to convince everyone that it was more than just another flavor of scientific creationism.[7] The strategy for achieving these aims was formalized in a Center for Science and Culture document, "Wedge."[8] The "Wedge" document listed five-year and twenty-year goals as well as five-year objectives.

From the very beginning, the strategy of the intelligent design movement has been to impact science and culture by providing a new paradigm for science at the university level and a new curriculum model for public school science courses.[9] The intelligence design movement has used conferences, books, research strategies, and the placement of scientists whose work is shaped by intelligent design at major research universities to accomplish its aims. Conferences featuring intelligent design ideas have been held at Southern Methodist University (1992), Biola University (1996), University of Texas at Austin (1997), Baylor University (2000), Concordia University–Wisconsin (2000), Yale University (2000), and Calvin College (2001).[10] The Baylor and Concordia conferences brought together ID proponents and their strongest critics. The Biola and Concordia conferences resulted in the publication of *Mere Creation: Science, Faith and Intelligent Design*, as well as *Debating Design: From Darwin to DNA*. In addition to Johnson's *Darwin on Trial*, other influential ID books are Behe's *Darwin's Black Box: The Biochemical Challenge to Evolution* (1996) and *The Edge of Evolution: The Search for the Limits of Darwinism* (2007); William Dembski's *The Design Interference* (1998), *Intelligent Design* (1999), and *No Free Lunch: Why Specified Complexity Cannot Be Purchased without Intelligence* (2001); and Wells' *Icons of Evolution* (2000).

Behe and Dembski have taken the lead in articulating how intelligent design might be detected empirically. As discussed in chapter six, Behe focuses on what he calls the irreducible complexity of biochemical systems— certain biochemical systems are too interrelated to be able to function without all their parts being present.

As discussed in chapter four, Dembski proposed specified complexity as the way to detect design mathematically. From the very beginning, ID proponents stated that they would do peer-reviewed research that would legitimize the ID paradigm.[11] During the early part of the ID movement, Center for Science and Culture fellows were found throughout the academy and included Francis J. Beckwith (associate professor of church-state studies, and associate director of the J. M. Dawson Institute of Church-State Studies, Baylor University); Behe (associate professor of biochemistry, Lehigh University); Dembski (associate research professor in the conceptual foundations of science and director of the Michael Polanyi Center, Baylor University); Guillermo Gonzalez (assistant professor of astronomy at Iowa State University); Dean H. Kenyon (professor emeritus of biology at San Francisco State University); and Henry F. Schaefer III (Graham Perdue Professor of Chemistry and director of the Center for Computational Chemistry at the University of Georgia). In 2001, Dembski and others established the International Society for Complexity, Information, and Design as "a cross-disciplinary professional society that investigates complex systems apart from external programmatic constraints like materialism, naturalism, or reductionism."[12] This society established a quarterly online peer-reviewed journal, *Progress in Complexity, Information, and Design*, for publication of ID research. In 2005, the Biologic Institute was founded to pursue research in protein and cell biology as well as computational biology.[13]

Now that over a decade has passed since the founding of the Discovery Institute, critics of the intelligent design movement continue to ask about the status of the scientific research projects promised by ID leaders.[14] Bruce Chapman, president of the Discovery Institute, has responded to these question by saying:

> So why aren't we talking more about them publicly? For several reasons: The most important is that the Darwinist establishment would like nothing better than to "out" research programs before they are finished. The idea is to shut down damaging evidence as early as possible. . . . There are too many examples of ID scientists and other scholars who have been hassled and harassed by the Dar-

winist Inquisition. . . . Friends of ID know the cases of a number of
ID-friendly scientists who have lost their lab privileges or otherwise
been discriminated against at universities here and in the UK.

Intelligent design supporters cite several examples of ID scholars who
have been discriminated against. Beckwith struggled to receive tenure at
Baylor University. Dembski was removed as director of the Michael Polanyi
Center at Baylor University. Gonzalez did not receive tenure at Iowa State
University. Kenyon was removed from teaching freshmen biology at San
Francisco State University.

One goal of the 1999 Wedge document was to help people "see intelligent design theory as an accepted alternative in the sciences. . . ."[15] by 2004.
In 2007, Phillip Johnson stated that his main disappointment was that ID
has not "made more headway in the mainstream scientific community."[16]
To date, the conferences, books, research strategies, and placement of scientists have not created a paradigm change in how science is practiced. Most
scientists not trained in philosophy focus on providing natural explanations
for their research (methodological naturalism) and do not worry about the
philosophical implications of their work.

ID PROPOSALS FOR DETECTING DESIGN

A key scientific question for the intelligent design movement is, How does
one detect design? It is relatively easy to detect design when one knows that
an object was made by humans—whether the object is a flint arrowhead or
the space shuttle. It is more challenging when one deals with an object found
in nature. For example, if a rock hound finds a piece of magnetic material,
how does he or she know if it is a human-made or naturally occurring lode-
stone? How can one distinguish between the two? The problem becomes
even more challenging when dealing with biological species. Species are
known to change in response to their environment; for example, disease-
causing organisms become drug resistant. Since species can change, is the
feature of the species being observed the result of design or natural change?
How can one distinguish between the two?

Michael Behe and William Dembski have taken the lead in formulating
how the intelligent design movement will detect design in the universe.

Behe argues in *Darwin's Black Box* that cellular biochemistry is too complex to be explained by a series of mutations. He argues that some biologi-

cal structures are irreducibly complex. As Behe states, "Life is in the details, and it is molecules that handle life's details. Darwin's idea might explain horse hoofs, but can it explain life's foundations?"[17] Behe is not a "young-earth creationist." He states, "I have no reason to doubt that the universe is the billions of years old that physicists say it is. Further, I find the idea of common descent (that all organisms share a common ancestor) fairly convincing, and have no particular reason to doubt it."[18] We need to quote Behe extensively to understand what he means by irreducibly complex:

> By *irreducibly complex* I mean a single system composed of several well-matched, interacting parts that contribute to the basic function, wherein the removal of one of the parts causes the system to effectively cease functioning. An irreducibly complex system cannot be produced directly (that is, by continuously improving the initial function, which continues to work by the same mechanism) by slight, successive modifications of a precursor system, because any precursor to an irreducibly complex system that is missing a part is by definition nonfunctional. An irreducibly complex biological system, if there is such a thing, would be a powerful challenge to Darwinian evolution. Since natural selection can only choose systems that are already working, then if a biological system cannot be produced gradually it would have to arise as an integrated unit, in one full swoop, for natural selection to have anything to work on.[19]

As we discussed in chapter six, the cell is a complicated place with many intricate parts. Does Behe propose that everything in the cell is designed? No, he does not. Behe states, "Some features of the cell appear to be the result of simple natural processes, others probably so. Still other features were almost certainly designed. And with some features, we can be as confident that they were designed as that anything was."[20] Since detecting design in natural systems is a challenging and controversial subject, we will review in detail one example that Behe considers to have resulted from natural process (hemoglobin) and one example that Behe considers to be the result of intelligent design (bacterial flagellum).

Behe presented several examples of natural macro-objects that could appear to be designed but are not: man in the moon, Italy as a boot, and the human face on Mars. Then, he turned to biological examples that could appear to be designed but are not: cell membranes and hemoglobin. Regarding hemoglobin, Behe says:

Or consider hemoglobin—the protein in our red blood cells that carries oxygen from the lungs to the peripheral tissue. Hemoglobin is made up of four individual proteins stuck together, and each of the four proteins can bind oxygen. Two of the proteins are identical to each other, as are the other two to each other (fig. 7.1).[21]

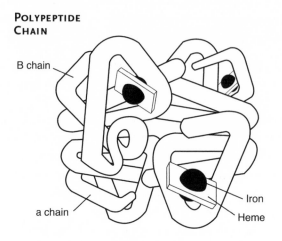

Fig. 7.1. The structure of hemoglobin

Behe further states, "There is another protein, called myoglobin, that is very similar to hemoglobin except that it has only one protein chain, not four, and therefore binds only one oxygen."[22] Myoglobin transports oxygen in the muscle (fig. 7.2).

Fig. 7.2. The structure of myoglobin

Then, Behe addresses design:

> The question is, if we assume that we already have an oxygen-binding protein like myoglobin, can we infer intelligent design from the function of hemoglobin? The case for design is weak. The starting point, myoglobin, already can bind oxygen. The behavior of hemoglobin can be achieved by a rather simple modification of the behavior of myoglobin, and the individual proteins of hemoglobin strongly resemble myoglobin. So although hemoglobin can be thought of as a system with interacting parts, the interaction does nothing much that is clearly beyond the individual components of the system. Given the starting point of myoglobin, I would say that hemoglobin shows the same evidence for design as does the man in the moon: intriguing, but far from convincing.

As an example of a human-made irreducibly complex object, Behe points to the mousetrap, which cannot function as a mousetrap if any of its parts (platform, catch, spring, hammer, and holding bar) are missing.[23] Behe presents the bacterial flagellum as an example of a biological irreducibly complex object (fig. 7.3).[24]

Fig. 7.3. Bacterial Flagellum

The bacterial flagellum consists of thirty proteins that allow many bacteria to swim. Behe states:

> [T]he flagellum is a propeller that is rotated by a motor. The mechanical requirements of such a system are quite complex . . . many discrete parts have to be in place to produce a functioning flagellum.

Clearly the necessary pieces of the flagellum itself have to be in place. If there is no whip protein, the bacterium cannot swim. If there is no rotary motor, then the flagellum lies in rigor mortis. If there is no base, then the flagellum has nothing to hang on to when it tries to turn. Furthermore, the parts themselves are multifunctional. The rotary motor uses a flow of acid to power it, like a hydroelectric dam uses a flow of water to power its turbines. . . . Thus, the flagellum itself is irreducibly complex.[25]

William Dembski has master's degrees in statistics and divinity as well as doctorates in philosophy and mathematics. He has written extensively on how people determine whether an event occurs by chance or by design.

Dembski has proposed that a mathematical test can be constructed that tests for the probability that a phenomenon has happened either by chance or by the design of some intelligent agent. He sets his probability limit by the use of three variables: number of elemental particles in the universe (10^{80}); the fastest time it takes transition from one physical state to another (10^{45}), which is the inverse of Planck time; and age of the universe (10^{25}). Multiplying these limits together results in what Dembski labels the "universal probability bound," with a value of 1 in 10^{150}. In Dembski's model, any event with a probability less than 1 in 10^{150} will be improbable.[26] Dembski calculated the probability of the twenty amino acids found in nature assembling in the correct sequence to form the thirty proteins found in the bacterial flagellum. His result was a probability of 1 in $10^{1,170}$, which is much less than his universal probability bound of 1 in 10^{150}. Thus, Dembski concluded that the bacterial flagellum could not have evolved and must be designed.[27]

Has the work of Behe on irreducible complexity and Dembski on specified complexity resulted in the acceptance of intelligent design as a new paradigm in science? Not yet. Many scientists have challenged the assumptions of both Behe and Dembski. An example is the work of the American biologist and Christian, Ken Miller. In regard to Dembski's probability calculation, Miller points out that Dembski assumes that the flagellum came about by the random assembly of amino acids into thirty different proteins. Further, Miller points out that Dembski assumes that no subset of the thirty proteins could have any biological activity.[28] Thus, according to Miller, Dembski's calculations can be mathematically correct but biologically irrelevant; the calculations do not reflect any mechanism that a biologist would propose.

Miller also challenges Behe's statement that the flagellum is irreducibly complex, as there would be no biological function if parts were removed. Some bacteria have a system for ejecting toxins into the cells of their hosts. Gram-negative bacteria use the type III secretory system (TTSS) for this purpose (fig. 7.4).

Fig. 7.4. Type III secretory system

As Miller states:

> At first glance, the existence of the TTSS, a nasty little device that allows bacteria to inject these toxins through cell membranes of their unsuspecting hosts, would seem to have little to do with the flagellum. However, molecular studies of proteins in the TTSS have revealed a surprising fact: the proteins of the TTSS are directly homologous to the proteins in the basal portion of the bacterial flagellum. . . . It is now clear, therefore, that a smaller subset of the full complement of proteins in the flagellum makes up the functional transmembrane portion of the TTSS. . . . If the flagellum is indeed irreducibly complex, then removing just one part, let alone ten or fifteen, should render what remains "by definition nonfunctional." Yet the TTSS is indeed fully functional, even though it is missing most of the parts of the flagellum.[29]

Were Miller's arguments sufficient to convince Dembski and Behe that the bacterial flagellum was not an example of intelligent design? No, they were not. Dembski responded:

> [I]t is not enough to point out that some genes for the bacterial flagellum are the same as those for a type III secretory system (a type of pump) and then to hand-wave that one was co-opted from the other.

Anyone can arrange complex systems in series based on some criterion of similarity. But such series do nothing to establish whether the
end evolved in Darwinian fashion from the beginning. . . .[30]

While Behe responded:

Miller uses the word "function" in two different senses. Recall that
the definition of irreducible complexity notes that a removal of a
part "causes the *system* to effectively cease functioning. . . ." Without
blinking, Miller asserted that the flagellum is not irreducibly complex because some proteins of the flagellum could be missing and
the remainder could still transport proteins. . . . He was equivocat-
ing, switching the focus from the function of the system, acting as
a rotary propulsion machine, to the ability of subset of the system
to transport proteins across a membrane. However, taking away the
parts of the flagellum certainly destroys the ability of the system to
act as a rotary propulsion machine, as I have argued. Thus, contra
Miller, the flagellum is indeed irreducibly complex.[31]

Behe's and Dembski's interpretations do not sway most biologists for several
reasons. Behe in his original definition of "irreducibly complex" used the
phrases "slight, successive modifications of a precursor system" and "natural selection can only choose systems that are already working."[32] Behe and
Dembski take these phrases to mean that the "already working" "precursor
system" must be doing the same thing as the final system. Thus, to them,
hemoglobin is not designed because myoglobin and hemoglobin have similar functions. To them, bacterial flagellum is designed because the already
working precursor system (type III secretory system) does not function the
same way as the final system (the bacterial flagellum). In contrast, Miller
takes these phrases to mean that the "already working" "precursor system"
is functioning, but not necessarily the same way the final system will function. Miller's interpretation of the phrases is in keeping with that of the
majority of biologists.

For the theist, the way Behe approaches design detection raises some challenging theological questions. As the Anglican vicar and geologist Michael
Roberts states, "Intelligent Design results in some of Creation being *design-
edly* created, whereas the rest is *undesignedly* created. We end up with a two-
tier Creation, with some life systems, which are due to the process of natural
laws, being undesigned, while the others are supernaturally designed."[33]

ID IN THE PUBLIC SQUARE

Dembski and others achieved widespread success in publicizing their work among Christians. Soon the movement took on a life of its own, with local and state school boards insisting that intelligent design be taught alongside or instead of natural selection. The Discovery Institute's Center for Science and Culture developed a document, "Teaching the Controversy: Darwinism, Design and the Public School Science Curriculum."[34] The curriculum proposed teaching the scientific arguments for and against Darwinian evolution, with students being tested on their understanding of these arguments. Although it does not advocate the teaching of intelligent design, the curriculum proposes that teachers should point out competing theories like that of Michael Behe.[35] Center for Science and Culture fellows were involved in many of these school board processes. Language endorsing critical analysis of evolution was enacted in Ohio (2002), New Mexico (2003), Minnesota (2004), Kansas (2005), South Carolina (2006), and Mississippi (2006). In 2001, the United States Senate adopted an amendment by then-Senator Rick Santorum (R-PA) to the Elementary and Secondary Education Act that stated, in part, ". . . where biological evolution is taught, the curriculum should help students understand why the subject generates so much continuing controversy. . . ."[36] Additionally, President Bush in 2005 endorsed the idea of exposing students to different ideas, such as intelligent design.[37]

Setbacks began with what appeared to be a major victory. In 2004, the school board of Dover, Pennsylvania, adopted intelligent design as part of its science curriculum. This adoption went against the advice of the Discovery Institute, which felt that ID theory was not developed enough for curriculum inclusion. In *Kitzmiller v. Dover Area School District*, eleven parents sued the Dover Area School District in U.S. District Court for the Middle District of Pennsylvania claiming a violation of the U.S. Constitution's establishment clause. The trial lasted from September 26 to November 4, 2005. Michael Behe was a witness for the defense. On December 20, Judge John E. Jones III ruled in favor of the plaintiffs. In a major blow to the inclusion of ID in public school science curricula, Judge Jones ruled:

> The overwhelming evidence at trial established that ID is a religious view, a mere re-labeling of creationism, and not a scientific theory. . . . ID is not science. We find that ID fails on three different levels, any one of which is sufficient to preclude a determination

that ID is science. They are (1) ID violates the centuries-old ground rules of science by invoking and permitting supernatural causation; (2) the argument of irreducible complexity, central to ID, employs the same flawed and illogical contrived dualism that doomed creation science in the 1980's; and (3) ID's negative attacks on evolution have been refuted by the scientific community. . . . The proper application of both the endorsement and Lemon tests to the facts of this case makes it abundantly clear that the Board's ID Policy violates the Establishment Clause."[38]

Four days after the end of the trial, all eight Dover School Board members up for reelection were defeated. In response to the election, Pat Robertson said, "I'd like to say to the good citizens of Dover: If there is a disaster in your area, don't turn to God. You just rejected him from your city. . . . If they have future problems in Dover, I recommend they call on Charles Darwin. Maybe he can help them."[39] After Judge Jones' decision, the newly elected school board voted not to appeal the decision and to pay the $1 million in legal fees and damages resulting from the verdict.[40]

The Ohio Board of Education voted on February 14, 2006, to remove the "Critical Analysis of Evolution" lesson plan. The board did ask its Achievement Committee, however, to consider whether it should adopt new lesson plans. Intelligent design supporters suggested a lesson plan that called for students to debate global warming and stem cell research along with evolution. This proposal was rejected by the board on October 10, 2006.[41] During the Ohio midterm elections of 2006, board candidates favoring "teaching the controversy" were defeated, along with the gubernatorial candidate who favored teaching ID. A similar occurrence happened in Kansas, with the state board candidates favoring teaching the controversy losing the 2006 midterm elections. On February 13, 2007, the newly elected board voted to remove the "teach the controversy" curriculum. Senator Rick Santorum of Pennsylvania was also defeated for reelection to the U.S. Senate.

What is the status of the intelligent design movement near the end of the first decade of the twentieth-first century? First, ID was more successful in philosophy, where its arguments influenced Antony Flew's decision to move from atheism to theism. Second, ID had not become accepted as a viable paradigm for the study of biological system. Third, its greatest setback was in the area of public school science curriculum when a court had ruled that ID was not science. ID's efforts in public school science curriculum made it appear to be another antievolution creationism crusade rather than a new approach to science.

WHO SHOULD DEFINE SCIENCE?

In 1973, the Supreme Court accepted the argument that the question of abortion is a private matter between a woman and her doctor. This reasoning follows from the notion that the question of when life begins is solely a medical question. Now the courts have ruled that intelligent design does not belong in the science classroom but that natural selection does. Both of these important cases illustrate the importance of understanding the relationship of science and religion in the public square.

For centuries, the kinds of questions that the courts have been deciding were debated within the academy until the intellectual disciplines involved reached a broad agreement. When life begins and whether or not intelligent design is science are questions that belong within the academy, but increasingly questions that involve the intersection of science and religion have been taken to political and judicial arenas for settlement. The recourse to nonacademic authorities suggests the breakdown in the modern academy's ability to carry on its own business.

Who in the academy should make these demarcation decisions? Some would say that the disciplines should set the demarcation criteria of what is science. Appealing to the disciplines will not necessarily result in one set of criteria. As an example, consider the term "observable," sometimes used to refer to science. Physics may say invisible subatomic particles are observable because of a meter reading, which is different from observables in biology. Anthropology, with its historical focus, would set different criteria than the laboratory science of chemistry. If not the disciplines, what about the philosophers of science? Philosophers of science have used terms such as "induction," "deduction," "hypothetico-deduction," and "falsification" to attempt to explain how science works.[42] Today, many philosophers of science feel that attempts to set demarcation criteria for science have failed.[43] As philosopher of science Del Ratzsch states:

> So any boundary (or zone) between scientific legitimacy and illegitimacy does not fall along a simple empirical/nonempirical divide, or along a human-free (objective) or human-tainted (subjective) break. It isn't nearly that easy. The implication of immediate relevance

is that blanket prohibitions on concepts or imposed limitations on content within science—such as stipulated bans on the supernatural—must have more behind them than merely the residual momentum of insufficiently nuanced empiricist conceptions of science. What must be sought is some separation running through the nonempirical and the human-shaded realms, and which distinguishes the scientifically legitimate from the scientifically illegitimate within those realms themselves.[44]

As the academy has struggled with demarcation criteria to separate science from non-science, there has been a tendency to turn to the federal courts to arbitrate the disputes in terms of the establishment clause of the first amendment of the United States Constitution. In 1982, in a creation science case, U.S. District Judge William R. Overton ruled in the case, *McLean v. Arkansas*:

> More precisely, the essential characteristics of science are:
> (1) It is guided by natural law;
> (2) It has to be explanatory by reference to nature law;
> (3) It is testable against the empirical world;
> (4) Its conclusions are tentative, i.e. are not necessarily the final word; and
> (5) It is falsifiable.[45]

Further, in the Dover intelligent design case in 2005, Judge John E. Jones III referred to the McLean decision when he used the following terms to refer to science: "explained by natural causes," "proven through empirical investigation," "testable," "falsifiable," and "limited to the search for natural causes to explain natural phenomena."[46]

Judge Jones also referenced a philosophical demarcation when he stated:

> Expert testimony reveals that since the scientific revolution of the 16th and 17th centuries, science has been limited to the search for natural causes to explain natural phenomena. . . . This self-imposed convention of science, which limits inquiry to testable, natural explanations about the natural world, is referred to by philosophers as "methodological naturalism" and is sometimes known as the scientific method. . . . Methodological naturalism is a "ground rule"

of science today which requires scientists to seek explanations in the world around us based upon what we can observe, test, replicate, and verify.[47]

What sets the origins of life debate apart from most scholarly debates within the academy, however, is the recourse to the popular press, the political arena, and the judicial sphere that has dogged the issue since Darwin. The famous debate between Huxley and Wilberforce in Oxford, and more importantly its "afterlife," played to the press and to the popular market. The Scopes trial a half century later was designed to boost the local economy of a backwoods Tennessee county seat. At the beginning of the twenty-first century, we see the issue of origins appearing in school board decisions by elected officials and finally in the federal court decision handed down December 20, 2005, in Pennsylvania that intelligent design belongs to religion rather than to science.[48] In his decision, Judge John E. Jones III declared that intelligent design was "nothing less than the progeny of *creationism*" [emphasis added].[49]

The allusion to creationism indicates the extent to which name-calling has entered the public debate. Some critics of intelligent design have labeled it "creationism," a term that has become shorthand for scientific creationism. The term crept into Judge Jones' ruling in the 2005 Dover school case. For the most part, scientific creationists have rejected the intelligent design project because of its acceptance of modern science. In his 1999 book *Intelligent Design*, William Dembski described the chasm between the intelligent design project and scientific creationism as a difference in perspective on the Bible. The scientific creationists view the Genesis account of creation as "scientifically accurate."[50] The agendas are quite distinct. Scientific creationism seeks to prove that the Bible is scientifically accurate and that modern science is not reliable. The intelligent design project seeks to demonstrate that naturalism is not a reliable philosophical foundation for modern science.

From a sociology-of-science perspective, however, creation science and intelligent design histories have a similarity that confuses the public. Both began with a best-selling book: *Flood Geology*[51] for creation science, and *Darwin on Trial* for ID. Both soon had think tanks: the Creation Research Society and the Institute for Creation Research (ICR) for creation science, and the Discovery Institute and the Center for Science and Culture for ID. Both promised a new paradigm that would revolutionize science; both promised research results to support this paradigm. Both became involved in the politics of local and state school board decisions. In both cases, the involvement with school boards made it appear that the respective movements were using politics to achieve what they could not achieve through scientific research. In both cases, involvement with school boards resulted in court cases that decided that neither creation science nor ID was science. In the public's mind (whether supporter or detractor), ID and creation science seem the same: an antievolution crusade. If ID can refocus its efforts on the science rather than the politics, the next decade might be better to it.

Meanwhile, in Kansas, Paul Mirecki stepped down as chair of the Religious Studies Department at the University of Kansas after the university cancelled his special topics course: Intelligent Design, Creationism and Other Religious Mythologies. Mirecki planned to offer the course after the Kansas Board of Education decided to criticize evolution in the science standards for public schools. In the meantime, two ruffians attacked Mirecki and sent him to the hospital with injuries.[52]

The origins controversy has been a media event largely because the issues operate at the emotional level as well as the cognitive. A recent Pew study revealed that 48 percent of the American public believes in some form of evolution, but by no means do all of these believe in natural selection. Only 28 percent believe in natural selection. On the other hand, 48 percent of Americans believe that life on Earth has existed in its present form since the beginning.[53] Intensity of belief involves the degree to which people hold to metaphysical commitments beyond the data of scientific research.

It is not unknown in the history of learning for scholars to be compelled by authorities to conduct their research in light of recognized metaphysical dogma. Galileo was punished by the academy for disagreeing with Aristotelian metaphysics. Scientists in the old Soviet Union were required to conform their science to the materialistic dialectic. The appeal to authorities outside the academy for support in the clash between natural selection and intelligent design represents the same kind of metaphysically driven controversy we have seen in the past.

One strand of the Western academic tradition has always valued debate as a means of arriving at truth. Disputation allowed for the presentation of different points of view on an issue that then made it possible for objective, impartial judges to make a reasoned decision. Another strand in the Western tradition has valued debate as an opportunity to slay one's opponent and win a popular following. Debate does not necessarily lead to the discovery of truth, as Augustine lamented fifteen hundred years ago. Debate plays an important role in deciding what action a group should take, but it does not always advance the discovery of truth.

In a conflict, debate can provide a means to rally support among those who agree with the position taken. This approach, however, ignores the responsibility to persuade others to that position. One rhetorical approach to debate involves posing the question in such a way as to heighten emotion without necessarily clarifying the issues. When a debate leaves the discipline of the academy and goes public, anyone can join the fray. Not all participants in a public debate have the same level of understanding of the issues involved; nor do they all pay attention to the careful nuances of the disciplines involved.

Evangelicals have recently entered the public debate over intelligent design and Darwinian natural selection. Until now, Evangelicals and mainline Christians in the United States have shown little interest in the issues lying at the intersection of science and religion. William Dembski, who has proposed the first important research program to bring a method to the question of intelligent design, has qualifications as both a mathematician and a philosopher. Across the American landscape, however, novices who do not have Dembski's training or background have rushed headlong into efforts to have intelligent design included in the science curriculum of local schools. Opponents of intelligent design have reacted with equal fervor by asking the courts to rule that intelligent design is religion rather than science.

Every discipline within the academy has the right and duty to define itself. The object and method of study for literature, anthropology, music, and economics are determined by those disciplines. The discipline of history cannot decide for political science what it will study or how it will study it. Neither is it reasonable to ask the courts to decide where history ends and political science begins.

The sciences can and should define themselves without the interference of other disciplines, including theology, philosophy, or poetry. Having defined itself, however, no discipline should be surprised if other disciplines question the validity of its truth claims or methodologies. In order to question the claims that emerge from a discipline such as evolutionary biology, someone from outside the field must first do some serious work. We cannot deal with abortion, embryonic stem cell research, cloning, genetic engineering, artificial intelligence, global warming, and a plethora of other technological and scientific issues if we ignore the basic spadework that must be done concerning the relationship between science and the Christian faith as expressed by the gospel of Jesus Christ.

Is ID Science?

In *Kitzmiller v. Dover Area School District*, Judge Jones ruled that ID was not science. Among Judge Jones' arguments was an appeal to the demarcation criteria of "testable" and "natural explanations": "It is therefore readily apparent to the Court that ID fails to meet the essential ground rules that limit science to testable, natural explanations."[54] Judge Jones' statement is interesting when one considers that others see ID proposing testable hypotheses. The physicist Loren Haarsma states, "Some activities of ID are clearly 'scientific' even under narrow definitions of that term, including modeling of evolutionary population dynamics, investigating the adequacy of known evolutionary mechanisms to account for specific instances of biological complexity, and investigating the general conditions under which self-organized complex is possible."[55] Dembski, with his specified complexity and universal probability formula, is proposing testable criteria to eliminate undirected natural causes before design is considered. Behe, with irreducible complexity, is also proposing testable criteria to determine if a biochemical structure can be explained by undirected natural causes. In fact, Judge Jones stated that Behe's irreducible complexity is "refutable and accordingly testable, unlike ID, by showing that there are intermediate structures with selectable functions that could have evolved into the allegedly irreducibly complex systems. Importantly, however, the fact that the negative argument of irreducible complexity is testable does not make testable the argument for ID."[56] Judge Jones is splitting hairs by stating that Behe's complex chemicals are science but the intelligence in ID is not. Even the anti-creationism, anti-ID philosopher of science Philip Kitcher disagrees with Judge Jones when Kitcher states, "Even postulating an unobserved Creator need be no more unscientific than postulating unobserved particles. What matters is the character of the proposals and the ways in which they are articulated and defended."[57]

Perhaps, for purposes of clarifying the issues at stake in the science and religion dialogue, intelligent design exposes the great failing of natural selection as a scientific theory. With his theory of natural selection, Darwin went beyond the bounds of what the scientific method can say. He did not simply say that organisms change from generation to generation. He said that God has nothing to do with the process. No one required Darwin to introduce

God into his theory. The concept of evolution had already been around for some time when he proposed natural selection. By making God part of the discussion, however, Darwin should have proposed a test for God's absence in order for his theory to pass as science. Dembski has proposed what such a test will look like for intelligent design, but Darwin proposed no such test. Dembski has a huge task ahead of him in arriving at the final form of his test. Darwinists, however, must first devise a way to test for the existence of God, the clarification of what kind of God exists, and a way to demonstrate that whatever God may or may not exist cannot be involved in an evolutionary process. Like Dembski's hypothesis, it would seem that any possible test that would advance the natural selection position to the realm of science would also have to be a probability analysis.

The age of the Earth is a proper question of scientific inquiry that involves the examination of physical evidence. The origin of the universe and the origin of life are proper questions of theological inquiry that involve the examination of the revelations of God. Science cannot go beyond the physical evidence in its enquiry and continue to be science. Another discipline must pick up where the methodology of science will not allow it to go. The methodology of philosophy allows it to probe beyond the physical, as does the methodology of theology. The confusion of disciplines occurs when people skip from the scientific method to philosophical and theological conjectures without recognizing that they have left the playing field. The confusion of the disciplines increases when a scientist makes a philosophical statement but expects it to be regarded as a scientific fact.

SCIENCE, RELIGION, OR PHILOSOPHY

Part of the confusion surrounding intelligent design arises because it truly intersects several disciplines in ways that suggest a unity of knowledge. At a time when the academy races headlong toward the disintegration of knowledge, the prospect of an integrated theory of knowledge seems unattractive to many who have established reputations on temporary schools of thought fashionable during the days of their ascendancy in the academy. It is enough to make a cynic observe that much more than truth is at stake; careers are at stake!

The cynic would be put to shame, however, in the face of Antony Flew, brilliant philosopher and principal Western critic of theism for the last fifty years. Since 1966, his *God and Philosophy* has enjoyed bestseller status in edition after edition. For almost forty years, this book presented belief in God as philosophically unwarranted as Flew steadfastly presented his own position of unbelief. In October 2004, however, Flew shocked the philosophical and religious worlds by announcing in a letter to *Philosophy Now* magazine that he had changed his mind about God. In light of what we have learned since Watson and Crick discovered the double helix structure of DNA, Flew declared flatly, "It has become inordinately difficult even to begin to think about constructing a naturalistic theory of the evolution of that first reproducing organism."[58]

In the introduction of what Flew declared would be the "final edition" of *God and Philosophy*, he described his famous book as "an historical relic."[59] Flew changed his mind because of the kinds of observations that many people in the scientific community had been making along the same lines as those discussed in previous chapters in this book. Flew had been in dialogue with several people on this issue before he changed his mind, including Gerald Schroeder, an Israeli physicist and Orthodox Jew, and Roy Abraham Varghese, an Eastern Rite Catholic. What the case of Flew and his non-Evangelical friends demonstrates is that the issues raised by the intelligent design movement have not arisen in one small corner of the world. These are not peculiar ideas to what some people confuse as a political group of sectarians in the United States. If intelligent design is not yet a scientific theory, it has more than succeeded as very good philosophy.

In many cases, the real issue in the science and religion debate is neither science nor religion, but philosophy. The problem facing Evangelical Christians when addressing science and religion issues in the public square may best be recognized when viewed from the other way around. For all his failings in understanding the philosophical problems with his point of view and in understanding the meaning of religious faith, Richard Dawkins understands what is really at stake in the public debate. In response to criticism from other "hardcore evolutionists" who would like him to tone down his rhetoric, Dawkins replies:

> And they could be right, in a political sense. It depends on whether you think the real war is over the teaching of evolution, as they do, or whether, as I do, think the real war is between supernaturalism and naturalism, between science and religion. If you think the war is between supernaturalism and naturalism, then the war over teaching evolution is just one skirmish, just one battle, in the war.[60]

Dawkins is a materialist who believes that no causes beyond physically observable causes can exist. He cares strongly about the question of the existence of a supreme being, and he insists that the question must be answered with scientific evidence. He insists upon some scientific proof for the existence of God because he acknowledges that "You cannot actually disprove the existence of God."[61]

Though C. S. Lewis disagreed strenuously with the position that Dawkins takes with regard to materialism and naturalism, he stood in complete agreement with him over the issue at stake. In *Miracles*, he said: "Some people believe that nothing exists except Nature; I call these people *Naturalists*. Others think that, besides Nature, there exists something else: I call them *Supernaturalists*."[62] A few years earlier, he had said in a radio broadcast later published as *Mere Christianity*:

> Ever since men were able to think they have been wondering what this universe really is and how it came to be there. And, very roughly, two views have been held. First, there is what is called the materialist view. People who take that view think that matter and space just happen to exist, and always have existed, nobody knows why; and that matter, behaving in certain fixed ways, has just happened, by a sort of fluke, to produce creatures like ourselves who are able to think. . . . The other view is the religious view. According to it, what is behind the universe is more like a mind than it is like anything else we know. That is to say, it is conscious, and has purposes, and prefers one thing to another. And on this view it made the universe, partly for purposes we do not know, but partly, at any rate, in order to produce creatures like itself—I mean, like itself to the extent of having minds.[63]

What Lewis recognized in 1941 and what Dawkins freely admits today is that the real issue at stake is not which particular scientific explanation will prevail on any particular question. The real issue at stake is whether anything exists besides the physically observable and whether anything can be known except through the scientific method.

BIBLICAL INTERPRETATION

Unfortunately, Christian theologians can confuse the science and religion discussion even when acting with the best of intentions. Confusion can occur when a theologian makes a statement that falls within the realm of science but expects it to be regarded as a theological statement. This confusion is heightened if the theologian believes that he or she speaks for God. In Western culture, which has been formed by the nurture of the Christian faith, all science and religion discussions eventually lead back to the Bible. Even though the science and religion dialogue has tended to be the domain of philosophers, the only real issue for the average secularist or Christian is whether the Bible disagrees with science.

Ever since the great Puritan prelate James Ussher, father of higher criticism, sought to ground biblical studies in Bacon's new scientific method, Evangelicals have tended to think that the Bible teaches a particular scientific understanding. The problem of deciding when a text should be taken literally and when it should be taken figuratively is one that has concerned Christians since Jesus Christ himself confounded the Sadducees and the Pharisees over their interpretation of the Law and the Prophets. Calvin and Luther took issue with the medieval tradition of interpreting virtually all of Scripture allegorically. A thousand years earlier, however, Augustine had warned of the danger of interpreting Scripture too literally.

Augustine's conversion to faith in Christ revolved around questions of science and religion. An ardent participant in the Manichaean religion, Augustine finally rejected Manichaeanism because its teachings about the world could not be reconciled with the best science of the day. He was unwilling to give Christianity a hearing, however, because the Bible seemed to teach that God is a physical being. Only after he heard the preaching of Ambrose of Milan did he realize that some portions of the Bible should be read poetically:

> And whilst I opened my heart to admit "how skillfully he spake," there also entered with it, but gradually, "and how truly he spake!" For first, these things also had begun to appear to me to be defensible; and the Catholic faith, for which I had fancied nothing could be said against the attacks of the Manichaeans, I now conceived might be maintained without presumption; especially after I had heard one or two parts of the Old Testament explained, and often allegorically—which when I accepted literally, I was "killed" spiritually. (1 Cor. 13:2; 2 Cor. 3:6)[64]

A literal reading of the entirety of Scripture had proven an obstacle to faith for Augustine, but when he learned that some passages should be read literally and some figuratively, he could receive them. This change in how he understood the Bible had a profound effect on his spiritual condition and formed an important step in his conversion. He observed:

> 6. I rejoiced also that the old Scriptures of the law and the prophets were laid before me, to be perused, not now with that eye to which they seemed most absurd before, when I censured Thy holy ones for so thinking, whereas in truth they thought not so; and with delight I heard Ambrose, in his sermons to the people, oftentimes most diligently recommend this text as a rule,—"The letter killeth, but the Spirit giveth life;" (2 Cor. 3:6) whilst, drawing aside the mystic veil, he spiritually laid open that which, accepted according to the "letter," seemed to teach perverse doctrines—teaching herein nothing that offended me, though he taught such things as I knew not as yet whether they were true.[65]

This understanding has important implications for the Christian engagement of the modern scientific world. In reflecting on his own experience and the Manichaean practice of making extravagant claims about the workings of the universe, Augustine advised Christians to be careful of what they assumed they knew about what we now call science. He said:

> When, therefore, it was discovered that his teaching concerning the heavens and stars, and the motions of sun and moon, was false, though these things do not relate to the doctrine of religion, yet his sacrilegious arrogance would become sufficiently evident, seeing that not only did he affirm things of which he knew nothing, but also perverted them, and with such egregious vanity of pride as to seek to attribute them to himself as to a divine being.
>
> 9. For when I hear a Christian brother ignorant of these things, or in error concerning them, I can bear with patience to see that man hold to his opinions; nor can I apprehend that any want of knowledge as to the situation or nature of material creation can be injurious to him, so long as he does not entertain belief in anything unworthy of Thee, O Lord, the Creator of all. But if he conceives it to pertain to the form of doctrine of piety, and presumes to affirm with great obstinacy that whereof he is ignorant, therein lies the injury.[66]

In modern times, Christians face the same danger of confusing a biblical reference to nature with a scientific teaching about nature. The logical fallacy seems to run something like this: Because the Bible is inerrant in all it affirms, if it speaks about anything pertaining to nature, it speaks scientifically. Behind this logical fallacy lies the modernist assumption appropriated, however unwittingly, by liberals and fundamentalists alike: that real truth must be scientific truth.

The irony of this assumption that has influenced Calvinists like Ussher, Arminians like Finney, and Dispensationalists like Scofield, as well as the wide variety of liberals like Barth, Bultmann, and Tillich, is that scientific truth is a fading flower. One scientific view gives way to another as Ptolemy's universe in which Augustine lived gave way to Kepler's universe in which Ussher lived. The universe of Newton in which Finney lived gave way to the universe of Einstein in which Tillich lived. If science is the real truth, one is left to wonder: which science? The science of today or the science of tomorrow?

God does not teach a particular science in the Bible. Rather, he speaks to a variety of cultures that understood the world in terms of the fading scientific views of their age. He spoke to people who lived in different technological ages: Stone Age, Bronze Age, and Iron Age. He spoke to people who lived in different kinds of societies: hunter/gatherer, nomadic shepherds, settled farmers, village craftsmen, and urban merchants. He spoke to people who lived in the spheres of the great ancient civilizations: Chaldean, Egyptian, Canaanite, Babylonian, Persian, Hellenistic, Roman. All of them had different understandings of how the world works, and God spoke to them all. God does not so much teach a particular science as he has spoken to people in terms they can understand. The miracle is that the terms in which God spoke make sense today in a highly sophisticated society like the United States and in an underdeveloped society like that of isolated tribes of New Guinea. The science can change and what God said still makes sense, unlike the teachings of Augustine's Manichaeans.

God tells us in the Bible, through the prophets and the apostles, what we cannot discover for ourselves. He has given us the means to understand our world and discover things about it. We can know him, however, only if he reveals himself. Science can take us only so far. Even Darwin recognized that his infinite regress of mutations back to an original life-form still left the greatest problem of all: accounting for life. Once Stephen Hawking persuaded the scientific community of the probability of a finite universe that had a beginning, he was struck by the awesome implications of explaining a beginning to everything. The explanation for everything is the foundational affirmation of biblical faith from Genesis to Jonah to John. Paul explained it to the Gentiles of Lystra and Athens: God made the heavens and the earth, and the seas, and everything in them.

Darwin and Scripture

We have seen that the concept of design has an ancient lineage and appears in a variety of forms in different cultural, philosophical, scientific, and faith settings. We have suggested that the affirmation of design has normally taken the shape of a faith statement rather than a scientific description. In other words, the "arguments" of Thomas Aquinas for the existence of God based on the appearance of design were never arguments at all. Thomas first assumed the orderliness of the universe, along with its purpose and goal.

A different world existed by the time of Charles Darwin. While Thomas and the ancient world saw a seamless interrelationship between the action of God and the action of the forces of nature, the seamless fabric of the universe was torn asunder by the Enlightenment view that drew a division between the natural and the supernatural. In a sense, the Enlightenment created the concept of the supernatural and then denied its existence or activity in the natural world. In his *The Origin of Species*, Darwin argues that if God has not created each species by a direct act, then God had nothing to do with the forms of life at all. In many ways, Darwin was an old-fashioned fundamentalist in his view of the Bible. He originally assumed a young Earth and creation of species by direct fiat. If Darwin discovered evidence that species arose over long periods, then in his eyes, the Bible was not true.

The nineteenth century was a great time for the development of either/or thinking. It was an age of naïve brilliance. The scientific discoveries of the previous two hundred years had proven so monumental that every branch of learning wanted to be "scientific." What the learned people of that day failed to recognize, however, is that not every field of study lends itself to the scientific method. Theology embraced a pseudoscientific approach to the study of the Bible and religion in general without recognizing the enormous false assumptions that it carried into the equation. Blind to its cultural and philosophical blinders, theology as a discipline grew charmed with its ability to ascribe "natural" explanations to religion. Conservative theologians also embraced pseudoscience as Charles Finney identified the "laws of revival" and C. I. Scofield, with his Dispensational reference Bible, laid out the scientific way to read the Bible. The underlying assumption for conservative and liberal theologians was that scientific truth is the real truth; therefore, the Bible must be scientific or false.

When Darwin discovered that he could explain the origin of the species without a direct act of creation by God, he reasoned that God had nothing to do with the species. At no point did he question his interpretation of Scripture.

Post Script

After Philip Johnson's book, *Darwin on Trial*, the irony of "intelligent design on trial" in Pennsylvania deserves notice. The greater irony of the trial, however, escaped notice until the broadcast of "Judgment Day: Intelligent Design on Trial," a two-hour episode of the PBS series NOVA. The textbook used in Pennsylvania to teach intelligent design was not an intelligent design text. *Of Pandas and People*[67] was written as a scientific creationism text that merely inserted some of the intelligent design language at strategic points. After distancing itself from scientific creationism, the Discovery Institute found itself tied to its adversary and judged on the basis of ideas with which it disagreed.

8. Awe and Wonder

Jimmy H. Davis and Harry Lee Poe

How much evidence does it take to prove a case? The question of evidence for a Designer of the universe is not like a normal scientific experiment in which observation leads to a description of how something happens. Ultimately, the question of design concerns why something has happened. In this case, the something is the entire universe and everything in it. We have seen that the intelligent design movement is concerned with developing criteria for demonstrating why the universe in general and life-forms in particular appear to be designed.

Why do people see patterns? Why do we gaze into the sky at the clouds passing overhead and see a ship in full sail or a Yorkshire terrier? Why do old ladies collect driftwood from a stream or seashore and give the different pieces names like Jonah's whale, the church mouse, or Dick Wittington's cat? They see a form or a pattern that resembles something else. They know it is not the thing they have named it, yet they see a pattern. They do not believe a sailing ship with full rigging is making its way across the sky. They do not believe an old, warped stick is actually a whale. Yet, they see correspondence and analogy. This is the stuff of poetry. Is this what people see when they say that the universe looks as though someone designed it?

On the surface, the situations seem the same, but they are quite different. It is one thing to say a stick looks like a snake and quite another to say that someone has fashioned a stick to look like a snake. The person who sees a ship in the clouds has a sense of satisfaction for being clever enough to "create" a ship where there was no ship. This sort of exercise in imagination rarely results in a sense of awe and wonder. It has more a self-congratulatory feel to it. The sense of awe and wonder comes when we gaze upon the clouds as clouds. Even when we know that they have resulted from a combination of relative humidity, temperature, barometric pressure, and wind, it is possible to lose ourselves in gazing at the clouds. No longer are we entranced with our ability to imagine a ship. We are drawn into the cloud as a work of art.

Awe and wonder involve more than merely the perception of a design, which is the experience of "seeing" the ship in the clouds. Awe and wonder involve knowing something lies behind the clouds. Merely seeing a pattern represents an act of human creativity. Awe and wonder, however, come with the recognition of the personal while observing the impersonal. They produce a surprise. The mind organizes what it sees to establish patterns. Worldviews also affect how we see or accept the patterns of life. Different worldviews give people different patterns of life, yet minds all over the world perceive design behind nature. Is this common occurrence the example of mind perceiving mind? Does this perception of design relate to the remarkable way that mathematics, a mental construct, corresponds to the world (as we saw in chapter four)? Rather than dismissing a phenomenon as "just" a mental construct, does the phenomenon not point to a relationship between the mind and what the mind perceives?

Worldviews and psychology can alter our perception. As we have seen, different cultures, theologies, and philosophies have spoken about design. The remarkable matter is not that they disagree over the meaning of design but that they agree over the fact of design. Psychology does not "work" like the hard sciences that have a clear advantage in how they observe their object of study. The subject that psychology studies is no more observable than God is observable. Psychology deals with secondary matters (affects). It gropes after the created intentions of the human mind, but the mind cannot be observed, only inferred. It can be revealed by itself, yet it cannot be verified as having truly revealed itself. This is the same problem with knowing God empirically: God can be perceived secondarily in nature and God can be self-revealing.

In his study of why people believe in God, Michael Shermer discovered that the most common reason people give for their own belief in God (28.6%) is the "good design" of the universe.[1] Oddly, they give quite a different answer for why they think other people believe in God. They most commonly believe that other people believe in God because belief gives them comfort or purpose (26.3%). Most people believe that very few people (6%) believe in God because of the good design of the universe. We may recognize God, but we doubt that others will!

A Changing Pattern

In the opening chapter of this book we saw that the idea of design has been present in most cultures all over the world, but the idea has rarely involved proving the existence of the Designer. The idea has more frequently involved knowing the Designer. It involves the difference between knowing something and proving something. It involves the difference between knowing something and reflecting on what one knows. The first three chapters of this book explored the better-known varieties of ways that people have thought about design, religiously, philosophically, and scientifically.

What about nature first made people think that it represented the handiwork of someone? The answer to that question lies buried in the past, but the history of the discussion reveals several dimensions in which the question of design operates. The religions of the world describe nature as revelatory of something or someone, or perhaps of many someones. In antiquity, people began to use the method of philosophy to reflect on the human experience of nature, as we saw with Plato and Aristotle. From the time of the Enlightenment, people began to utilize science to reflect on the human experience of nature. To understand the underlying and fundamental consideration of design, however, we need to recall that the discussions began with people who already believed something about what or who was responsible for nature. In the West, the tools of philosophy and science were employed to help believers gain a deeper grasp of faith rather than to prove the existence of the one in whom they had faith. At least this situation prevailed until the Age of Reason, when so many scientists adopted a mechanical model of the universe in keeping with the technological and scientific advances of the day.

The mechanical model coincided with a growing tradition in natural theology to view empiricism as the dominant and only certain means to true knowledge. People of devout piety pushed this understanding, including Bishop Butler and the authors of the *Bridgewater Treatises*. An earlier taxonomy of knowledge would have given place to revelation, experience, tradition, rationalism, and empiricism. By the time of Tennant in the twentieth century, however, we find Christians who no longer recognized the validity of any of these ways of knowing except empiricism.

The last three centuries have witnessed a loss in the variety of the palette of ways of knowing. The palette has shrunk from many complementary ways of knowing that mutually informed one another to only one or two recognized ways of knowing. This transition corresponds to a general frag-mentation of knowledge. We have witnessed an explosion in some kinds of knowledge, but poverty in other areas of knowledge.

In compiling the *Bridgewater Treatises*, the authors believed that by the sheer accumulation of data, the force of their argument would prove over-whelming. The complexity of the question, however, suggests that evi-dence must be drawn from a wider range of experience. For three hundred years, however, Christians have abandoned the interrelated fabric of human knowledge. Calvin planted the seeds of modern skepticism with his dichot-omy of specific revelation and general revelation. He considered the general revelation of God found in nature unhelpful to people as a result of their fallen minds. Descartes succeeded in separating considerations of the spiri-tual from the physical with his dichotomy of mind and body. Pascal suc-ceeded in separating spiritual experience from the domain of reason with his dichotomy of reason and feelings. Butler despised religious experience and looked to empiricism alone as the only legitimate basis of knowledge. On this basis, the natural theology tradition entered into dialogue with sci-ence. One might argue, however, that it had nothing left to bring to the conversation.

In John Wisdom's parable of the gardener that we introduced in chap-ter three, we saw the gridlock that occurs when two people presented with the same evidence have different responses to the data. One person looked about and said that a gardener had been at work. Another person looked about and simply saw an old garden. Both people saw the pattern of a gar-den, but one of the people raised the issue of the presence of personality. In all of the discussion of design, it is possible to lose sight of the reason for the discussion. That design has evoked in people an awareness of the personal. Not everyone acknowledges this experience of the personal, but an over-whelming number of people do experience it. Sheer numbers do not prove the case, but it does help focus the question. Empiricism is a valid and help-ful means of gathering data, yet the data require interpretation.

The design argument does not operate the way a scientific experiment works. First, it has been developed and used for centuries by people who already know what it is they hope to demonstrate. Thus, it does not have as its primary purpose the discovery of new truth. People who already had firm convictions about the origin of the physical world developed the argu-ment. On the other hand, the argument has a compelling staying power that has survived many scientific revolutions. The argument transcends the scientific frameworks in which it has been stated as well as the philosophical frameworks in which it has been rationalized.

The argument from design is not really a proof for the existence of God. Design rarely operates as a proof in any culture. It usually operates as a declaration of faith. The Bible and other religious traditions do not prove God's existence by design even though they affirm the evidence of design. Instead, design explains what kind of God exists and what kind of universe exists. Different religious traditions have differing views of what kind of God exists and what kind of universe exists. Their differing accounts of the nature of design reflect these variations.

Even Aristotle's proofs are not really proofs at all for the existence of God. Instead, they are aspects of his explanation of the workings of the physical world. He is not so much concerned with proving the existence of God as he is concerned with disproving Plato's understanding of universal ideas. Design is merely an aspect of one extended argument in Aristotle, and perhaps the least important.

Belief in an intelligent Designer forms the foundational article of faith for Islam, Judaism, and Christianity. Within these faiths, design does not function as a proof but as a "self-evident truth." The act of design and creation bestows a sacredness on the physical world (often forgotten in the modern period) such that it is wrong to deface (pollute) what God has made or to act in a way contrary to God's design. Even in non-theistic religions we find a strong awareness of the sacredness of the physical world, though often this awareness comes through the perception of the divine within the physical order rather than through the perception of the physical order as the result of the creativity of the divine.

Since the eighteenth century, the design argument has had strong opposition. Certainly, Augustine and Calvin held that one could never come to true knowledge of God through philosophical arguments, but they did not oppose the argument as Hume did. They opposed the argument as people of faith who believed that God had designed the world and that the world gave compelling evidence of its design. They simply believed that people who did not already believe in God as Creator could not discover this truth from their own interpretation of the evidence. Thus, even those who opposed the argument affirmed its conclusion as well as its premises! People believed in and experienced design even if they did not believe it could prove the existence of God.

Now the entire playing field has changed. Aristotle and Aquinas pointed to the design of nature that everyone could see and accept. From the self-evident truth of design they argued toward the Designer, even though they had entirely different concepts of God and of the nature of the universe. In the twentieth century, however, the argument has added an additional step. The culture no longer publicly accepts the notion of design and direction, goal and purpose for nature. Now the argument focuses on the demonstration of *intelligent* design. People may still perceive what has the appearance of design, but they question the validity of their own experience of nature. In the breakdown of knowledge spurred on by Descartes' dichotomy of mind and body, design became enmeshed with the empirical dimension of science. With the growth of deism and the adoption of empiricism as a primary method of theology at the same time that specific revelation diminished in importance, the need to prove design itself became of greater concern than proving the Designer.

Plato, Augustine, Calvin, Descartes, and Pascal all understood the fundamental flaw of empiricism. Sensory experience does not lead to the absolute certainty we might wish as the quantum physicists have pointed out in the twentieth century. Science has a history of "proving" things that in the end are later disproved by alternative theories and evidence that is replaced by new breakthroughs. Jesus discussed the inadequacy of empirical evidence to establish his identity because of the mental framework within which people evaluated the evidence. Though the Gospels contain many instances in which he performed miraculous deeds, Jesus refused to provide a sign as evidence of his identity. In response to Peter's famous statement of faith in him as Christ, Jesus remarked, "Flesh and blood has not revealed this to you, but my Father which is in heaven" (Mt. 16:17).

Yet, we find that God always gives a tangible, observable, concrete basis for faith. For Thomas, faith came through touching (Jn. 20:24–28). For the two disciples on the road to Emmaus, faith came by seeing (Lk. 24:28–31). In the Bible, God consistently provided a concrete basis for faith that related the spiritual experience to the bodily experience; as Paul said, "Faith comes by hearing..." (Rm. 10:17). Aristotle, Aquinas, Butler, Buchland, and Tennant understood the flaw of ignoring sensory experience as the Eastern religions tend to do. Do we need a new synthesis of the two great evolutionary species of descent from Plato and Aristotle? Probably not, because that would suggest that Plato and Aristotle represent the original thesis and antithesis of knowledge when, from a biblical perspective, they more accurately represent the beginnings of the Western tradition to fragment knowledge.

Beauty

"Beauty itself doeth of itself persuade
The eyes of men without an orator."
–William Shakespeare, *The Rape of Lucrece*

"Beauty is in the eye of the beholder."
–Margaret Wolfe Hungerford, *Molly Brown*

As discussed in chapter five, Newton's success came from using one set of equations to describe motion both on the Earth and in the heavens. Many educated people began to look at the universe as a deterministic, clockwork universe. To many people, nature was no longer warm and fuzzy; nature was now a cold machine. The poets of the Romantic Movement revolted against this view of nature and against science. To the Romantics, scientists were heartless cads who had cut beauty out of nature. As William Wordsworth (1770–1850) wrote in "The Tables Turned":

> Sweet is the lore which nature brings;
> Our meddling intellect
> Misshapes the beauteous form of things
> We murder to dissect.

Or as Johann Wolfgang von Goethe (1749–1832) wrote in *Faust:*

> Unless you feel it, you will never achieve it.
> If it doesn't flow from your soul . . .
> Your listener will not believe it . . .
> Gray and ashen . . . is every science,
> And only the golden tree of life is green.

The life of Charles Darwin can be cited as an example of how science destroyed the enjoyment of nature. In his letters, Darwin laments the loss of his enjoyment of literature, poetry, music, and natural beauty.[2] Darwin states, "I am a withered leaf for every subject except Science. It sometime makes me hate Science."[3] Also, a quick examination of some recent introductory astronomy, biology, chemistry, and physics texts reveals no listings of the words "awe," "beauty," "splendor," or "wonder" in their indexes.[4] Is there no beauty or wonder in modern astronomy, biology, chemistry, or

physics? Surprisingly, these terms also were not found in many texts dealing with the interaction of science and faith.[5]

Natural Philosophical Beauty. As the historian of science John Brooke
has pointed out, earlier forms of the design argument did include the appreciation of beauty.[6] The German astronomer Johannes Kepler (1571–1630)
searched for harmony in the relationships of the planets. When he discovered that the planets followed an elliptical orbit, he felt that he was hearing
the music of God. The beauty of gemstones captivated the English chemist Robert Boyle (1627–1691). Boyle, believing that nature was constructed
along a plan of simplicity and economy, envisioned that the external shape
of crystals resulted from a regular arrangement of particles. The English scientist Robert Hooke (1635–1703) used the microscope to explore nature.
Hooke was impressed by his observation that at the microscopic level,
nature was not only functional but also beautiful. The ornamental beauty of
fish scales or fly eyes impressed him. He was amazed that under the microscope human artifacts (edge of a razor) looked imperfect compared to the
artifacts of nature. For Hooke, this beauty and perfection pointed toward
a Designer. The English physicist Isaac Newton (1642–1727) looked for
beauty in a mathematical undergirding of nature. He felt that the beauty of
colors or of the solar system was based on simplicity of mathematical ratios.
The Swedish naturalist Carolus Linnaeus (1707–1778) used the principles
of economy and beauty to develop a classification scheme for living organisms. British geologists William Buckland (1784–1856) and Hugh Miller
(1802–1856) were attracted to the beauty of fossils. One fossil that attracted
them was that of the ammonite, an extinct marine mollusk with a coiled
shell containing a series of chambers. The shapes of these fossils reminded
the geologists of human architecture. As Buckland wrote:

> The general principle of dividing and subdividing the ribs, in order
> to multiply supports as the vault [of the shell] enlarges, is conducted
> nearly on the same plan, and for the same purpose, as the divi-
> sions and subdivisions of the ribs beneath the groin work, in the flat
> vaulted roofs of the florid Gothic Architecture.[7]

Buckland and Miller believed that since the artifacts of nature and humans
shared architecture principles, there was a Designer of nature. Even Darwin (1809–1882) in the early part of his career was attracted to beauty.
Biographers Adrian Desmond and James Moore describe Darwin in the
Brazilian rain forest: "Seated on a mossy log . . . his feelings flowed. 'Twin-

ers entwining twiners,' his pencil twitched, 'trees like hair—beautiful lepidoptera—Silence—hosannah.'"[8]

Physical Beauty. Modern physics continues this emphasis on beauty. Particle physics studies the properties of the particles found inside atoms. Particle physicists depend heavily on mathematical formulations to "describe" the subatomic world. In many cases, there are no instruments powerful enough to test some of the predictions of these mathematical formulations. A challenge for modern science is to determine the criteria for verifying particle physics theories. Ideas proposed and used have included "agreement with data," "coherence with other accepted theories," "simplicity," and "beauty." Beauty! To paraphrase Tina Turner, "What has beauty got to do with it?" The British physicist and Nobel laureate Paul Dirac (1902–1984) was a hard-nosed empiricist; it was reported that if you asked Dirac about the weather, he would go open the door and check before answering! Yet, Dirac is famous for using beauty as a criterion for truth. He stated:

> [I]t is more important to have beauty in one's equations than to have them fit experiment. . . . It seems that if one is working from the point of view of getting beauty in one's equations, and if one has a really sound instinct, one is on a sure line of progress. If there is not complete agreement between the results of one's work and experiment, one should not allow oneself to be too discouraged, because the discrepancy may be due to minor features that are not properly taken into account and that will get cleared up with further developments of the theory.[9]

The American physicist and Nobel laureate Steven Weinberg (1933–) included the chapter "Beautiful Theories" in his recent book *Dreams of a Final Theory.*[10] Weinberg wrote that it is "rather spooky . . . that something as personal and subjective as our sense of beauty helps us not only to invent physical theories but even to judge the validity of theories."[11] For Weinberg and others, a beautiful theory is one that displays simplicity and inevitability. We have all seen a painting or heard a musical score to which we would not want to add or remove anything. This feeling that it was inevitable that all the components would be there is what physicists mean by beauty.

The chemist and philosopher Michael Polanyi believed that a great theory is one that has "an inarticulate component acclaiming its beauty, and this is essential to the belief that the theory is true."[12] For example, Weinberg (1933–) remarked: "I believe that the general acceptance of general relativity was due in large part to the attractions of the theory itself—to its beauty."[13] Weinberg won the Nobel Prize for proposing the electroweak theory uniting the weak nuclear force with the electromagnetic force. When this theory was proposed, it clashed with experimental results. Its beauty encouraged scientists to continue to check to see if their experimental results were in error. The superstring theory is convincing to many not because someone has seen a string (which they have not), but because of its beauty. Science appears to be converging with the Romantic poets. In the poem "Ode on a Grecian Urn," John Keats (1795–1821) said, "Beauty is truth, and truth beauty." This statement is reflected in the remarks of the American physicist and Nobel laureate Charles H. Townes (1915–):

> The beauty of nature elicits a response from both our scientific and our poetic modes of understanding. . . . We scientists, seeing a simple relationship that seems beautiful, intuitively think it likely to be true. Both scientists and theologians give themselves to the truth that transcends and invites us.[14]

The British physicist and Anglican priest John Polkinghorne agrees with Townes that the beauty of a scientific theory points to the Creator's joy in the creation.

False Beauty. Sometimes, one's taste leads to a preference for "tacky paintings" or for false theories. As Weinberg stated, "[J]ust as in our appreciation of music or painting or poetry, this sense of [beauty] is a matter of taste and experience. . . ."[15] The Dane Tycho Brahe (1546–1601) was the greatest astronomer of his day, yet he rejected the Copernican model of the solar system in part because the model had an "ugly" gap between the planets and the nearest stars. Although Kepler wasted years trying to find a model of the solar system based on the "beautiful" shapes of the five Platonic solids, his search resulted in the discovery that planets move in elliptical orbits.[16] The British chemist Humphry Davy (1778–1829) opposed John Dalton's atomic theory because Davy thought it was more beautiful to have one type of matter; ironically, Davy continued to discover elements, thereby supporting Dalton's theory that matter was divided into several building blocks. More recently, Albert Einstein, Louis de Broglie, and Erwin Schrodinger (key players in the founding of quantum mechanics) opposed the probabilities associated with quantum mechanics. It did not fit their sense of the aesthetic, to paraphrase Einstein, for God to play dice. As the examples in this section reveal, a sense of beauty does not always point toward how nature behaves. The other criteria discussed in the previous section also must be applied.

Not a Natural Beauty. If the aesthetic was a topic in natural philosophy and is a topic in particle physics, why do we not find the aesthetic in many introductory science books? One reason that many texts do not index words such as "awe," "beauty," "splendor," or "wonder" could be because of the view that science should be objective, rational, and empirical. In this view, scientists are to remove their emotions, be objective, and be logical. Each type of literature has its own style of writing. In many cases, scientific writing appears in the unemotional and precise style that the Romantic poets hated. Yet, this cannot be the only reason for not mentioning the aesthetic, because there are emotions and hunches in science. Einstein stated, "When I examine myself and my methods of thought, I come close to the conclusion that the gift of fantasy has meant more to me than my talent for absorbing positive knowledge."[17] Einstein also stated, "I'm enough of an artist to draw freely on my imagination. Imagination is more important than knowledge. Knowledge is limited. Imagination encircles the world."[18] In the essay "What I Believe," Einstein addressed beauty, awe, and wonder:

> The most beautiful emotion we can experience is the mysterious. It is the fundamental emotion that stands at the cradle of all true art and science. He to whom this emotion is a stranger, who can no longer wonder and stand rapt in awe, is as good as dead, a snuffed-out candle. To sense that behind anything that can be experienced there is something that our minds cannot grasp, whose beauty and sublimity reaches us only indirectly: this is religiousness. In this sense, and in this sense only, I am a devoutly religious man.[19]

Another reason that the aesthetic is not found in many modern texts could result from the new view of the "beautiful" in light of Darwin's theory of evolution. Characteristics of organisms are now discussed in terms of the utility that resulted from natural selection, not in terms of their awe and wonder reflecting a designer. The ammonite structures that impressed Buckland and Miller as beautiful architectural forms are now described as forms that were useful in the ammonite's struggle for survival:

> The reduction of beauty to utility, orchestrated by the Darwinians, marked the passage of an era: "Those colours which so fascinated the poet or artist, and which seem to be spread in such royal lavishment

over copse and meadow and heath, have all their purpose to fulfil;
they have to serve as an attraction to insects which effect the fertili-
sation of the flower."[20]

Another challenge to beauty is the presence of what some say are imperfect
forms. Those wonderfully beautiful structures of the natural philosophers
are considered imperfectly designed by evolutionists. An example of this
common argument is given by the American biologist Kenneth Miller:

> Because intelligent design works from a clean sheet of paper, it
> should produce organisms that have been optimally designed for
> the tasks they perform. . . .[21]

> To adopt the explanation of design, we are forced to attribute a
> host of flaws and imperfections to the designer. Our appendix, for
> example, seems to serve only to make us sick; our feet are poorly
> constructed to take the full force of walking and running; and even
> our eyes are prone to optical errors and lose their ability for close
> focus as we age.[22]

In chapter six we discussed the American biochemist Michael Behe's concept of irreducible complexity. Since Behe has written some of the best criticisms of the perfect design argument, we will quote him extensively:

> The most basic problem is that the argument demands perfection
> at all. Clearly, designers who have the ability to make better designs
> do not necessarily do so. For example, in manufacturing, "built-in
> obsolescence" is common—a product is intentionally made so it
> will not last as long as it might, for reasons that supersede the sim-
> ple goal of engineering excellence. Another example is a personal
> one: I do not give my children the best, fanciest toys because I don't
> want to spoil them, and because I want them to learn the value of
> a dollar. The argument from imperfection overlooks the possibility
> that the designer might have motives, with engineering excellence
> oftentimes relegated to a secondary role. Most people throughout
> history have thought that life was designed despite sickness, death,
> and other obvious imperfections.[23]

The perfection critique also naïvely assumes that organisms do not change
over time. Miller implies that what we see today is what we would have

seen yesterday. In chapter six, we discussed how some organisms could be adapted by changing environmental conditions. Thus, because an organism may show a history of adaptation does not rule out the possibility of design.

A FLAWED DESIGN?

A friend who serves as president of a denominationally related Christian college has occasion to attend meetings of pastors. At one of these meetings, the preacher of the day waxed eloquent about the loveliness and serenity of nature as he referenced the manicured lawns and well-kept flowerbeds outside. On such a day, he asked, how could anyone doubt the existence of God? Upon leaving the meeting, the college president chanced to notice an adorable little baby squirrel playing in the grass. At that moment, down from the heights, a hawk dove and scooped up the little squirrel for its lunch! The president observed that the preacher had not noticed episodes like the demise of the squirrel in his sermon.

A common argument against awe, wonder, and beauty is the presence of cruelty and evil. Nature is viewed as "red in tooth and claw": herbivores always being stalked by carnivores, aging alpha males being thrown out of the tribe by youthful challengers, terrible parasites, or devastating plagues. This critique also has a personal tone. Weinberg writes, "I have seen a mother die painfully of cancer, a father's personality destroyed by Alzheimer's disease, and scores of second and third cousins murdered in the Holocaust. Signs of a benevolent designer are pretty well hidden."[24] Weinberg's arguments have an emotional tone, rather than the objective, rational, and empirical tone of science. It is interesting that this critique appeals to a sense of justice, of right and wrong. Yet, the alternative proposed to design is a materialist account based on the interaction of forces and matter. What does cruelty, evil, or injustice mean in this materialist account? Why should one event be "better" if all organisms are adapting to the "neutral dictates" of natural selection?

Those who oppose the idea of design because of the presence of "evil" or bad things that happen have undergone a subtle shift in their own response from one of intellect to emotion. The fact that ugliness, thorns, death, pain, suffering, and chaos are present in the world does not disprove design. Infestation by termites does not prove a house did not have an architect. Vandalism does not prove a house did not have an architect. Arson does not prove a house did not have an architect. Sloppy homeowners who do not paint or carry out the garbage do not prove a house did not have an architect. These matters simply raise questions about the situation of the house since it was built. The presence of suffering in the world appears to be a recurring theme of people who oppose the idea that the world bears evidence of design. The presence of suffering may raise questions about the adequacy of the design or the character of the architect, but not about the issue of design itself. As to what the presence of suffering tells us about the designer, we must look to other sources of evidence to explore the character of the designer, but only after establishing the existence of such a being. It does no good to jump the gun and argue against such a being based on the being's character. The recognition of ugliness, pain, and evil, however, suggests an equally perplexing problem. How do we account for goodness, truth, and beauty? Some would say that these qualities are only mental constructs in the mind. If so, we are left to explain ugliness, pain, and evil in the same way. The Buddha accepted this conclusion and resolved that all of physical existence is an illusion. He accepted the reality of the perception of design, but he denied the reality of the design that we perceive!

Hume raised the issue of pain and suffering as evidence against design in the eighteenth century, when the mechanical model of the universe was all the rage. The design Butler saw and that Paley would describe was that of a machine. Hume argued that the presence of bad things in the universe demonstrates a flaw in the design of the machine. He argued that a good, all-powerful God would not design a machine with such a serious flaw. Those who bring up the flaw usually do so as if it were a secret that religious people somehow seek to ignore or deny. Actually, the heart of religion involves the acknowledgement of the flaw. Plato spoke of the flaw as a shadow. Aristotle spoke of it as the problem of change and decay as opposed to the eternal perfection of the heavenly realm. The Buddha spoke of it as an illusion and the entire focus of his approach to religion is to get over the illusion. For Muslims, Jews, and Christians, the problem is sin, and the purpose of religion is to solve the problem of sin. In contrast to the popular view of sin as merely "breaking the rules," these religions view sin as cosmic in scope, striking at the very heart of the nature of physical and spiritual reality.

The Christian religion is the story of nature, including people, from creation to completion. Page after page of the Bible deals with the flawed nature of people and their impact on each other and nature. It is the story of intimate contact between the Creator and the creature toward an ultimate goal that has not yet been accomplished. It is a story in which the struggle has meaning and represents an aspect of the goal. The coming of Christ into the world to participate in physical, human life defined by the experiences of both birth and death forms the focal point of the completion of people.

The Christian worldview, which Weinberg has attacked, does provide the basis for judging events. The life of Jesus provides the basis for judging human actions. While demanding that evil be opposed, this worldview explains why human actions alone cannot overcome evil. As the science writer Kitty Ferguson states, "[T]hose who believe in the biblical God point out that the biblical description of the world situation is, sadly, on target, and that the biblical explanation for our human predicament and the problem of evil—though we may not like or accept the explanation—fits."[25]

If the universe is seen as a completed work at its inception, then the complaint of flawed design has merit. If the universe is a vast machine, then the static idea of creation makes sense. It was made and started. Now it runs on its own. The deists held to this view, but they also popularized this view as a reading of the first chapter of Genesis in which God created the heavens and the earth. As a work of art in progress, however, the complaint of flawed design does not hold. The universe is not finished and neither are people. As we demonstrated in *Science and Faith: An Evangelical Dialogue*, the first chapter of Genesis as written in Hebrew stresses that God *began* to bring the creation about, which is a continuous action.[26] It also stresses the completed action of creation. English translations tend to deal with this seeming contradiction by placing all of creation in the past tense as completed action in the past. Hebrew has no tense—neither past, present, nor future. It has completed action and continuing action. Genesis stresses that in the ages of creation, God continues to be involved in creation. It also stresses, however, that in the totality of creation, God completes the work.

Thus, the problem of pain and suffering is the problem of incompletion. The presence of pain and suffering does not preclude design. It is the design of the artist, however, rather than the design of the engineer. It is the artist painting on a great canvas; the sculptor chipping away at an enormous block of marble until all of the roughness is gone and only the design in the artist's mind remains. It is the play in progress. It is the song being sung. The Hindu might say that it is the dance of the dancer that exists only as the body of the dancer moves.

Perceiving the Personal

The power of nature to evoke awe and wonder in people constitutes the primary way that people experience the personal through nature. In gazing upon a brilliant sunset, a terrible electric storm, or a serene mountain pool, people often speak of an experience of wonder. Some would identify it with the experience of worship. Yet, others who have a purely materialistic orientation will claim to have had similar experiences listening to a Beethoven symphony or observing a painting by Botticelli. This similarity of experiences can be explained in at least two ways. Reference to the moving, rapturous experience in response to some form of creative, artistic expression by humans suggests that the "religious" experience people have in response to nature is merely an internal human response to certain sensory stimuli. It also suggests, however, that what people dub a "religious" experience should more properly be called a "personal" experience in which a human responds to a perception of the personal behind a collection of sensory stimuli. The music of Beethoven and the sunset suggest an artist. A random set of noises at different frequencies does not produce the same effect in a person that a carefully designed set of tones by Beethoven produces. Rather than evidence for the absence of an artist for nature, the experience of rapture over human artistic expression provides evidence that similar effects have similar causes.

An entire stream of philosophers and theologians of the nineteenth and twentieth centuries devoted themselves to exploring the experiential dimension of faith. They had no interest in the exploration of natural philosophy. People like Søren Kierkegaard, Friedrich Schleiermacher, Rudolf Otto, and William Hocking continued a trajectory away from sensory experience that dates back to Descartes and Pascal. They were concerned with religious experience without cognitive content. The fact that they abandoned the idea of revelation as well as empiricism does not in any way diminish the significance of the insights they had into the narrow realm of experience that they separated from other ways of knowing. Otto in particular explored the universal phenomenon of religious experience. He referred to the encounter between people and the personality behind nature by the Latin term *"mysterium, tremendum, et fascinans."* By these terms, he meant that people have a mysterious encounter in the context of sensory experience that takes them beyond the sensory. This experience has a tremendous dimension to it that elicits fear. Yet, the perception of the other fascinates so much that we feel drawn to it. These terms may prove helpful in considering how the notion of intelligent design involves more than just the observable facts.

Mysterium: *Modest Personality*

The human response to nature as design involves more than the mere recognition of pattern, order, system, regularity, probability, and predictability. When people perceive the world as an artifact, is it the artifact that they perceive or the personality behind the artifact that they perceive? Does the world serve as a mediator of the personality responsible for the world? This is a different question than, Does the world give evidence of design? The second question may be an attempt to rationalize the first question and resolve it with an empirical methodology. As we have seen in chapters one and two, peoples all over the world assumed the answer to the first question until relatively recently.

So much of the discussion of design since the time of Newton has focused on the perception of the universe as a great machine. In this model, the perception of design has increasingly depended on the power to demonstrate how the universe is like a machine rather than to see how the universe is the result of creativity. The two are not quite the same thing. Is the universe more like a machine as the deists suggested, or a body as Plato suggested, or a work of art as the Bible suggested? Is God an engineer or an artist?

Tremendum: *The Problem of Evil*

The imperfection in the universe represents one of the major objections to the idea that some intelligence designed the universe. Hume objected to design on these grounds. Darwin was driven to find a naturalistic explanation for life that would let God off the hook. Following the Holocaust, this issue has contributed to theological conversation about God's possible involvement in the world. Many have reasoned that it is better not to have a God at all than to have one who could allow evil. Why would a great intelligence create a world in which evil and suffering occur? Notice that the question involves emotion and values more than it involves a simple empirical inquiry into whether the universe shows evidence of design.

At a recent international gathering of scientists and theologians at Oxford, we engaged a prominent physicist and a prominent molecular biologist in conversation about God's relationship to time. In independent conversations, both men—who hold scientific and theological degrees—opted against the notion that God stands outside time. The conversations took quite some time to work through all of the issues, but the final determining issue for both men, and they both used the same language, was that they "feel uncomfortable" with the idea that God knows what is going to happen. The emotional concern for human freedom governed the terms in which they considered the question.

Freedom and suffering have an intrinsic relationship to each other. In order for the possibility of freedom or non-determinacy, the possibility of pain and suffering must also be present. Without this basic openness of the universe that we can detect at the subatomic level in quantum mechanics and in the relationships of systems found in chaos theory, humanity as we know it could not exist. Perhaps life could not exist. Pain is the price the universe pays for existing. In the end, pain and suffering provide an easy exit from the discussion.

The true difficulty with the problem of pain is to explain the problem of pleasure. Why should pleasure, joy, and beauty be within the realm of experience?

Fascinans: *Attraction*

Life both attracts and conceals. A walk through the zoo will tell us so. We can see some animals whose coloration and form attract a mate. We can see other animals whose coloration and form conceal them from other animals that would eat them. Animals attract their own kind for reproduction, yet they conceal themselves from danger. Darwin's theory offers an explanation for this feature of life. The animals that adapted in such a way as to appear attractive or "beautiful" to another of their kind had greater success in reproduction. The animals that adapted in such a way as to conceal themselves within their environment had greater success in surviving ambush from a predator. The theory certainly makes good sense, but it does not provide a full explanation. Adaptation to appeal to the "beauty" impulse does not explain the origin of the "beauty" impulse. The presence of the "beauty" impulse implies preference in comparing the relative merits of potential suitors. Preference implies values. Values may be quite utilitarian and pragmatic, such as *better* as a protector, *worse* as a food provider, *better* as a reproducing mate.

Within nature we see the principle of attraction related to sexual reproduction. The features that operate in the "beauty" impulse may not have any correlation to the potential of the prospective mate to reproduce in the most favorable way. Human history is full of stories of people smitten by beauty who fail to produce an acceptable offspring. Henry VIII divorced his wife, suffered excommunication from the church he had defended against Martin Luther, risked war with the Continental powers, risked civil war in his own country, and all to marry Anne Boleyn. He wanted a wife who would produce a suitable child, but he was attracted by beauty. One might argue that Henry's wives did produce three children. To this remark, we observe that none of his children produced heirs. Physical features that animals find attractive may work to insure that the attractive animal gets a mate, but this situation does not explain why physical features would make any difference at all for reproduction.

At the fundamental level of the atomic structures that compose the universe, we find the principles of attraction and repulsion at work. Does this fact provide us with a natural explanation for these features at the level of complex organisms? No. It merely provides a description of the complete pervasiveness of the phenomenon. It offers no explanation. At every point in which God does something in nature, we must necessarily see a physical cause, because the action takes place in the observable physical world. To identify a physical cause does not preclude the action of God. A physical, describable event should not be confused with a naturalistic event.

Awe and wonder compose a human response to nature. Not all people respond to nature in this way. Design is an idea based on the analysis of what produced the awe and wonder in a person. It might most approximate an art or music appreciation course. Awe and wonder represent knowledge of the Creator without the cognitive content of knowing the Creator. Even the discovery of an awe and wonder gene, or the religion gene as some call it, would not prove that the appreciation of beauty or the apprehension of the personal mediated through creativity is merely a naturalistic event. It might describe the physical domain through which people experience such things, but Descartes' insistence upon the separation of the physical and the spiritual does not make it so. We have drunk deeply of the dualistic wine in the West.

Any action by God in the physical world can be described according to the laws of physics; otherwise, it could not occur physically. To describe a phenomenon is quite different, however, from explaining a phenomenon. In the same way, any spiritual experience of a person related to the physical world will have a biological context through which the person had access to the physical world. It lies within the realm of science to describe the processes at work when a person responds to the physical world in a way often spoken of as "religious" experience. It is quite another thing, however, to explain the cause of the experience. The fact that drugs can produce similar experiences by no means suggests that the other experiences have no merit. Drugs can produce a similar experience to the tongue of tasting sugar. This fact does not suggest that sugar has no reality. It merely points out that all sources of knowledge are susceptible to distortion.

The ancient Hebrews described the interplay of the human body and spirit as the *nephish hayah* (living being). It was quite a different concept from Plato's view of the *psyche* (life principle). It is most unfortunate for Western civilization that centuries ago scholars translated both words as *soul*. For the Hebrew, the soul represented the unity of life that involved both a physical and a spiritual dimension. For Plato, the soul was the life principle of the universe that became embodied in flesh until it could cast off the physical shell. Physical life was a hindrance to the soul. Aristotle reacted to his teacher and suggested that the spirit had nothing to say to the body. Unfortunately, philosophers and theologians for over two thousand years have played off Plato and Aristotle while paying little heed to the ancient Hebrew understanding of the relationship between physical and spiritual reality. The Hebrew concept of the Creator and the Christian concept of the Incarnation of God in Jesus Christ affirm the dynamic relationship between the spiritual and the physical realms.

The Eye of the Beholder

At the moment of perhaps the greatest triumph of science over the forces of nature, some of the men involved in the effort expressed their own sense of awe and wonder at the experience. John Glenn was the first American to orbit the Earth. On February 20, 1962, Glenn was launched into orbit around the Earth. He orbited the Earth three times in a flight that lasted almost five hours. Only two others, the Russians Yuri Gagarin and Gherman Titov, had orbited the Earth. Some of Glenn's observations during his flight included:[27]

> Oh, that view is tremendous. . . .
> Can see clear back, a big cloud pattern way back across toward the
> Cape. Beautiful sight. . . .
> The horizon now is a brilliant blue. . . .

I have the Cape in sight. I can see the whole State of Florida just laid
out like a map. Beautiful.

After his historic flight, Glenn wrote about his experiences in light of his
faith in God.[28] Glenn's comments were based on his studies about the nature
of the universe as well as his observations during his spaceflight. Glenn was
awed with the wonderful structure of the universe:

> It is the *orderliness* of the whole universe about us—from the smallest
> atomic structure to the most enormous thing we can imagine: galax-
> ies millions of light-years across, all traveling in prescribed orbits in
> relation to one another. Could this have just happened? Was it an
> accident that a bunch of flotsam and jetsam suddenly started mak-
> ing these orbits of its own accord? I can't believe that. This was a
> definite Plan. This is one big thing in space that shows me there is a
> God. Some Power put all this into orbit and keeps it there.[29]

Through a worldview shaped by his military experiences, Glenn saw design
in terms of order and structure.

Apollo 8 was launched on December 21, 1968, and was the first manned
mission to orbit the moon. The crew of *Apollo 8* included Frank Borman,
James A. Lovell Jr., and William A. Anders. They arrived at the moon on
December 24. The *Apollo* astronauts were the first humans to directly see
the backside of the moon as well as the Earth rising over the moon's surface.
They orbited the moon ten times before returning to Earth. Their photographs of the Earth are some of the most famous of the space age. One striking photograph shows the vibrant, blue jewel of the Earth hovering over the
barren moon against the blackness of space.

On Christmas Eve, as they approached a lunar sunrise, Anders began to
read:

> In the beginning God created the heaven and the earth. And the
> earth was without form, and void; and darkness was upon the face
> of the deep. And the Spirit of God moved upon the face of the
> waters. And God said, Let there be light: and there was light. And
> God saw the light, that it was good: and God divided the light from
> the darkness. And God called the light Day, and the darkness he
> called Night. And the evening and the morning were the first day.
> (Gen. 1:1–5 KJV)

Lovell continuing the reading:

> And God said, Let there be a firmament in the midst of the waters, and let it divide the waters from the waters. And God made the firmament, and divided the waters which were under the firmament from the waters which were above the firmament: and it was so. And God called the firmament Heaven. And the evening and the morning were the second day. (Gen. 1:6–8 KJV)

Borman concluded the reading:

> And God said, Let the waters under the heaven be gathered together unto one place, and let the dry land appear: and it was so. And God called the dry land Earth; and the gathering together of the waters he called Seas: and God saw that it was good. (Gen. 1:9–10 KJV)

Borman finished by saying: "And from the crew of Apollo 8 we close with good night, good luck, a Merry Christmas, and God bless all of you—all of you on the good Earth."[30]

As Anders said, "The more I see of God's universe, the deeper will be my belief in God."[31]

9. EPILOGUE

W E HAVE SEEN that over a span of three thousand years, in different places and cultures, the notion of the design of the universe is an idea that has enjoyed remarkable resilience. This remarkable fact may not prove the thesis of design, but it certainly gives occasion for awe. Not only has this idea of design survived changes in religious context; it has survived changes in philosophical and scientific worldview as well. It has survived the changes in worldview from Moses to Plato (via Augustine) to Aristotle (via Aquinas) to Copernicus and Newton to Einstein and Bohr.

In light of this resilience and the unending changes in science and philosophy, this book has no conclusion. We simply add this epilogue to a question that is easily settled for many, but remains an open matter of discussion for others.

We began the preface with a brief account of two conferences concerned with the design question. The sole bridge between the two meetings was Cliff Matthews, a prominent biologist and atheist who is remarkably inquisitive enough to be fascinated with the question of the existence of God. Matthews somehow violated the laws of physics, or at least managed to attend parts of both conferences. He gave a fair-minded report of the Concordia meeting, which included the leaders of the intelligent design movement, during a general question-and-answer period. In his remarks, however, he reported that Ken Miller (professor of biology at Brown, author of *Finding Darwin's God*, and critic of intelligent design) took up Michael Behe's challenge of irreducible complexity. Behe gives the mousetrap as a mechanical example of intelligent design that requires all the pieces in place in order to work. The mousetrap is irreducibly complex: remove one element and it will not function. According to Matthews, Miller produced a mousetrap and began removing pieces to show that it would still work! The brief report seemed more like an account of a carnival show, with Miller perhaps ready to pull a rabbit out of his hat for the next trick. As it turned out, Miller actually used conceptual drawings of mousetraps rather than a working model.

Michael Behe responded to Miller in an article posted on the Web site of the Discovery Institute. He defended the mousetrap analogy and critiqued Miller's slight-of-hand use of a series of drawings of mousetraps of decreasing complexity. Behe demonstrated that even in Miller's drawings of conceptual traps rather than actual traps, multiple alterations must occur in the design of the traps at each stage of complexity for the traps to function.[1] Behe points out that a naturalistic explanation of the changes in complexity may have a satisfactory feel to it, but it collapses upon examination of the details. This explanatory power gives naturalism its charm because it provides science with what the postmodernists would call a "metanarrative."

Gayle Woloschak has pointed out the problem of the argument of irreducible complexity in terms of biology. As recently as the 1980s, the immune system was considered irreducibly complex, but now it is not. Woloschak, a genetic biologist, has observed that the human body has so much redundancy that we can live with a remarkable amount missing in each system. On the other hand, at lower levels of life irreducible complexity becomes a greater issue because redundancy is not present at those levels.

Irreducible complexity may be an example of the infinite regress so feared by the philosophers of old. Take the case of the steam engine. Steam power represents one of the greatest achievements of the industrial revolution, but the first steam engine was nothing more complex than steam escaping from a boiling kettle: a one-cell system! The great airships of the 1930s with their rigid skeletons and massive gondolas that transported passengers in luxury across the Atlantic Ocean began simply as bits of ash sailing up a chimney in the late 1700s. The fact that such complex machines came from such simple origins, however, does not disprove the element of design that went into their formation over time. In fact, the analogy suggests the presence of intelligence that responds to the changing situation as it guides the development of complexity over time.

The argument of natural selection through the survival of the fittest in the competition for the resources of life makes sense at a certain level. As metanarrative, it served to justify the imperialistic ambitions of Western Europe at the end of the nineteenth century. It provided Hitler with a scientifically based political philosophy with which he could rebuild Germany after the devastation of World War I. On a day-to-day basis, we see animals and humans behaving according to an eat-or-be-eaten mentality. We see how it could be so at the functional level. The urge not only to survive but also to prevail, as Faulkner would say, seems apparent at the cognitive level—so much so that it corresponds to our experience with other people. At the lower levels of life, however, it appears that Darwin's natural selection actually operates as a metaphysical principle. He has not supplied a simpler explanation than the God hypothesis. He has merely camouflaged his metaphysics in the trappings of naturalism, as Hegel and Marx had done with their dialectics of history.

The desirability of pursuing design as either theology or science remains a heated topic of discussion. Controversy has surrounded the intelligent design movement for reasons that often sound more emotional than intellectual. Intelligent design represents a throwback to an earlier time before the great fragmentation of knowledge through specialization that has engulfed the West. The fragmentation has occurred in theological and philosophical circles as much or more than within scientific circles. It represents the norm of academic culture in which the disciplines no longer speak to each other. The intelligent design movement has made clear that it hopes to make design a recognized part of science. This hope has raised a specter of horror for many who fear the blur of interdisciplinary contact.

The intelligent design movement has arisen at a time when the scientific community faces a major philosophical crisis related to the certainty of empirical observation as a result of the advances in quantum theory during the twentieth century. In the context of postmodern views toward empiricism and rationalism, science faces a significant challenge in terms of what we can know of reality. Theology faces the same challenge after three hundred years of modernity, during which the mainstream of theological thought grew increasingly suspicious of objective revelation from God and of subjective religious experience as well. The renewed interest in design creates an opportunity for a new discussion of the nature of human knowledge that could lead to an integration of ways of knowing which has been largely absent from Western thought since Aristotle disagreed with Plato.

In his book *Darwin on Trial*, Phillip Johnson argued that the scientific community was dominated by a materialistic philosophy, and he called for a public discussion about the difference between science and any philosophy that may come alongside it. Unfortunately, this important discussion has been overshadowed by the public drama surrounding the intelligent design movement. Though the intelligent design movement made scientific claims for intelligent design, its critics dismissed it outright as creationism, and its supporters focused more on public policy than on the scientific work necessary to prove it.

We have seen that both a more liberal branch of Christianity that is drawn toward naturalistic explanations of religious experience and a more conservative branch of Christianity that relies upon Scripture for all religious content view the design argument with suspicion. Has anyone ever actually come to faith through the contemplation of science and creation? As a matter of fact, this dynamic consideration led Augustine to faith. Ironically, the suspicion of natural theology held by the Reformed tradition owes its origin to Augustine, who had failed to notice God prior to his conversion. Augustine rejected natural theology as sufficient to arrive at an adequate knowledge of God on its own; Calvin would do the same after him. He did not, however, reject what truth can come through natural theology. Science and philosophy helped Augustine come to faith, but once he knew the Creator, he realized that he had spent his life in ignorance of God. He thought that this could not be possible if our senses alone can give us knowledge of God unaided by the intervention of God. The problem lies in the interplay of the various ways of knowing and the human danger of giving priority to one way of knowing without recognizing that the other ways continue to operate whether we acknowledge them or not.

Many Christians fervently affirm that God created the world but just as fervently deny that people could come to this knowledge through observation of the world. Intelligent design presents these Christians with a dilemma. They know as a matter of faith that life cannot be explained purely by appeal to naturalistic forces. On the other hand, they refrain from endorsing the intelligent design movement's attempt to establish an empirical method for demonstrating design. The heavens may "declare the glory of the Lord," but "we walk by faith and not by sight."

The Western tradition since Plato and Aristotle has taught us to choose between alternatives rather than to recognize how alternatives inform one another. The dilemma arises largely because of the philosophical fragmentation of reality and knowledge that occurred centuries ago and left its mark on all aspects of culture: religious, scientific, political, artistic, economic, and philosophical alike. Satisfactory empirical evidence may be present to conclude that a Designer made the universe, but we receive this knowledge by faith.

Stephen Jay Gould has articulated this fragmentation of knowledge and experience with his insistence that science and religion belong to Non-Overlapping Magisteria (NOMA). "East is East, and West is West, and never the twain shall meet." The discussion of design raises the possibility that spiritual reality and physical reality are intrinsically related. The old fragmentation may give way to an older integration. As the old West fades, the emerging "postmodern" culture has a thirst for spirituality and wholeness. Perhaps in this climate a new understanding of the nature of reality and the possibilities of human knowledge rooted in the ancient Hebrew understanding of the soul made in the image of God may emerge.

Notes

Preface

1. We explore this problem at length in our earlier book. See Harry L. Poe and Jimmy H. Davis, *Science and Faith: An Evangelical Dialogue* (Nashville: Broadman & Holman, 2000).

Chapter 1: The Appearance of Design

1. S. A. Nigosian, *World Religions: A Historical Approach*, 3rd edition (Boston: Bedford/St. Martin's, 2000), 37–42.
2. Ibid., 45.
3. Ibid., 31.
4. Ibid., 60.
5. Thomas Bulfinch, *Bulfinch's Mythology* (New York: Avenel Books, 1978), 12.
6. Ibid., 4.
7. Nigosian, *World Religions*, 196.
8. Bulfinch, *Mythology*, 329–30.
9. Ibid., 348–49.
10. Plato, *Timaeus*, in *Plato: Selections*, ed. Raphael Demos (New York: Charles Scribner's Sons, 1955), 391.
11. Ibid., 394.
12. Ibid., 396.

Chapter 2: The Design Argument

1. Tertullian *Apology* 46.
2. Tertullian *The Prescription against Heretics* 7.
3. R. M. Wilson, "Mani and Manichaeism," *The Encyclopedia of Philosophy*, vol. 5 (New York: Macmillan, 1972), 149–50.
4. Augustine *Confessions* 3.4.7.
5. Ibid., 5.3.4.
6. Ibid., 5.14.25.
7. Ibid.
8. Ibid., 5.10.20.
9. Ibid., 4.7.12.

10. Ibid., 5.10.20.
11. Ibid., 7.12.18.
12. Ibid., 7.14.20–21.
13. Ibid., 5.10.20.
14. Ibid., 5.14.24; 6.3.4.
15. Ibid., 7.17.23.
16. Ibid., 8.11.27.
17. Ibid., 11.4.6.
18. Ibid., 2.5.10.
19. Ibid., 2.3.6.
20. Ibid., 2.6.14.
21. The five proofs of Thomas Aquinas may be found in his *Summa Theologica*, Part I, question 2, article 3.
22. Thomas Aquinas, *Aquinas on Creation: Writings on the "Sentences" of Peter Lombard*, trans. Steven E. Baldner and William E. Carroll, Medieval Sources in Translation 35 (Toronto: Pontifical Institute of Medieval Studies, 1997), 134–35.
23. Aquinas, *Summa Theologica* 1.2.3.
24. Ibid.
25. Aquinas, *Aquinas on Creation*, 54.
26. Stephen W. Hawking, *A Brief History of Time* (New York: Bantam Books, 1988), 140–41.
27. John Calvin, *The Institutes of the Christian Religion*, trans. Henry Beveridge, vol. 2 (Grand Rapids, MI: Eerdmans, 1957), 43.
28. Ibid., 51.
29. Ibid., 51–53.
30. Ibid., 53.
31. Ibid., 59.
32. Ibid., 62.
33. For a concise summary of Descartes' principal ideas, see Bernard Williams, "René Descartes," *Encyclopedia of Philosophy*, vol. 1 (New York: Macmillan, 1972), 344–54.
34. Matt. 11:27: "Neither knoweth any man the Father, save the Son, and he to whomsoever the Son will reveal him."
35. Isa. 45:15: "Verily, thou art a God that hidest thyself." Blaise Pascal, *Pensées*, trans. W. F. Trotter, Great Books of the World, vol. 33 (Chicago: Encyclopedia Britannica, 1955), 4.242. C. S. Lewis quotes from this section of the *Pensées* in the introduction of *The Problem of Pain*.
36. Pascal, *Pensées*, 3.233.

CHAPTER 3: THE MECHANICAL UNIVERSE

1. Amos Funkenstein, *Theology and the Scientific Imagination: from the Middle Ages to the Seventeenth Century* (Princeton: Princeton University Press, 1986), 3.
2. Ernest Campbell Mossner, "Deism," in *The Encyclopedia of Philosophy*, vol. 2 (New York: Macmillan, 1967), 330-31.
3. Bernard Ramm, *Varieties of Christian Apologetics* (Grand Rapids, MI: Baker, 1979), 113.
4. Isaac Newton, *Mathematical Principles of Natural Philosophy*, trans. Andrew Motte,

rev. and ed. Florian Cajori (1714; Berkeley: University of California Press, 1934), 32, as quoted in John C. Hutchison, "Darwin's Evolutionary Theory and 19ᵗʰ Century Natural Theology," *Bibliotheca Sacra* 152 (July–September 1995): 335.

5. Though published in 1779 after Hume's death, the manuscript had been finished in rough draft since 1751. See J. C. A. Gaskin, ed., "Introduction," *Dialogues Concerning Natural Religion by David Hume*, Oxford World's Classics (Oxford: Oxford University Press, 1998), xviii.

6. Hume, *Dialogues Concerning Natural Religion*, Part II.

7. Ibid., Part IV.

8. Ibid.

9. Ibid., Part V.

10. Ibid., Part VI.

11. Ibid., Part VII.

12. Ibid., Part VIII.

13. Ibid., Part IX.

14. Ibid., Part X.

15. Ibid.

16. Ibid.

17. William Paley, *Natural Theology; or Evidences of the Existence and Attributes of the Deity, Collected from the Appearances of Nature*, 2nd ed., vol. 1 (Oxford: J. Vincent, 1828), 1–4.

18. See John Hick, *Philosophy of Religion*, 2nd ed. (Englewood Cliffs, NJ: Prentice-Hall, 1973), 25; Hugh Ross, *The Creator and the Cosmos* (Colorado Springs: NavPress, 1995), 106.

19. Ibid., 65.

20. The eight contributors were Thomas Chalmers, John Kidd, William Whewell, Sir Charles Bell, Peter Mark Roget, William Buckland, William Kirby, and William Prout.

21. William Buckland, *Geology and Mineralogy Considered with Reference to Natural Theology*, vol. 1 (London: William Pickering, 1836), viii.

22. Ibid., 130–31.

23. John Hadley Brooke and Geoffrey Cantor, *Reconstructing Nature: The Engagement of Science and Religion*, Glasgow Gifford Lectures (Edinburgh: T & T Clark, 1998), 147.

24. Morton O. Beckner, "Darwinism," *The Encyclopedia of Philosophy*, vol. 2 (New York: Macmillan, 1972), 300.

25. Ibid.

26. John Wisdom, *Philosophy and Psychoanalysis* (Oxford: Basil Blackwell, 1953), 154–55, as quoted in Hick, *Philosophy of Religion*, 86.

CHAPTER 4: A FINE-TUNED UNIVERSE

1. For a more detailed discussion of this topic, please see Harry L. Poe and Jimmy H. Davis, *Science and Faith: An Evangelical Dialogue* (Nashville: Broadman & Holman, 2000), 65–69.

2. George Greenstein, *The Symbiotic Universe: Life and Mind in the Cosmos* (New York: William Morrow, 1988), 93.

3. In fusion reactions, nuclei are identified by the name of the atom followed by a number. The number represents the number of protons and neutrons present in that nucleus.

For example, helium-4 is the name for a helium nucleus whose total number of protons plus neutrons is four.

4. Fred Hoyle, "The Universe: Past and Present Reflection," *Annual Reviews of Astronomy and Astrophysics* 20 (1982): 16.

5. Carl Sagan, *Cosmos* (New York: Random House, 1980), 298–302.

6. When NASA funding was cut off, SETI quickly raised more than $4 million from technology leaders such as Hewlett-Packard co-founders William Hewlett and David Packard, Intel co-founder Gordon Moore, and Microsoft co-founder Paul Allen.

7. In August 2000, astronomers announced discovering a Jupiter-size planet orbiting the star Epsilon Eridani, 10.5 light years from Earth and the home star of *Star Trek*'s Mr. Spock.

8. Greenstein, *The Symbiotic Universe,* 27–28.

9. Martin Gardner, "WAP, SAP, PAP, & FAP," *New York Times Review of Books*, May 8, 1986, 23.

10. John Archibald Wheeler, "Bohr, Einstein, and the Strange Lesson of the Quantum," in *Mind in Nature*, ed. Richard Q. Elvee (New York: Harper & Row, 1981), 18.

11. John D. Barrow and Frank J. Tipler, *The Anthropic Cosmological Principle* (New York: Oxford University Press, 1986), 677.

12. Ibid., 682.

13. Gardner, "WAP, SAP, PAP, & FAP," 25.

14. Quoted in Heinz R. Pagels, "A Cozy Cosmology," *The Sciences* (March/April 1985): 37.

15. Quoted in Marcus Chown, "Out in the Cold," *New Scientist* 166 (2000): 32.

16. Ibid.

17. Hugh Ross, "Big Bang Model Refined by Fire," in *Mere Creation: Science, Faith and Intelligent Design*, ed. William A. Dembski (Downers Grove, IL: InterVarsity Press, 1998), 372–80.

18. Peter D. Ward and Donald Brownlee, *Rare Earth: Why Complex Life Is Uncommon in the Universe* (New York: Copernicus, 2000). The authors did an excellent job of presenting the scientific evidence of why the Earth is a unique planet.

19. Quoted in Guillermo Gonzalez, "No Other Eden," *Touchstone* (June 2000): 37.

20. William A. Dembski, *Intelligent Design: The Bridge Between Science and Theology* (Downers Grove, IL: InterVarsity Press, 1999), 90–91.

21. Michael J. Behe, "Foreword," in Dembski, *Intelligent Design*, 10.

22. Hugh Ross, *The Creator and the Cosmos* (Colorado Springs: NavPress, 1993), 125.

CHAPTER 5: THE COMPREHENSIBLE UNIVERSE

1. A representation of the plaque can be seen on the NASA Web site: http://spaceprojects. arc.nasa.gov/Space_Projects/pioneer/PN10&11.html.

2. Carl Sagan, *The Cosmic Connection: An Extraterrestrial Perspective* (New York: Anchor Press, 1973), 30.

3. NASA included a much more ambitious message on the *Voyager 1* and *2* spacecrafts. These spacecrafts carried a 12-inch gold-plated copper phonograph record containing the sounds and images of Earth. Instructions again include the "common mathematics."

4. It is interesting how current scholars deal with Newton's beliefs. In the Microsoft *Encarta 98 Encyclopedia* article entitled "Newton, Sir Isaac," author Richard S. Westfall

states, "In addition to science, Newton also showed an interest in alchemy, mysticism, and theology. Many pages of his notes and writings—especially from the later years of his career—are devoted to these topics. However, historians have found little connection between these interests and Newton's scientific work."

5. All the atoms making up an element have the same number of protons but can have different numbers of neutrons.

6. The exception is helium, which has only two electrons.

7. The arrangement is actually more complicated than this. The second shell is divided into two subshells or orbitals. The third shell is divided into three subshells, and so forth. For the purpose of this book, the shell arrangement is adequate.

8. Whether a covalent molecule is nonpolar or polar also depends on the three-dimensional structure of the molecule. Considering the three-dimensional structure is beyond the scope of this book.

9. Intergovernmental Panel on Climate Change, "Climate Change 2007: Mitigation of Climate Change—Summary for Policy Makers," www.ipcc.ch.

10. Samuel Taylor Coleridge, *The Rime of the Ancient Mariner*, st. 9.

11. An interesting discussion of the different ways to pack cannonballs (molecules) appears in the science fiction novel *Cat's Cradle* by Kurt Vonnegut Jr. (New York: Dell, 1963).

12. Philip J. Davis, Reuben Hersh, and Elena Anne Marchisotto, *The Mathematical Experience* (Boston: Birkhauser, 1995).

13. Ibid., 84.

14. Richard W. Hamming, "The Unreasonable Effectiveness of Mathematics," *American Mathematics Monthly* 87 (1980): 81–90. Eugene P. Wigner, "The Unreasonable Effectiveness of Mathematics in the Natural Sciences," in *Symmetries and Reflections: Scientific Essays of Eugene P. Wigner* (Bloomington: Indiana University Press, 1967), 222–37.

15. Hamming, "The Unreasonable Effectiveness of Mathematics," 84.

16. Ibid., 82.

Chapter 6: The Complexity of Life

1. Sylvia Mader, *Inquiry into Life*, 8th ed. (Dubuque, IA: Wm. C. Brown, 1997), 81.

2. Quoted in Maitland A. Edey and Donald C. Johanson, *Blueprints* (Boston: Little, Brown, 1989), 235.

3. The two other RNA molecules, tRNA and rRNA, are synthesized in a similar manner.

4. If the codon on the mRNA is AUG, the anticodon on the tRNA would be UAC. This tRNA would be transporting the amino acid Met or methionine.

5. *Science* 316 (May 25, 2007): 1113.

6. For a more thorough discussion of Darwin's theory of evolution, see Harry L. Poe and Jimmy H. Davis, *Science and Faith: An Evangelical Dialogue* (Nashville, TN: Broadman & Holman, 2000), chaps. 7–9.

7. Jacques Barzum, *Darwin, Marx, Wagner: Critique of a Heritage*, 2nd ed. (Chicago: University of Chicago Press, 1941, 1958, 1981), 11.

8. Charles Darwin, *On the Origin of Species*, ed. Charles Eliot, Harvard Classics, vol. 11 (New York: P. F. Collins & Son, 1909), 511.

9. Ibid., 517.

10. Ibid., 210.

11. Ibid., 523.

12. *Teaching Science in a Climate of Controversy: A View from the American Scientific Affiliation* (Ipswich, MA: American Scientific Affiliation, 1986, 1987, 1989, 1993).

13. The Grants' findings are discussed in a Pulitzer Prize–winning book by Jonathan Weiner, *The Beak of the Finch: A Story of Evolution in Our Time* (New York: Knopf, 1994).

14. Robert T. Pennock, *Tower of Babel: The Evidence against the New Creationism* (Cambridge, MA: MIT Press, 1999), 271.

15. For a further discussion of this topic, please see Ian G. Barbour, *Religion and Science: Historical and Contemporary Issues* (New York: HarperSanFrancisco, 1997), 106–36.

16. Michael Polanyi, "Life Transcending Physics and Chemistry," *Chemical and Engineering News* 45, no. 35 (August 21, 1967): 54–66.

17. Mader, *Inquiry into Life*, 40.

18. H. H. Pattee, quoted in Nancy R. Pearcey and Charles B. Thaxton, *The Soul of Science: Christian Faith and Natural Philosophy* (Wheaton, IL: Crossway Books, 1994), 241.

19. David Hull, "The Limits of Cladism," *Systematic Zoology* 28 (1979): 419.

20. David Hume, "An Enquiry Concerning Human Understanding," sec. 11, in *Principle Writings on Religion*, ed. J. C. A. Gaskin (Oxford: Oxford University Press, 1988), 14.

CHAPTER 7: THE INTELLIGENT DESIGN PROJECT

1. The book published by InterVarsity Press was a recipient of a *Christianity Today* 1992 Readers' Choice Award and was Book of the Year runner-up. In 2006, *Christianity Today* selected this book to be one of the top fifty books that have shaped Evangelicals. The term "intelligent design" is attributed to the Oxford scholar F. C. S. Schiller in his 1897 essay in *Contemporary Review*. The emergence of the intelligent design movement in the 1990s was built on works such as Michael Polanyi, "Life Transcending Physics and Chemistry," *Chemical and Engineering News* 45, no. 35 (August 21, 1967): 54–66; Charles B. Thaxton, Walter L. Bradley, and Roger L. Olsen, *The Mystery of Life's Origin* (Dallas: Lewis & Stanley, 1984); and Michael Denton, *Evolution: A Theory in Crisis* (Great Britain, Burnett Books, 1985).

2. Donald A. Yerza, "Phillip Johnson and the Origins of the Intelligent Design Movement, 1997–1991," *Perspectives on Science and Christian Faith*, March 2002, 47–52.

3. William A. Dembski and Michael Ruse, "General Introduction," in *Debating Design: From Darwin to DNA*, ed. William A. Dembski and Michael Ruse (Cambridge: Cambridge University Press, 2006), 3.

4. The Discovery Institute was founded in 1990 by Bruce Chapman, who served as director of the Census Bureau, deputy assistant to the president, director of the White House Office of Planning and Evaluation, and ambassador to United Nations Organizations in Vienna during the Reagan administration. The Discovery Institute (see http:www. discovery.org) focuses include: Technology and Democracy Project, Center for Science and Culture, the Cascadia transportation system, bioethics, and economics.

5. The Center for Science and Culture was founded in 1996.

6. "About Discovery: How Discovery Institute Functions," http://www.discovery.org/aboutFunctions.php.

7. Scientific creationism seeks to prove that the Bible is scientifically accurate and that modern science is not reliable.

8. The "Wedge" document was prepared in 1999 as a fundraising proposal by the Center for Science and Culture. It became a controversial document after it was leaked on the Internet. Opponents claimed that the "Wedge strategy" was a religious conspiracy to "substitute 'theistic science' for natural science in the public mind. . . ." This quote is from the dust jacket of Barbara Forrest and Paul R. Gross, *Creationism's Trojan Horse: The Wedge of Intelligent Design* (New York: Oxford University Press, 2003). Others claim that Forrest may herself have a hidden agenda, since she does not disclose in her writings that she is member of the board of directors of the New Orleans Secular Humanist Association. See Angus Menuge, "Who's Afraid of ID?" in Dembski and Ruse, eds. *Debating Design*. The Center for Science and Culture at first ignored the attacks on the "Wedge" document but did respond in 2003 with "The 'Wedge Document': So What?" See http://www.discovery.org/scripts/viewDB/filesDB-download.php?id=349.

9. Phillip E. Johnson, *Darwin on Trial* (Downers Grove, IL: Intervarsity Press, 1991), 165; and Phillip E. Johnson, "Afterword: How to Sink a Battleship," in William A. Dembski, ed., *Mere Creation: Science Faith & Intelligent Design* (Downers Grove, IL: InterVarsity Press, 1998), 452.

10. Angus Menuge, "Who's Afraid of ID?" in Dembski and Ruse, eds., *Debating Design*, 41.

11. Michael Behe and William Dembsi presentations at Union University, Jackson, TN, February 1998 and 2000.

12. From http://www.iscid.org/.

13. Celeste Biever, "Intelligent Design: The God Lab," *New Scientist* 15 (December 2006): 8–11; John West, "Intelligent Design Research Lab Highlighted in *New Scientist*," http://www.evolutionnews.org/2006/12/intelligent_design_research_la.html.

14. Bruce Chapman, "The State of Scientific Research on Intelligent Design," http://www.evolutionnews.org/2006/10/the_state_of_scientific_resear.html.

15. Wedge document.

16. Kim Minugh, "Father of Intelligent Design," *Sacramento Bee*, http://dwb.sacbee.com/content/news/education/v-print/story/14254103p-15069795c.html, May 11, 2006.

17. Michael J. Behe, *Darwin's Black Box: The Biochemical Challenge to Evolution* (New York: Free Press, 1996), 4.

18. Ibid., 5.

19. Ibid., 39.

20. Ibid, 208.

21. Ibid., 206.

22. Ibid., 207.

23. Ibid., 42.

24. Ibid., 69–73; and Michael J. Behe, "Intelligent Design Theory as a Tool for Analyzing Biochemical Systems," in Dembski, ed., *Mere Creation*, 180–81.

25. Behe, "Intelligent Design Theory" 180–81.

26. William A. Dembski, *The Design Interference: Eliminating Chance through Small Probabilities* (Cambridge: Cambridge University Press, 1998).

27. William A. Dembski, *No Free Lunch: Why Specified Complexity Cannot Be Purchased without Intelligence* (Lanham, MD: Rowman & Littlefield, 2002).

28. Kenneth R. Miller, "The Flagellum Unspun: The Collapse of 'Irreducible Complexity,'" in Dembski and Ruse, eds. *Debating Design*.

29. Ibid., 86–87.

30. William A. Dembski, "The Logical Underpinnings of Intelligent Design," in Dembski and Ruse, eds., *Debating Design*, 326.

31. Michael J. Behe, "Irreducible Complexity: Obstacle to Darwinian Evolution," in Dembski and Ruse, eds. *Debating Design*, 359–60.

32. Behe, *Darwin's Black Box*, 39.

33. Michael Roberts, "Intelligent Design: Some Geological, Historical, and Theological Questions," in Dembski and Ruse, eds. *Debating Design*, 289.

34. David K. DeWolf, Stephen C. Meyer, Mark E. DeForrest, *Teaching the Controversy: Darwinism, Design and the Public School Science Curriculum* (Foundation for Thought and Ethics, 1999).

35. Stephen C. Meyer, "Teach the Controversy," *Cincinnati Enquirer*, March 30, 2002.

36. Congressional Record Proceedings of the 107th Congress, 1st ed., 147:82 (June 13, 2001), s6148

37. "President Bush's Support for Free Speech on Evolution and Intelligent Design Draws Praise from Discovery Institute," http://www.discovery.org/scripts/viewDB/index.php?command=view&id=2764.

38. Judge John E. Jones III, "United States District Court Opinion *Kitzmiller v. Dover Area School District*, http://www.pamd.uscourts.gov/kitzmiller/kitzmiller_342.pdf.

39. See http://www.cbsnews.com/stories/2005/11/10/politics/main1036232.shtml.

40. See http://www.yorkdispatch.com/searchresults/ci_3535139.

41. See http://www.ncseweb.org/resources/news/2006/OH/636_a_clean_break_from_creationis_10_17_2006.asp.

42. Del Ratzsch, *Nature, Design and Science: The Status of Design in Natural Science* (Albany: State University of New York Press, 2001).

43. Larry Laudan, "The Demise of the Demarcation Problem," in Michael Ruse, ed., *But Is It Science?* (Amherst, NY: Prometheus Books, 1996), 337–50.

44. Ratzsch, *Nature, Design and Science*, 91.

45. Judge William R. Overton, "United States District Court Opinion *McLean v. Arkansas*," in Ruse, ed., *But Is It Science?* 307–31.

46. Jones, "United States District Court Opinion *Kitzmiller v. Dover Area School District*."

47. Ibid., 64–65.

48. Larry Witham, "Intelligent Design Goes on Trial," *Science & Theology News*, January 2006, 12–15.

49. Ibid., 12.

50. Dembski, *Intelligent Design*, 247.

51. John C. Whitcomb and Henry M. Morris, *The Genesis Flood: The Biblical Record and Its Scientific Implications* (Phillipsburg, NJ: Presbyterian and Reformed Publishing Co., 1961).

52. John Milburn, "Class Dismissed," *Science & Theology News*, January 2006, 17.

53. "Measuring Perceptions about Evolution," *Science & Theology News*, January 2006, 17. The poll was conducted between July 7 and July 17, 2005. The data for the *Science & Theology News* article came from the Pew Research Center for the People and the Press and the Pew Forum on Religion and Public Life.

54. Jones, "United States District Court Opinion *Kitzmiller vs. Dover Area School District*."

55. Loren Haarsma, "Is Intelligent Design 'Scientific'?" *Perspectives on Science and Christian Faith* 59 (March 2007): 55.

56. Ibid., 76.
57. Philip Kitcher, *Abusing Science: The Case Against Creationism* (Cambridge: MIT Press, 1982), 125.
58. See Flew's letter at www.philosophynow.org/issue47/47flew.htm.
59. Ibid.
60. Steve Paulson, interview with Richard Dawkins, October 13, 2006, www.salon.com/books/int/2006/10/13/dawkins.
61. Ibid.
62. C. S. Lewis, *Miracles* (London: Fontana, 1960), 9.
63. C. S. Lewis, *Mere Christianity* (New York: Macmillan, 1952), 17–18.
64. Augustine *Confessions* 5:24 (Nicene and Post-Nicene Fathers).
65. Ibid., 6:6.
66. Ibid., 5:8–9.
67. Percival Davis and Michael Keaton, *Of Pandas and People: The Central Question of Biological Origins*, 2nd ed. (Richardson, TX: Foundation for Thought and Ethics, 1989, 1993).

Chapter 8: Awe and Wonder

1. Michael Shermer, "Why People Believe in God: An Empirical Study on a Deep Question," *The Humanist*, 59, no. 6 (November/December 1999): 20–26. This article comes from Shermer's book *How We Believe: The Search for God in an Age of Science* (New York: W. H. Freeman, 1999).
2. Ian G. Barbour, *Religion and Science: Historical and Contemporary Issues* (New York: HarperSanFrancisco, 1997), 59.
3. Francis Darwin, ed., *Life and Letters of Charles Darwin* (New York: D. Appleton, 1887), 2:273.
4. The scientific books reviewed were Darrell D. Ebbing, *General Chemistry*, 5th ed. (Boston: Houghton Mifflin, 1996); W. Thomas Griffith, *The Physics of Everyday Phenomena*, 2nd ed. (Dubuque, IA: Wm. C. Brown, 1998); Sylvia Mader, *Inquiry into Life*, 8th ed. (Dubuque, IA: Wm. C. Brown, 1997); and Michael A. Seeds, *Foundations of Astronomy*, 2nd ed. (Belmont, CA: Wadsworth Publishing, 1988).
5. These texts did not contain the words "awe," "beauty," or "wonder" in their indexes: Michael J. Behe, *Darwin's Black Box: The Biochemical Challenge to Evolution* (New York: Free Press, 1996); Charles Colson and Nancy Pearcey, *How Now Shall We Live?* (Wheaton, IL: Tyndale House, 1999); William Dembski, ed., *Mere Creation: Science, Faith & Intelligent Design* (Downers Grove, IL: InterVarsity Press, 1998); Hugh Ross, *The Creator and the Cosmos: How the Greatest Scientific Discoveries of the Century Reveal God* (Colorado Springs: NavPress, 1993; and Robert T. Pennock, *Tower of Babel: The Evidence against the New Creationism* (Cambridge, MA: The MIT Press, 1999). Beauty was mentioned in Kitty Ferguson, *The Fire in the Equations: Science, Religion and the Search for God* (Philadelphia: Templeton Foundation Press, 2004); and Ted Peters, ed., *Science and Theology: The New Consonance* (Boulder, CO: Westview Press, 1998).
6. John Brooke and Geoffrey Cantor, *Reconstructing Nature: The Engagement of Science and Religion* (Edinburgh: T & T Clark, 1998), 185–87.
7. William Buckland, *Geology and Mineralogy Considered with Reference to Natural Theology* (London: William Pickering, 1836), 341.

8. Adrian Desmond and James Moore, *Darwin* (New York: Warner Books, 1991), 122.
9. Paul Dirac, "The Evolution of the Physicist's Picture of Nature," *Scientific American* (May 1963): 47.
10. Steven Weinberg, *Dreams of a Final Theory: The Search for the Fundamental Laws of Nature* (New York: Pantheon Books, 1992).
11. Ibid., 133.
12. Michael Polanyi, *Personal Knowledge: Towards a Post-Critical Philosophy* (Chicago: University of Chicago Press, 1962), 133.
13. Weinberg, *Dreams of a Final Theory*, 98.
14. Charles H. Townes, "Logic and Uncertainties in Science and Religion," in Peters, ed., *Science and Theology*, 45.
15. Weinberg, *Dreams of a Final Theory*, 148.
16. A Platonic solid or regular solid is a three-dimensional body with identical faces. The five Platonic solids are the cube, the tetrahedron, the dodecahedron, the icosahedron, and the octahedron.
17. Albert Einstein, quoted in John Winokur, *Einstein: A Portrait* (California: Pomegranate Art Books, 1983).
18. Albert Einstein, quoted in Walter Isaacson, *Einstein: His Life and Universe* (New York: Simon & Schuster, 2007), 387.
19. Ibid.
20. Brook and Cantor, *Reconstructing Nature*, 226. They quoted Anon., "Is Nature Perfect?" *Monthly Journal of Science*, London (1879): 271–76.
21. Kenneth R. Miller, "Life's Grand Design," *Technology Review* (February/March, 1994): 29.
22. Kenneth R. Miller, *Finding Darwin's God* (New York: Cliff Street Books, 1999), 101.
23. Michael J. Behe, *Darwin's Black Box: The Biochemical Challenge to Evolution* (New York: Free Press, 1996), 223.
24. Steven Weinberg, "A Designer Universe?" http://www.physlink.com/essay_weinberg.cfm. This article is based on a talk Weinberg gave in April 1999 at the Conference on Cosmic Design of the American Association for the Advancement of Science.
25. Ferguson, *The Fire in the Equations*, 274.
26. Harry L. Poe and Jimmy H. Davis, *Science and Faith: An Evangelical Dialogue* (Nashville: Broadman & Holman, 2000), 79–81.
27. John Glenn, quoted in "An American in Orbit Talks to His Planet," *U.S. News & World Report*, March 5, 1962, 42–44.
28. John Glenn, "Why I Know There Is a God," *Reader's Digest*, July 1962, 37–39.
29. Ibid., 38.
30. "'Modern Magi' Put Moon Flight into Scriptural Perspective," *Christianity Today*, January 17, 1969, 36–37.
31. Ibid.

CHAPTER 9: EPILOGUE

1. Michael J. Behe, "A Mousetrap Defended: Response to Critics," http://www.discovery.org. Miller's argument and his drawings as well as Behe's response may also be found in William A. Dembski and Michael Ruse, eds., *Debating Design: From Darwin to DNA* (Cambridge: Cambridge University Press, 2006).

Index